The African American Resource Guide to the Internet and Online Services

The African American Resource Guide to the Internet and Online Services

Stafford L. Battle

Rey O. Harris

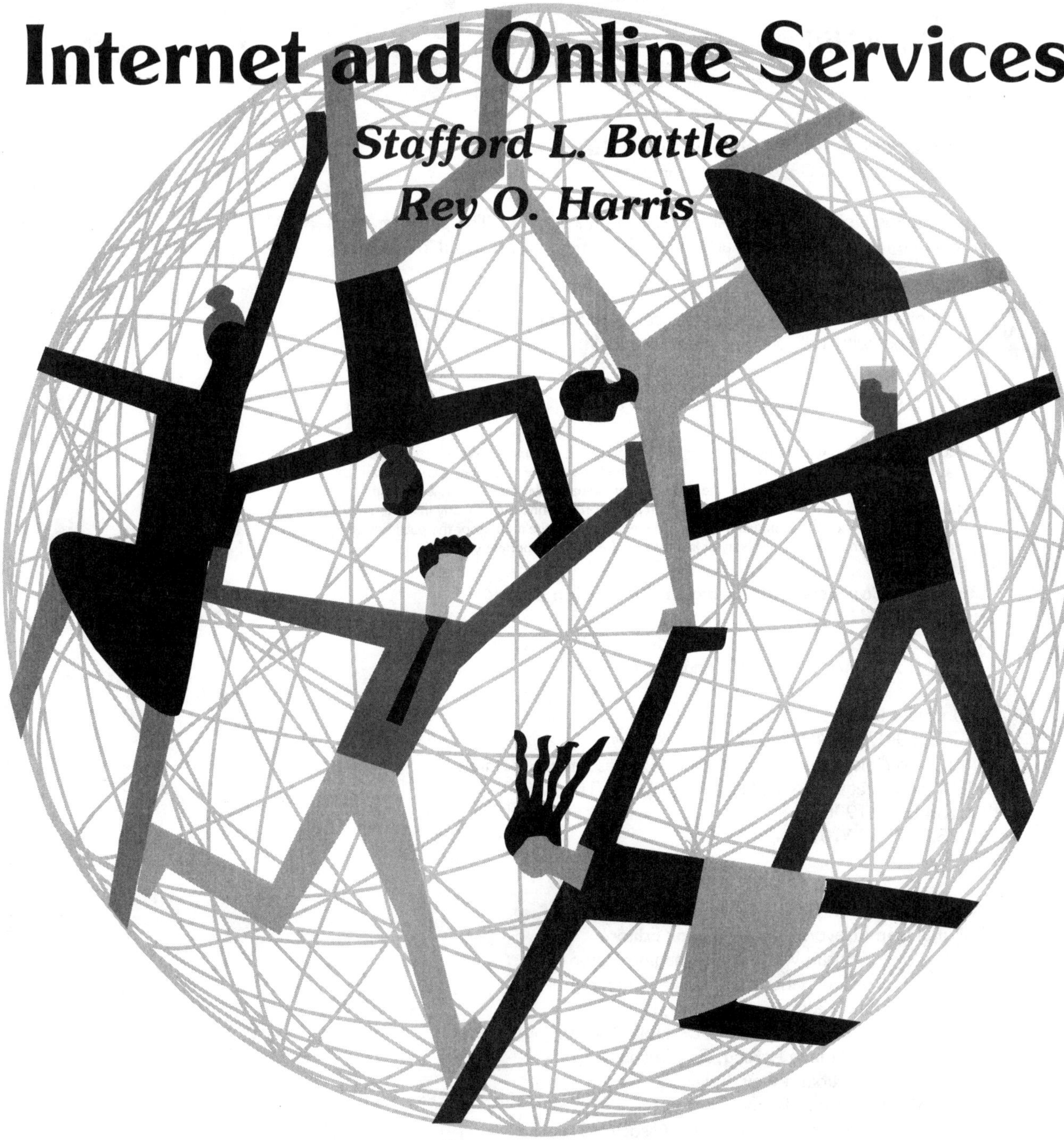

McGraw-Hill

New York San Francisco Washington, D.C. Auckland Bogotá Caracas Lisbon London Madrid Mexico City Milan Montreal New Delhi San Juan Singapore Sydney Tokyo Toronto

McGraw-Hill

A Division of The McGraw-Hill Companies

Published by The McGraw-Hill Companies.

This book is printed on recycled paper containing a minimum of 50% total recycled fiber with 15% postconsumer de-inked fiber.

pbk 1 2 3 4 5 6 7 8 9 BBC/BBC 9 0 0 9 8 7 6

Library of Congress Cataloging-in-Publication Data

Battle, Stafford L.

The African American resource guide to the Internet and online services / by Stafford L. Battle and Rey O. Harris.

p. cm.

Includes index.

ISBN 0-07-005499-1 (pbk.)

1. Afro-Americans—Computer network resources. 2. Internet (Computer network) I. Harris, Rey O. II. Title.

E185.B33 1996

025.06'305896'073—dc20 96-11964

CIP

Acquisitions editor: Brad J. Schepp

Editorial team: Navorn Johnson, Book Editor
Susan W. Kagey, Managing Editor
Lori Flaherty, Executive Editor

Production team: Katherine G. Brown, Director
Lisa M. Mellott, Desktop Operator
Linda L. King, Proofreading
Joann Woy, Indexer

Design team: Jaclyn J. Boone, Designer
Katherine Lukaszewicz, Associate Designer

0054991
WK1*

This book is dedicated to Stephanie, William, and Aaron.
They represent our future and, among all the people we know,
are the least computer-phobic.

Contents

Foreword

We have done everything in our power to provide information that is as up to date as possible. However, due to the fluid nature of telecommunications technology, we realize that information will change quickly. Therefore, computer bulletin boards, Internet addresses, telephone numbers, and individuals mentioned in this book may have changed.

We will continue to publish updates to this work in order to bring you the latest information possible. Also, we welcome any comments, suggestions, or additions.

Stafford L. Battle, *sbattle@aol.com* or *sbattle@cityofnewelam.com*

Rey O. Harris, *elam@mnsinc.com*

Preface

America is unique among many nations because of the cultural diversity in its creation. A colorful variety of races, cultures, and societies from the entire planet reside within the United States and its territories.

Like other groups, African Americans have played key roles throughout this country's history and will continue to contribute to the building of a 21st-century America. Unfortunately, unlike the African American presence in music, sports, and other forms of popular entertainment, African-American technological contributions have never received extensive recognition.

Via the Net, we hope to see this oversight corrected.

The purpose of this book is twofold. First, it is to highlight some of the Internet and online service activities in which black Americans are engaged. Contrary to some critics, African Americans are not "road kill" on the information superhighway. Indeed, along with others, Blacks are builders and drivers on that global computer communications network loosely called the Internet.

Secondly, this book was written to encourage more African Americans to get involved with computers and modems. The future is now, and in order to help cure some of the ills that are afflicting the black community, it is critical that black America go online. The Internet is rapidly becoming an essential communications medium for corporations, universities, federal government, entrepreneurs, and private individuals. Jobs, education, civil rights, community activism, and all facets of modern life soon will be directly linked to the Internet or some advanced form of the super i-way.

Acknowledgments

It is a very painstaking but also a very pleasurable undertaking to thank the people that touch your life in so many different ways, from the beautiful Ethiopian street vendor sisters, to the extremely articulate homeless brother we refer to as "Mr. Wendell." Thanks for your smiles, thoughts, words, deeds, and gestures of support and encouragement, and for taking the time to spend some time even if it was only a few seconds.

Acknowledgments and kudos are so very rare among us. We are so very quick to criticize and ever so slow to praise or say hello, have a good day, or please and thank you. The networks work, but we have got to work them. When someone provides some assistance or aid to you, acknowledge it.

We must first and always give thanks to the Creator for continually bestowing His blessings on our lives. It is true that the Creator makes no mistakes and that everything happens for a reason. We have been challenged on all fronts, but we will prevail.

We want to thank Reba Barnes, who, though fairly new at the task, took on the role of publicist to help spread the word about the first edition of the book. Also, a warm thanks must go to Winfred Battle, who used his household money to help publish and distribute the first edition.

We want to send our appreciation to Ron Yarborough and Anita Brown for their backbone and help in some difficult times.

Also, we send many thanks to our families, friends, colleagues, and even the ne'er-do-wells and our enemies—peace and blessings from the authors.

The following is the rest of our thank-you list. In the African tradition, we have included everyone who has helped to influence, encourage, or improve our efforts. It is exhaustive; we tried to remember all who have made a difference to us. If we overlooked you, please call us and let us know.

Alyce Alexander
Carol Alexander
Zattura Amenua-El
Kent Amos
Wally Amos
Monique Anderson
Sandra Ansah
John Austin
Jessica Barbour
Joe Barbour
Joseph Barbour
Mildred Barbour
Vickie Barbour
Marion S. Barry
Lila F. Battle
Stephanie L. Battle
Winfred Battle
Larry Bland
Alvin Boss
Otis Bowman
Johnetta Bozeman
Juanita Britton
Edgar Brookins
Shirley Brookins
Anita K. Brown
Les Brown
Billy Butler
Maurice Calhoun
George Carter
James Carter
Rita Carter
Steve Carter
Alice Chandler
Benjamin Chavis
Michelle Cobbin
Bruce Codrington
Joan Collins
Marilyn Cooper
Delacy Cox
Keith Crawford
Theresa Crawford
Thomas Crawford
Algernon Daly
Jeanne Daly
Leonard Dechamps
Christine Dotson
Bernard Evans
David Faucette
Linda Faucette
George Fraser
Melvin Foote
Barry L. Ford
Elton Ghee
Lee Green
Dick Gregory
Geraldine Hailes
Aaron V. Harris
Doris E. Harris
Joe Harris
William M. Harris
William O. Harris
Cynthia Harvey
Reggie Harvey
Toni Hawkins
Earlene Haynes
Lisa Hines
Tim Hines
Wanda Hopkins
Cathy Hughes
Alicia Johns
Charles Jolley
Sheila Jones
Marshall Joseph
Mike Julius
Odis Kenton
Dennis Kimbro
Richard Knight
Gary Larson
Lester Lee
Lorna Leone
Wilbert Lewis
Levi Lipscomb
Roland Liverpool
Linda May
Michael May
Bernie McCane
Arthur McGee
Jacqueline Brown Moore

Ed Murphy
Frances Murphy
Pearl Murphy
Winston Murray
Lorna Newton
Nzinga Norman-Bey
Brimmy Olaghere
Les Parsons
Yvette Pearson
T.J. Perry
Walter Pickett
Russell Price, Jr.
Constance Ragsdale
Eldridge Ragsdale
Kya Ragsdale
William Reed
Deborah Riley
Jim Roberts
T. Robinson
Ifa Sango
David Saunders
Siobahn Scott
Nia Shabazz
Dennette Smith
Rochelle Smith
Akilah I. Spencer
Ralph Spencer
Eric St. James
Debbie Stepp
Bree Taylor
Steve Taylor
Kenneth L. Thompson
Beatrice Tignor
Ernesto Vance
Devance Walker
Cheryl Walton
Clif Ward
Debbie Ware
Akeem Washington
Al Washington
Garrett Washington
Gibran Washington
Theodore Watkins
Angela West
Laverne Wilkins
Roy Wilkins
Diane Williams
Terri Williams
Trina Williams
Melba Williams-Taylor
Debbie Wood
Ron Yarborough
Beverly Young
Muhammad Zahir

Introduction

In the 1960s and 1970s, it was Gil Scott-Heron; the revolution will not be televised; black was beautiful; and we were watching out for Big Brother. El-Hajj Malik El Shabazz, better known as Malcolm X, was chiding "If you want to keep something from the Negro, hide it between the pages of a book."

Now, in the 1990s, Gil is back with "Message to the Messenger"; we are still beautiful; Big Brother is still here; and Brother Rey's spin on Malcolm is "If you want to keep usable, pertinent information away from black people, hide it on the computer."

The Internet is a vast and fertile land rich with information, data, and mega, mega, megabytes of useful tools for the so-called "minority" community. True, racism is alive and well, but when you ask the right questions, you will receive the right responses out of a sense of surprise, guilt, or respect. We know that in the scheme of things, we are not minorities on the planet, but on the information superhighway, we're just a few hoboes and lame hitchhikers at this point. But,

Bam!

Here comes *The African American Resource Guide to the Internet and Online Services*. Find out about the World Wide Web, gophers, Archie, Veronica, chat, CD-ROM, modems, spamming, telecommuting, IP address, gateways, newsgroups, FEDWORLD, clipper chip, e-mail, frequently asked questions, teleconferencing, download, upload, digitial, analog, net etiquette, headers, net domains, top BBSs, 386, 486, Pentium chip, 686, virtual reality, tele-medicine, tele-law, IRS, CIA, CDC, FDA, EPA, DOD, DOL, SBA, MBDA, SBDC, OPM, GSA, HUD, DOJ, DOT, DOE, HHS, NASA, FAA, and the White House online crew. You can discover education, games, travel, extensive business information at little or no cost, if you know where and how to check out the Net. Like Prego spaghetti sauce, it's in there, and

Whoomp, here it is!!!!!!!

The revolution will not be televised, it will be digitized, and we are bringing you the modus operandi to function within it.

Please enjoy *The African American Resource Guide to the Internet and Online Services*. Have fun with it, as we did. And more important, learn and take control.

Peace and many blessings.

Stafford L. Battle, *sbattle@aol.com*
Rey O. Harris, *elam@mnsinc.com*

1

The Internet and the New Black Power

MANY African Americans have expressed the concern that although nearly 400 years have passed since the first African was brought to this country in chains, the long-term effects of that appalling human degradation are still felt by blacks in the United States.

During the centuries following the arrival of that unfortunate black man, numerous bloody revolts and slaughters originating from both sides of the color barrier eventually led to the Civil War between the industrial northern states and agricultural southern regions. Subsequently, slavery was abolished in theory, but harmful human indignities continued.

Yet black people, despite the lack of acknowledgment in most American history textbooks, never passively accepted their condition. Instead, they constantly refined their survival techniques and quietly changed their weapons and tactics.

In the 1920s and 1930s, the National Association for the Advancement of Colored People (NAACP) rose in prominence to challenge the lawfulness of American apartheid. During that time, black people also banded together to promote the arts, culture, and their identity in the form of the Harlem Renaissance. The achievements and talents of African Americans gained recognition and praise throughout various sections of America and the world.

Lynching, race riots, and Jim Crow practices were formidable foes, and black leaders eventually rallied behind the civil rights movement—the new battlefield. During the 1950s and 1960s, there were many martyrs, both black and white, who died for the simple belief that all people were created equal.

In the 1960s, Dr. Martin Luther King, Jr., organized millions of supporters from all walks of life. Black Power screamed across the headlines—the Nation of Islam, the Black Panthers, and other "radical" groups were feared, not solely because of their guns and rhetoric, but because of their ideas. America was in the midst of a social revolution.

During the 1970s and 1980s, many more significant battles were won, but most blacks still felt that the struggle was far from over. New weapons, new ideas, and new battle lines were formulated. African Americans were going corporate, banging on glass ceilings, forging new alliances, and healing old wounds, but most important, contrary to popular notions, by the 1990s a small segment of the African-American population began embracing futuristic technology to further the cause.

It has been more than 130 years since the Civil War officially ended and slavery was abolished in this country. Yet a large segment of

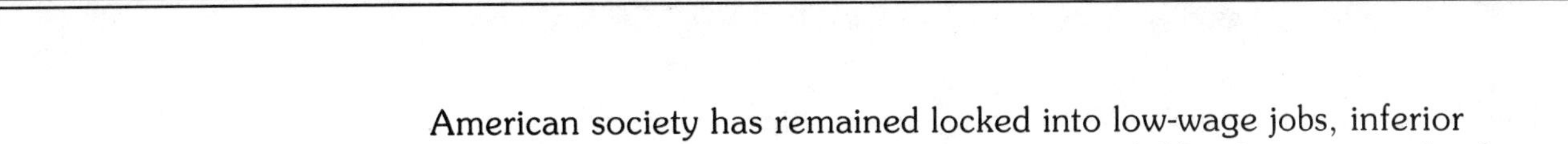

American society has remained locked into low-wage jobs, inferior schools, and destitute living conditions—much like the poor souls of the antebellum cotton plantations and northern factory workers of the late 1800s.

But we now are on the verge of a new era, and the tools for social change again are being modified. As we enter the 21st century, not only will our industrial machines and household gadgets be transformed, the way people interact with each other will be drastically altered and improved. One of the most significant changes will be the rise of the New Black Power.

The New Black Power does not rely solely on clenched fists or pithy slogans. The New Black Power is not a rapper's chant.

The New Black Power is knowledge: how to get it and how to use it wisely, profitably. The New Black Power can set fire to a million minds, instantaneously, but it does not burn. It can build. It can bring together people separated by oceans and dialects. It can uplift. And the best exchange of knowledge is through that vast, worldwide river of information known as the Internet, or the information superhighway.

The effective use of information is to gain power. Those who possess it are powerful. Rich. In the black. African Americans have the New Black Power within their grasp. With a few strokes of the keyboard, the whirr of a CD drive, and the synchronization of fingertips, black people are creating jazz on the Internet, with a serious message in the music.

Perhaps the most basic explanation of the Internet is that it is a computerized method of sending messages (e-mail) to one or a million possible individuals or organizations around the world for only a few dollars a month. Compared to the United States Postal Service or telephone charges, the convenience of the Internet is light-years ahead. You post a message on the Net and receive answers:

"Small black business, 8A certified, available for subcontract work."

"Fortune 500 company is seeking minority entrepreneurs for African development project."

"Investment dollars are available for smart businesspeople with a solid business plan. All inquiries are welcome."

"Seeking recipes for new cookbook on West African cuisine for nonprofit fund-raisers."

People respond to e-mail. Partnerships, friendships, and business alliances are formed. And this is just the tip of the information iceberg. It has been an inconspicuous message for nearly a decade among large corporations and universities that the Internet is not just the current of the future; it is the information tidal wave of things to come. Businesses and universities have been conducting transactions and reaping huge profits for years. Long-distance telephone fees are way down, expensive travel and hotel costs are being reduced, and employees are being encouraged to stay home and telecommute through the Internet.

Moreover, the best part of the Internet for companies and individuals is that it is basically *free*. The average connection cost is only $25 a month or less. Now there are *Gateways* (computer connections to the Internet) supported by local and national governments that cost less than a pay phone call to your neighbor across the street. Is it any surprise that the Internet has received so much coverage and attention in the news media?

Yet, in spite of the reporters and their sound bites, there remains considerable confusion about the Internet. To add to that confusion, many Net experts confess that nobody knows exactly of what the Internet is comprised. Among the majority of African Americans, the situation on the surface appears to be bleak. Other than Congressmen Kweisi Mfume, John Conyers, Dr. Julian Bond, and a few others, most black leaders simply shake their heads in bewilderment at the flood of technobabble and geekspeak about the Net. The Internet is so large and is connected to so many computers and has access to so much information that even the average rocket scientist is baffled. John and Jane Six-Pack have been frightened away—until now.

There are enough books and magazines about the Internet to fill the trunks of 10 gold Cadillacs. Most of the books are loaded with excessive technical jargon that changes from month to month, or they simply overwhelm the reader into various states of information overload.

One of the easiest books to read is the *Big Dummy's Guide to the Internet*, published and distributed online by the Electronic Frontier Foundation. The book states that "much of the confusion comes from the technodescription of an Internet connection versus the functional description of Internet connectivity." *Huh?!*

The book goes on to explain more clearly:

> E-mail is perhaps the easiest and most ubiquitous method of connection to the Internet. It is easy to connect different e-mail systems to the Internet, making it the de facto minimal standard for e-mail networks communication. Despite all the excitement over other Internet services like USENET Newsgroups, Gopher, WAIS,

IRC, WWW, MUDs/MOOs, and MIME, simple old e-mail still dominates usage on the Internet. E-mail connections to the Internet probably number higher than the commonly quoted 20–30 million Internet users. America Online, Prodigy, and CompuServe alone result in many millions of users accessible over Internet e-mail.

Using the Net can be as simple as writing a letter to a close friend. Moreover, it's like presenting a question at a meeting where the whole world is in attendance.

Big Dummy's Guide to the Internet

The Web version of the Big Dummy's Guide to the Internet *was produced from a book by the same title written by Adam Gaffin for a joint project of Apple Computer, Inc., and The Electronic Frontier Foundation (EFF). An online version is available free from the EFF. It is split up in more than 300 pieces, so you do not have to download the complete document at once. The best way to read this rather large and comprehensive document is to browse through the table of contents and read interesting chapters.*

The Guide contains a number of topics that will interest and amaze almost anyone. In one location, you can find out more about the history, growth, and use of the Internet. The following is a brief sample.

- *Education and the Net*
- *Hardcover & Softcover Publications*
- *Interesting FTP Sites*
- *Internet Country Codes*
- *Internet Mailing Lists*
- *Internet Origins and Facts*
- *IRC, MUDs and other things that are more fun than they sound*
- *Journal Articles and Paper*
- *Project Gutenberg—Electronic Books*
- *Public-Access Internet Providers by State*
- *The Unofficial Smiley Dictionary*
- *Usenet: The Global Watering Hole*
- *Using Electronic Mail via Various Internet Services*

About the EFF

Every day decisions are made that affect life online—decisions about what sorts of technology you can use to protect the privacy of your communications, decisions about what services you can receive over the emerging national information infrastructure, decisions that are made before you even know that there are choices. The Electronic Frontier Foundation has been working since July 1990 to ensure that the civil liberties guaranteed in the Constitution and the Bill of Rights are applied to new communications technologies.

EFF members receive the following benefits:

- *Subscription to a biweekly electronic newsletter, EFFector Online*
- *Online bulletins about the key legal, legislative, and policy developments affecting your online communications;*
- *An online response mechanism for key issues.*

You can contact the EFF at

The Electronic Frontier Foundation
1550 Bryant St., Suite 725
San Francisco, CA 94103
415-436-9333 (voice)
415-436-9993 (fax)

Send e-mail to: membership@eff.org. *EFF's Web site is located at* http://www.eff.org.

Other online publications about the Net

As far as African American online publications go, there is a rapidly growing selection. One of the first black publications to reach the Net was Black on Black Communications, *otherwise known as* BOBC News. *BOBC is an electronic newsletter that covers issues of importance to African Americans. Twice a month BOBC brings its readers vignettes on issues related to the arts, business, medicine, law, technology, sports, entertainment, health, the political process, education, and finance.*

It is a positive, concise, powerful, and relevant read for busy people who don't have time to search for this information but who can benefit from it. As an electronic newsletter, BOBC is available to anyone with an e-mail address. BOBC can also be found on the World Wide Web at http://www.i-media.com/BOBC.

Not to be outdone, other black publications are rushing to the Web. Some of the more notable pubs include:

The Afro-American Newspaper *at http://www.afroam.com*

Black Enterprise *at http://www.blackenterprise.com*

Emerge Magazine *at http://www.betnetworks.com*

YSB Magazine *at http://www.betnetworks.com*

Essence Magazine *at essenceonline.@nyo.com*

Why Black America must be online

Once you understand that the Internet is simply a computerized message system, it is easier to see practical uses. An electronic

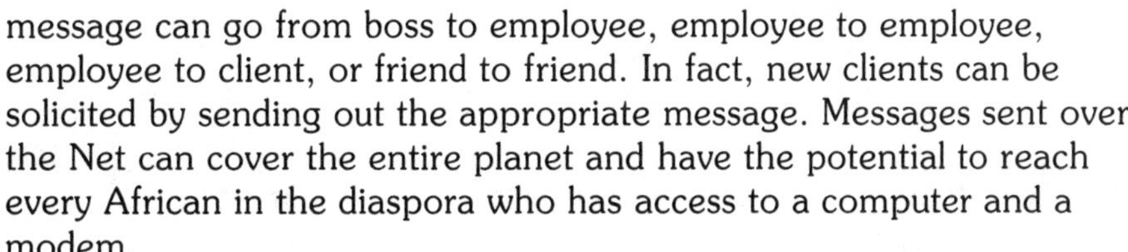

message can go from boss to employee, employee to employee, employee to client, or friend to friend. In fact, new clients can be solicited by sending out the appropriate message. Messages sent over the Net can cover the entire planet and have the potential to reach every African in the diaspora who has access to a computer and a modem.

That's the real advantage to using the Net. African Americans can send specific messages that pertain to their unique concerns more efficiently and effectively. Information exchange can help locate jobs, promote political platforms, solicit buyers, train and educate, and help to form a unified voice.

There is a newsgroup called "soc.culture.african.american" on the Net. Essentially, a newsgroup is a location in cyberspace where people who are concerned about a particular issue gather to send e-mail messages and read responses. Hundreds of messages might be posted regarding a particular issue, such as The Million Man March. The dialogue can be fast and furious, but everybody has a chance to participate.

Other topics might range from the O.J. Simpson trial to why black women shouldn't dye their hair blond. What is opened here is a window on the pulse of black America. Messages from hundreds of black professors, engineers, students, homemakers, and others can be sorted and read. Opinions, advice, referrals, and personal experiences are freely exchanged.

Some newsgroups might contain only a hundred messages at one time. (After a predetermined period of time, old or unanswered messages are erased by the sysops (system operators, or "computer gods") who oversee their particular area of the Net.) The black newsgroup soc.culture.african.american, however, has thousands of messages posted at any one time.

This represents the long-sought-after black buying dollar worth billions in revenue and spending power. Also, nonprofit organizations that are seeking to increase their membership can reach thousands of interested individuals around the world for under $25 a month.

African-American consultants are already online, communicating with e-mail that advertises their capabilities. (Services such as research and writing are easily conducted over the Net.)

Small vendors and craftspeople can communicate around the world to promote their products. Every black national organization has at least one major event a year. On the Net, someone is usually willing to take the time to announce special events and offer news coverage of the event.

The Internet is rapidly becoming the communications medium of choice. Soon it will be the only choice, because, essentially, the entire country is going "digital."

Every major telecommunications-related industry is gearing up to switch from traditional "analog" technology to computer "digital" technology. For instance, the record industry transformed literally overnight from analog LPs to digital CDs. Entire industries disappeared as new ones were born. Across the country, existing music retailers could no longer be called "record stores." A change in the way we purchased music was thrust upon us in the blink of an industrial eye.

The United States government likewise has already put into motion legislation to allow broadcast television signals to go digital. The television manufacturers already have been alerted that a big change is on the way. Inconspicuously, they have begun to redesign their factories and products. Consumers will soon be faced with the realization that all the expensive big-screen TVs they recently purchased may be obsolete before the warranties expire.

According to the 1994 edition of *The State of Black America* published by the National Urban League, African Americans purchased more than four billion dollars of consumer electronics. When TV goes digital, black wallets will be forced wide open again.

Telephone companies are retooling to allow their signals to be transmitted in digital formats. African Americans purchase a considerable amount of telephone services and equipment. Again, when the change from analog to digital arrives, black families will be lining up at their local Radio Shack store.

This major modification in our way of life can be compared roughly to the switch from horse and buggy technology to the widespread use of the automobile and its related industries. Horses can't compete on high-speed interchanges, and blacksmiths can do nothing with fuel-injected engines.

That is why black America must be online. It is not simply a matter of equality, it is a matter of survival. If African Americans, or in fact Americans of any background, do not embrace the new technologies, they will find themselves picking cotton somewhere deep in Mexico on a plantation.

Black community networks

In Cleveland, Ohio, a not-for-profit computer network called Cleveland Community Freenet provides e-mail, Internet access, and other similar amenities to people who often are not well served by online commercial services that require credit cards and bank accounts. This service has discussion groups and information about locally available opportunities.

Cleveland Freenet is considered by many to be a standard-bearer in the community network movement. The Blacksburg Electronic Village, which also has received considerable coverage in major newspapers such as *The Washington Post* and on The Discovery Channel, demonstrates the positive results of an alliance among business, civic, and educational institutions.

Community networks can become the primary information repositories to empower African Americans across the country in their move to embrace the information superhighway. Community networks can provide low-cost access to electronic mail, education, new technology, government, recreation, or just about anything else the host operators would like to place online.

According to some sources, a standard network for a medium-size city can cost in the six-figure range. The smaller systems appropriate to the needs of small local neighborhoods can be had for a tiny fraction of that cost. In fact, some community-based systems can fully serve local residents and still offer Internet access for free.

These community networks can address some of the disparities within the mainstream information infrastructure. Many communities in America cannot afford fully stocked public libraries or model school facilities. Books and buildings may be beyond the economic reach of these poorer communities. But low-cost computers, such as refurbished 386-based machines, are affordable for under $200.

Local computer networks can be repositories of knowledge accessible to low-income citizens who are bypassed by the commercialization of the information superhighway, as well as educational facilities. Like libraries, community nets can be controlled by the citizens of the local community and not by external economic interests. Even the most inexpensive community nets can offer interesting educational, social, political, and economic communication. No prior computer experience is required to access the system.

Remember, the Internet, despite its high-tech birth, can be useful to the most disadvantaged in our communities. Homeless individuals can connect with and successfully lobby the local government to fund basic amenities.

Public libraries can provide low-income individuals with access to local community freenets that contain information about housing, training, and employment. Schoolchildren can access educational resources at MIT, Harvard, Howard, or in fact nearly any university on the planet.

Users can be shown a menu of items analogous to institutions common to a community—a post office, a government municipal branch office, local health practitioners, banks, and nearby merchants. If, for instance, the user wanted information about various elected officials, accessing the municipal branch office could offer a list of menus that take the user along a path toward the information he or she needs.

The Internet offers local black communities and individuals real power to interact effectively with their government and educational institutions, health facilities, and local commerce. And, in order to interact with 21st century government, corporations, and universities, Black America must be online. Jobs, education, and political movements will all be online. Anyone who does not have access will be a non-citizen—a Neanderthal living on the fringes of human society. Black power, people power, in the future will rely heavily on access to the Internet and information.

The New Black Power movement

The New Black Power movement is growing rapidly. Within two years, a "global black family" will be a reality. It is important to note that the New Black Power will not be violent. The Reverend Dr. Martin Luther King, Jr., would be proud to see what Africans and African Americans are doing to promote their causes, improve their economic conditions, and form tangible links not only with each other but with other ethnic groups that are seeking their fair share of the American pie without resorting to open civil war.

The New Black Power doesn't exclude white people. In fact, it encourages other racial groups to listen in and see what is happening in the global black family. There are no racial boundaries on the Internet. Freedom of speech is highly valued.

Yes, the white supremacists and neo-Nazis are on the Net. And yes, someone once posted a series of racist jokes aimed at blacks. In every human society, there will always be at least one or more frightened individuals lacking in intellectual maturity and good judgment. But the Net takes care of itself. One miscreant Net user was "flamed" (electronically swamped with angry e-mail) so severely that his host mainframe computer was overloaded and temporarily shut down.

The positive aspects of the Net far outweigh the negative. And there is more than just e-mail! A Net user can tap into public databases to do research, download images for reproduction, chat in live conversations, and even receive voice or televised images. Many Net users frequently cruise the Net, traveling from computer to computer around the world, simply to see what information is available.

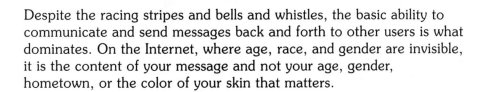

Despite the racing stripes and bells and whistles, the basic ability to communicate and send messages back and forth to other users is what dominates. On the Internet, where age, race, and gender are invisible, it is the content of your message and not your age, gender, hometown, or the color of your skin that matters.

Black Americans have been wanting, asking for, and demanding a level playing field for generations. Well, at the risk of sounding like a car commercial: We asked for it. We got it! Internet. All that remains is to make the best possible use of it. And that is up to every one of us.

2

How to Use the Internet

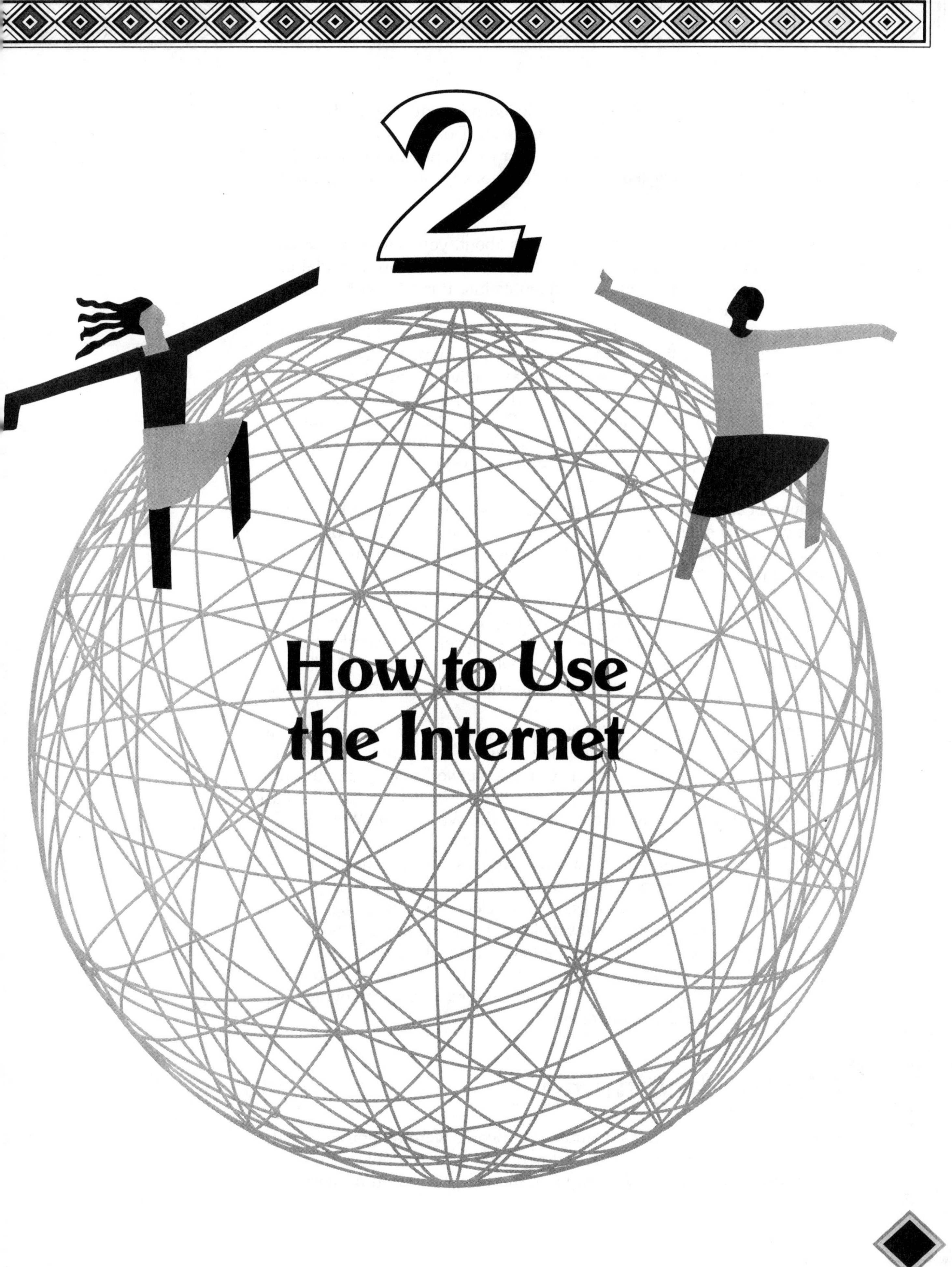

THERE is only one way to truly learn how to use the Internet: You must experience it for yourself. Dozens of books, videos, audio tapes, maps, and guides can offer excellent explanations of what the Net is, as well as provide directions to places to visit in cyberspace.

But to discover what all the shouting is about, you have to place your fingers on the computer keyboard, move the mouse around, dial in, then merge with and pour your thoughts into this all-encompassing electronic melting pot.

The Internet is so large, and connected to so many places, no one is absolutely sure how many individuals are actively using it at any given time. Estimates range from 30 to 50 million people. Business researchers have calculated that in 1995, the Net grew by as much as 160,000 new subscribers a month. By the year 2000, it is estimated that one billion people will be cruising the i-way.

Anyone can join the millions of Africans and African Americans who are currently online around the world. You only need plain old telephone service (POTS), an inexpensive personal computer, a modem, and a "gateway."

The Internet (a.k.a. information superhighway, a.k.a. the i-way, a.k.a. the Net, a.k.a. the Infobahn, a.k.a. cyberspace) is constantly changing; and there is an ongoing debate about which ramps, parallel toll roads, side streets, and back alleys should be considered legitimate parts of it.

There is a lot of misunderstanding as to what the Internet really is. In the simplest terms, it is a worldwide network of computer networks. Any computer connected to any of these networks can communicate with any other connected system. This communication can be as basic as electronic mail or as sophisticated as the World Wide Web.

It appears certain that as the world embraces digital technology, the computer will be the backbone for all modern communications. Telephones, personal digital assistants, television, radio, pagers, and other communication devices will all use the same compatible technology. The Internet, or some form of it, will be our most important window to the outside world. It will be an intimate part of our day-to-day lives. We will rely on it for education, employment, entertainment, and enlightenment.

In the beginning

In the 1970s, the earliest computer networks were tenuously linked together through Defense Department and state-run university mainframe computers. At that time, the i-way was used primarily for

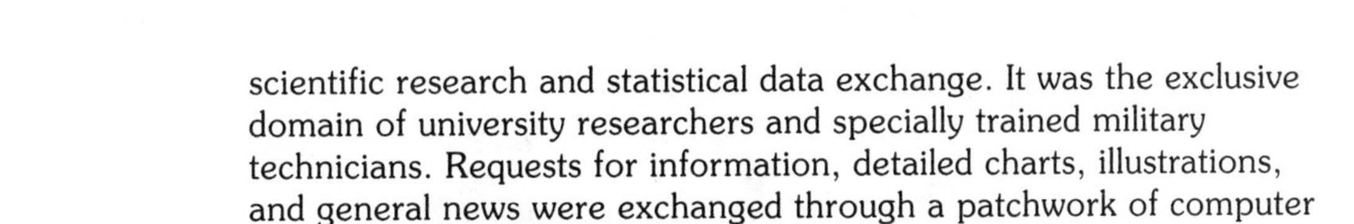

scientific research and statistical data exchange. It was the exclusive domain of university researchers and specially trained military technicians. Requests for information, detailed charts, illustrations, and general news were exchanged through a patchwork of computer connections. The designers' goal was to be able to quickly disseminate critical knowledge in the event of a nuclear attack on certain sections of the United States.

Since scientists and high-level planners were the principle players, everyone using the Net had some expertise with obscure computer commands and resolving conflicting communication problems. Because of the lack of established procedures and standardization from computer to computer, using the Net required a hatful of collegiate degrees, several buckets of patience, and a mountain of guesswork.

A decade ago, when ordinary people began to venture onto the Net, significant changes began to occur. User-friendly Internet tools began to appear. Services such as Gopher, Archie, Veronica, and others made finding information as well as connecting with other computers simpler and faster. E-mail became the most heavily used and navigable lane on the information superhighway.

Common Internet Tools

In the bad old days, before the World Wide Web, some of the common Internet tools first developed were Telnet, FTP, Archie, Gopher, Veronica, and Jughead. Today, you might never encounter any of these tools, but occasionally, you might find it useful (perhaps at cocktail parties) to have a deeper understanding of what the true pioneers had to deal with.

Telnet

Telnet is one of the original Internet tools. It allows you, a computer user in one location, to establish an online connection with another computer elsewhere. The other (remote) computer might be across town or around the world—it doesn't matter.

Once a connection has been established, you can use the resources of the remote computer system as if you are physically colocated with it. The Telnet process is completely transparent to you, the user. The remote host computer "thinks" your computer is connected dirrectly to it and responds accordingly. When you Telnet, you might need to use your password and ID for the remote computer.

File Transfer Protocol

File Transfer Protocol (FTP) is an Internet tool that lets you transfer (send and receive) files from one Internet-connected computer to another. It is an important tool because it enables you to find the data or information of interest to you and transfer it back to your individual computer for later use.

A variety of files can be retrieved and transferred, including text files, software programs, graphic images, sound, video, and photographs. FTP is especially useful when transferring large data files over the Internet. Unfortunately, with FTP, you are unable to look at the contents of a file while you are online. You need to transfer a copy of the file to your computer and then view it. Also, in most instances, files are compressed to help speed transmission. Once you receive the file, you have to decompress the files using decompression tools that are available for free from your Internet service provider. The good news is that, today, most files automatically decompress themselves.

Many Internet sites have publicly accessible areas where files can be retrieved and transferred by any Internet user. These are known as "anonymous FTP sites," To access the site, you need to know its FTP address. You then generally login (also referred to as userid) as "anonymous." Use your e-mail address as your password.

Archie

Archie is a tool that searches all registered FTP sites that are indexed by title and keyword. The easiest way to initiate this type of search is by logging into a remote Archie site via a Telnet connection. Once you have established a successful connection, type "archie" at the login or userid prompt.

Some of the common Archie addresses are:

telnet archie.sura.net

telnet archie.rutgers.edu

telnet archie.ans.net

telnet archie.unl.net

telnet archie.ds.internic.net

Gopher

While FTP is an important tool that allows you to transfer files across the Internet, it doesn't let you easily "browse" a site to see what type of information and data is available. Gopher, another Internet tool, was designed to do just that.

In "gopher space," data and information are organized in broad categories. With this tool, you literally "burrow" through lists of menus with increasing specificity until you reach your level of interest.

Developed at the University of Minnesota in 1991 (the university's mascot is a gopher), Gopher was the Internet's most user-friendly tool, until the recent emergence of the World Wide Web. Gopher allows you to go out, select, and view the information.

As with other Internet tools, to access a gopher site, you must know its address. For example, if you want to connect to the gopher site at the Bureau of Transportation Statistics, you would type:

gopher.bts.gov

You would then receive the main menu in the form of a list of folders. When you click on a folder, you receive more specific information in other folders. Eventually, you see your destination in the form of a text document that you can open and read online.

There are thousands of gopher locations containing valuable information and data. But several "meta" sites offer good starting points to begin your exploration of gopher space. One of these is the "Mother Gopher" at the University of Minnesota, accessible at the following address:

gopher.boombox.micro.umn.edu

Veronica and Jughead

Veronica helps you search gopher space by filtering through directories or documents. Many gopher sites have a Veronica search capability embedded as a menu selection. Jughead is similar to Veronica, but it only searches a particular site rather than all of gopher space. Both these tools might require a tiny knowledge of UNIX commands if you wander down a back alley and can't find your way home.

The advantages of using the Net to transfer information was clearly evident among novices and experts alike. Long or detailed documents such as computer software, which may contain thousands of lines of code, could travel directly from computer to computer. Many tedious hours of rekeying academic reports or business proposals or transporting bulky computer tapes could be avoided.

The early Net was a great resource as long as you had access to a mainframe computer. But mainframes cost millions of dollars, and only major universities, large corporations, or government facilities had them. For years, the number of users on the Net remained small and elite.

When the personal computer was introduced to the general public in the 1980s, the door to the Internet was kicked wide open. A much larger segment of society could afford to purchase its way onto the Internet. Now that you've heard the sizzle, let's get down to the steak. Getting onto the Net is as easy as one, two, three:

Step one: Purchasing a personal computer

Step two: Selecting a gateway

Step three: Starting to cruise!

Step one: Purchasing a personal computer

The earliest computers, in the 1950s, were mechanical monstrosities jammed with vacuum tubes, clicky-clock switches, miles of wire, springs, prongs, and other moving parts. By the 1960s and the beginning of the Space Age, the transistor had replaced vacuum tubes, and computers no longer filled entire warehouses, just a corner of a large conference room. These updated mainframe computers were the computational marvels that put men on the moon, sized up the American population, and calculated our growing national debt.

As technology improved, machines got faster, smaller, and more powerful. In fact, today's wristwatch calculator has as much power as the 1950s' powerhouse mainframes.

Hardware and software

Almost everything you need to know about computers will fall under the description of hardware or software. Computer hardware consists of the physical components of a computer system such as the monitor, keyboard, mouse, CPU, printer, and scanner.

Computer software (or programs) consists of coded instructions telling the computer how to perform the wide variety of duties of which it is capable. There are software packages created to let you write letters, fax documents, draw pictures, publish magazines, calculate business expenses, and thousands of other functions.

Most software is accompanied by a manual of instructions. But software manuals are notoriously difficult to read. There also are videotapes, books, and magazines that can provide clearer advice on how to get the best from your software. You might want to invest in one of these if you are having difficulty with a new program.

As this book goes to press, the IBM compatibles (often called "clones") and Apple Macintoshes are far and away the two most popular personal computers. The IBM clones are also known as DOS- (disk operating system) or Windows-based machines. Many people refer to IBM clones as PCs. Macintoshes are called Macs or Power PCs, depending on their level of sophistication.

Macintosh machines have gained popularity due to their reputation for ease of use and superior graphics capabilities. Until recently, Macs also had the edge in what is referred to as "multimedia" software. With the advent of multimedia PCs, the gap has narrowed dramatically. Multimedia involves the use of a computer to manipulate

sound, video, photography, and typography for movies, animated features, and other presentations. For this and other reasons, Mac users are fiercely loyal and can point out dozens of other advantages over rival PCs.

PCs, on the other hand, can boast that they outnumber Macs in use by roughly 10 to 1. Because of the size of the PC market, it is more profitable for software developers to focus on products for them. There are considerably more software packages and hardware accessories for PCs than Macs. Moreover, PCs have always cost much less than Macs. PCs also can be hand-built from kits, thus lowering the price even more.

Regardless of which computer you choose, any minimally equipped PC or Mac is more than adequate to access the Net. To cruise in any degree of style, however, requires a bit more horsepower. You need a computer with a processor running at a minimum of 40 MHz, 8MB of RAM, and 300–400MB of disk storage. Most machines sold in stores these days are in that range, so we're not talking about anything too exotic.

You can purchase a new machine for as little as $900. But after adding accessories and "racing stripes"—larger hard drive, more RAM, faster modem, CD-ROM drive—you will probably spend closer to $1500 for your new system. The best prices will be found in mail-order catalogs. First-time computer buyers, however, should consider buying from a local retail outlet that has a knowledgeable sales staff and nearby service and repair center, or from a large company that offers technical support. Be warned, your darling new machine will one day "crash," break down and/or malfunction. That is why you must always back up your work on diskettes or tape drives.

Backing up your information

One of the greatest mistakes you can make is failing to maintain current backup copies of your entire system, especially critical files. Until lately, doing a full backup has required a large number of time and diskettes, or a tape backup system. Neither of these alternatives is anything close to ideal. Recently, new technology has become available that makes the process much easier and less expensive. For under $200 you can purchase a disk drive with removable cartridges.

These removable disks are much like floppy disks, though slightly larger, but are able to store 100 megabytes of information or more. The cartridges are very inexpensive (only about $15 each) and are nearly as fast as a conventional hard disk. Best of all, when you're not using this device for backup purposes, it is available to supplement your main storage system. You can purchase cartridges at about a tenth the cost of an equivalent amount of ordinary hard disk storage.

Be sure to include such a device on your shopping list if you can. It is one of the best bargains in the computer industry. Perhaps best of all, it encourages the practice of frequently creating backups, rather than discourage it. Compared to diskette or tape backup, it is a tremendous improvement.

Many microcomputers are "bundled" packages. Some come with everything you need—hardware and software—to get online immediately already installed on the system. Be sure to inform the salesperson of what you plan to do with your machine before you purchase. This way, you'll have a better chance of getting the best package for your needs and your budget.

While "bundled" systems are convenient, there are also some pitfalls. First and foremost, they tend to be an overpriced collection of about-to-become-out-of-date technology. There is a better than even chance that you could buy something more current for the same or even less money.

The software bundled with these systems is almost always of minimal functionality. It may look like the greatest thing since sliced bread when you see it at the store, but when you start using it, you may find there are important things it won't do. With that said, if your needs are not too demanding and you don't know exactly what you want to do, then take what you can get knowing that it is more of a learning experience than a permanent solution. Later, when you are more familiar with what you do and don't need, go out and buy software that is better suited to your tasks.

Desktop computers are better buys than laptop or notebook computers because it is expensive to reduce the size and power consumption of all the components. Laptops and notebook computers are extremely useful if you must be able to take your computer, and the data stored in it, with you frequently. Otherwise, they are an expensive luxury. If your circumstance requires, you may want to have both a desktop and portable system.

One last word on bundles. Most of the stores selling such systems are of the supermarket variety—department stores, electronic outlets, etc. Too often, they are not equipped to answer your questions well when you are buying and even less equipped to support you after the sale. (A riddle: What's the difference between a computer salesman and a used car salesman? Answer: The used car salesman knows when he's lying to you.)

Laptops cost hundreds of dollars more than desktops, and you get fewer accessories. When you purchase your desktop machine, you can expect to receive the following components.

Essential hardware

CPU

Technically, the CPU (central processing unit) is a single computer chip that functions as the brain of your computer. The term has also come to mean the box that contains, in addition to the actual CPU chip itself, all the supporting circuits, a power supply, modems, disk drives, and everything else that is built into the system. The actual CPU chip represents the limit of the amount of work your computer can do in a given period of time. The faster the CPU, the faster it can get work done. You need to choose a computer with a CPU that is capable of doing everything you need it to do. In the Apple world, your best choice is the Mac Performa or Quadra Series. If you buy a PC, get one with a 486 or Pentium CPU chip.

RAM (random access memory)

RAM is computer memory used by the CPU to manipulate data and programs. The more RAM you have, the more programs your computer can run at once. In order to fully utilize most modern system software, you will need a minimum of 8 megabytes (MB) of RAM. The amount of RAM you have can also affect the speed at which your software operates. Be prepared to add more memory as new memory-hungry software products reach the marketplace.

Hard drive

Your computer's hard disk drive is its primary storage device. Everything you want to store on your computer—programs, data files, pictures, etc.—takes up space on your hard drive. As PC software become more sophisticated and "user friendly," it also becomes larger. As a result, the amount of space required to store it increases. Only a few years ago, 40MB of storage was considered adequate. Nowadays, if you have less than 400MB, you are considered a poverty case. In the next few years, 1 gigabyte (GB) (1000MB) will be the norm.

Color monitor

Monitors come in a variety of sizes and resolutions. A 14" VGA monitor is adequate for most purposes. However, because many of the graphics on the Net contain millions of colors with high resolution, a Super VGA (SVGA) monitor can be very useful. It's not that you can't view images that are beyond the capacities of your monitor. It's just that a sunset over Cape Town isn't much to look at when it is reduced to 16 colors. And that's most likely exactly what you'll get when viewing it on a standard VGA monitor. Ultimately, the best advice when choosing a monitor is to let your wallet do the talking.

Modem

Modems connect your computer to the telephone lines which in turn connect you to an Internet service provider and the Internet itself. The speed of a modem is proportionate to the "baud rate" at which it operates. The baud rate is roughly equivalent to the number of bits-per-second at which it is able to send and receive information over the phone. The higher the baud rate, the faster you can send and receive information. In order to view online graphics or retrieve large files in a reasonable amount of time (less than an hour), you must have a 14.4 modem (14,400 baud) or above. If you can afford it, purchase a 28.8 (28,800 baud) modem. If your job depends on state-of-the-art Internet connections, you should request that your employer install an ultra-fast ISDN line. Using an ISDN connection, you can receive Internet information much faster than POTS.

Printer

You will always need a printer for a number of reasons. For one, there may never be a completely paperless office. Until and unless there is, your paper output needs to look as good as possible. The good news is that many relatively inexpensive printers produce very high-quality documents. At the low end of the spectrum are ink jet and bubble jet printers. These start at around $200 in today's market and produce documents that rival those of more expensive laser printers. Many are also available in color models or have add-on modules to provide full color capabilities. The main differences between these and their laser-based counterparts is cost and speed. If the difference between three pages a minute and eight pages a minute is important, then spring for a laser printer. Otherwise, put your money into something that will do you more good (like a faster modem, more memory, or a bigger hard drive).

CD-ROM drive

The basic technology used in CD-ROM devices is virtually identical to the CD player connected to your stereo system. The difference is that one is used to store only music and the other is used to store almost anything. Unlike ordinary magnetic disks, CD-ROMs store information as tiny pits in the smooth surface of the disk. The information is then read by a laser light beam. The other difference is that you cannot ordinarily modify the information on a CD-ROM disk. There are drives that allow this, but they are extremely expensive (20–50 times as much as a read-only drive). CD-ROM drives can be installed in your CPU or as an external unit. Most multimedia software is available only on CD. Movies, encyclopedias, cartoons, games, software, and everything you can imagine can be found on CDs.

Keyboard and mouse

Keyboards and mouse input devices also come in many styles. Sit down and test drive several models before you purchase. A keyboard should be comfortable, with support for your wrists. The mouse should glide easily but remain under control. Since they all work about the same, your choice should ultimately be the one that feels right.

First kid on the block syndrome

Some people are afflicted with the need to be the first to try new technologies. This can be a risky proposition. The trouble is that often new products, especially if they are in some way revolutionary, are a little green around the edges. There may be problems with them for which solutions are not immediately available. Sometimes you may have to pay to make them work even after a fix is provided. Unless you have a crying need for some exotic new feature, try to steer clear of these tempting new revelations. It could save you a lot of heartache later.

Optional but fun stuff to have

Stereo speakers

Hey! Did you know you can play your favorite music CDs on your computer while you work? Well, you can. And it's true stereo too. For the best sound, you will want to connect your computer directly to your stereo system. You will, of course, need a multimedia-capable computer to do this. Be sure to make that clear when buying the unit.

Microphone

You can send voice announcements along with your written notes, or dub your own music soundtracks. Also, with the advent of new telephone-like software, you can actually talk to people all over the world through the Internet. At present, this type of software is very new and is more like a two-way radio in actual practice, but there are no long-distance charges. You will need a multimedia-capable machine.

Video camera

Yes! If you already have a camera, you can hook it up to your computer for as little as $100, though more powerful products can cost several times that much. Video images also can be transmitted along with text files over the Net. Video phones and video conferencing are becoming common in cyberspace. Expect even more of that in the near future.

Essential software

Software packages perform specific functions such as word-processing, mailing list management, or graphic designing. You can purchase individual programs for particular needs or acquire a multipurpose software package, such as Claris Works or Microsoft Works, which provide software for word-processing, spreadsheets, telecommunications, database management, and more. Often, one of these combination packages will be bundled with your hardware purchase.

You need some kind of telecommunication software to access the Internet. Depending on how you connect to and use the Internet, you may need anything from a single terminal program to a whole library of specialized applications.

The so-called Big Three commercial online companies will provide you with all the software you need to access their services. The software provided by such a service, however, is only usable for that service.

For a simple UNIX "shell" account, almost any program with terminal emulation will get the job done. For an IP (Internet protocol) account, you need separate programs for the World Wide Web, Telnet, FTP, e-mail, and other purposes. Your Internet service provider can recommend a collection of programs with which it has experience. Most will provide them to you either online or on disk. Virtually all modems come with some kind of terminal emulation software with which you can download whatever else you need. (For a more detailed discussion of these issues, read the sidebar at the end of the section on Small Commercial Internet Providers.)

In addition to the software needed to actually access the Internet or other online services, you need a collection of utility programs. These are small, specialized programs used for purposes such as these:

- Compress/decompress files to reduce their size for storage and transmission.
- Encode files for security or other purposes.
- Viewers to allow you to view various graphics formats, movie clips, and other specialized data.

All of these programs can be downloaded from the Net once you are online and may even be provided by your service provider as part of a "start-up" software package.

The bottom line for choosing a computer

If you are starting from scratch, your first of many choices to make will be which computer to buy. Although Macintosh has for years enjoyed the reputation of being more user-friendly than the PC, the differences between them have become increasingly blurred. Now, the differences are minimal for most purposes. Even Mac devotees are calling Windows 95 "the best Mac clone so far."

Perhaps more important than the actual capabilities of the computers themselves are questions like: What do my friends and coworkers use? What am I already familiar with? What have I always wanted?

If you are a "newbie" (anyone new to the Internet) or are unfamiliar with using microcomputers, you may want to select one of the mid-range Macintosh Performa series and start with the following configuration: Performa CPU; 8MB of RAM; a 260MB hard drive; 28.8 baud fax/modem. The alternative is a similarly equipped Pentium-based PC.

If you're on a tight budget, you can make do with an inexpensive used machine. If at all possible, get a PC with at least an 80386 CPU that either has or can be expanded to at least 4MB of RAM. This will let you use a World Wide Web browser, though at a sacrifice in speed. You should be able to find a system like this for around $300–500.

For those who are on an even more limited budget, DOS-based PCs are around for about $100. Most computers at that kind of price won't be exactly overflowing with horsepower, but they can be quite serviceable for a UNIX shell account (see p. 30), especially with a fairly fast modem. One good strategy in such a case is to get whatever you can afford and find some way to make the computer pay for its replacement. It can and has been done, though it may take some imagination, effort, and time.

If you plan to use the Internet for your small business, select a Pentium-based PC with the following equipment: Pentium-based CPU; 16MB of RAM; 1GB (gigabyte) hard drive; 28.8 baud modem; quad speed CD-ROM drive.

Step two: Choosing an Internet gateway

Before you can start traveling on the information superhighway, you must find an "on-ramp." All this really means is that you must connect your computer to one that is already permanently connected to the

Internet. There are thousands of computers that are capable of connecting others in this fashion. They are operated by schools, government agencies, large online services, small local companies, and private institutions of all kinds. Your job is to find one that will provide a connection for you with the services you want and at a price you are willing and able to pay. What follows will help you in that process.

There are five types of on-ramps that will be discussed here:

- Major commercial online services
- Small commercial Internet providers
- Corporations on the Internet
- Government and nonprofit systems
- Computer bulletin boards (BBSs)

Major commercial online services

Commercial online services can be thought of as toll roads on the information superhighway. Though each of them has their own payment schedules which change periodically due to competition and other factors, the basic scheme is usually about the same. You pay a flat monthly fee to have an account on their system. For that fee you receive access to some basic services and a number of hours of free use of additional "premium" services. Once your monthly allotment of free time is used up, you must pay an hourly fee for additional time. Most Internet services usually are considered in the premium category. This means that after the first few hours, the meter goes on and the price starts climbing. The largest of these services, sometimes called the Big Three, are America Online (AOL), Prodigy, and CompuServe. Although the numbers change almost daily, all these services have in the neighborhood of two or three million users and are growing at a breathtaking pace. Lest you think that these guys are just plain ripping you off, there are several advantages to being connected to one of them.

Friendly software and customer support

The Big Three each offer their own proprietary software. It may even come already installed on your computer when you bring it home. If not, it is (theoretically) easy to install and use. It offers a single, integrated interface to all of their own services as well as the Internet.

Each also offers user support to help you get what you want out of their system. They have a strong preference for helping you through various online help functions. These can range from documentation available online to e-mail support services, to online "live" chat rooms in which you can interact directly with real, living humans. All provide forums in which users can help each other. In most cases, the meter stops running while you are consulting user support.

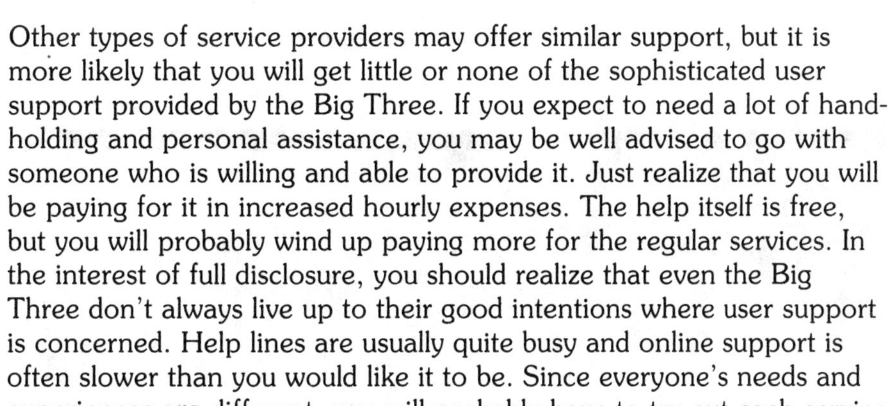

Other types of service providers may offer similar support, but it is more likely that you will get little or none of the sophisticated user support provided by the Big Three. If you expect to need a lot of hand-holding and personal assistance, you may be well advised to go with someone who is willing and able to provide it. Just realize that you will be paying for it in increased hourly expenses. The help itself is free, but you will probably wind up paying more for the regular services. In the interest of full disclosure, you should realize that even the Big Three don't always live up to their good intentions where user support is concerned. Help lines are usually quite busy and online support is often slower than you would like it to be. Since everyone's needs and experiences are different, you will probably have to try out each service and make your own decision. That is one reason to take advantage of the "free introductory offer" offered by all of them. If you aren't happy with the fees or service after a few weeks, cancel and move on. It won't cost you anything to experiment that way.

Proprietary content

All of these services provide huge amounts of information that is available only to their subscribers. This includes news, weather, and sports, as well as software databases, product reviews, encyclopedias, and thousands of other offerings. Much of this information is now available on the Internet for free, but each service has certain content that is unique to them. The real question becomes one of what you are willing to pay for and how much.

The Big Three travel well

If you travel and want to stay connected, you will probably want an account on one of the major services. They all have local phone numbers in hundreds of cities nationwide, and in some cases worldwide. In the unlikely event that you are visiting your Aunt Sally in Toad Suck, Arkansas (yes, there really is such a place), you can call an 800-number and still be connected at a cost that is probably less than calling long-distance to a larger city. If you don't need this convenience, you may not want to pay for it.

Local availability

If you live in an area where the major services are the only ones that offer a local access number, you may have little choice but to pay their hourly rates. They will probably be about half the cost of calling long-distance to the nearest city offering an alternative. With Internet providers popping up everywhere, this consideration is becoming less common every day. There are local Internet providers in towns with as few as 8000 people in fairly isolated places.

Newcomers to the ranks of commercial service providers include the Microsoft Network, Digital Link from the Washington Post, the ImagiNation Network for AT&T, and Apple's E-World.

Figures 2-1, 2-2, and 2-3 show the opening screens of the Big Three.

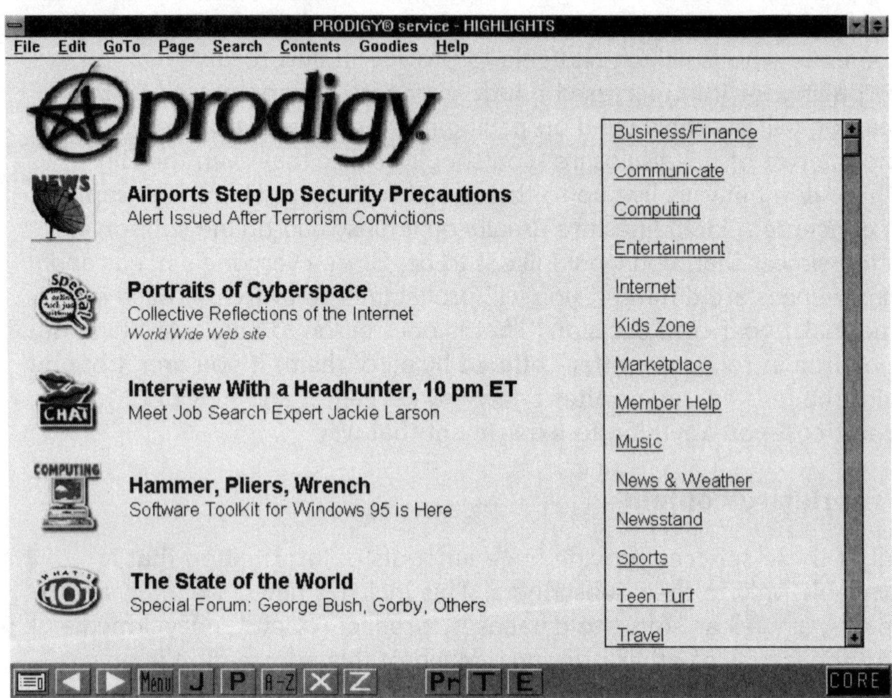

Fig. 2-1 *Prodigy's opening screen*

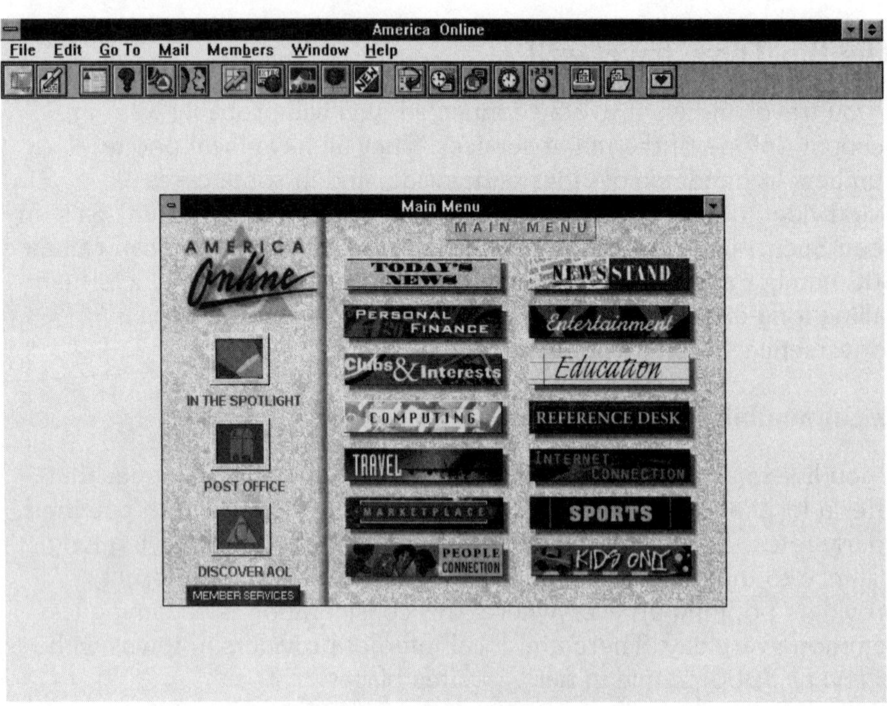

Fig. 2-2 *America Online's opening screen*

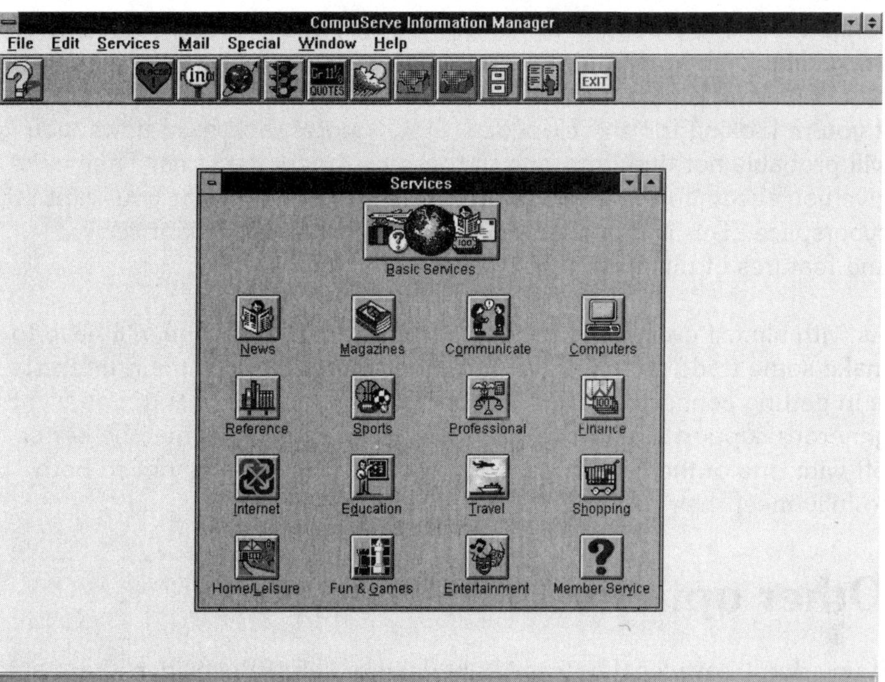

Fig. 2-3 *CompuServe's opening screen*

Small commercial Internet providers

The fastest-growing segment of online companies are relatively small Internet service providers (ISPs). These may have anywhere from a few dozen to tens of thousands of subscribers. Unlike the large commercial networks such as AOL, Prodigy, and CompuServe, they don't generally provide original content. Their primary job is to provide you with an on-ramp to the i-way and not with news, entertainment, and other value-added features.

More often than not, ISPs are considerably less expensive for anything beyond minimal use than are the big networks. Many of them will sell you unlimited access for a flat fee of around $25 a month. This basic fee is somewhat higher than the big networks, but if you are online more than a few hours a month, you soon will more than make up the difference in savings.

There are several potential disadvantages to using these private providers. You may not be able to find one suitable for your needs within your local calling area. This is unlikely to happen unless you are well outside even a modest population center, but it can.

If you want a lot of hand-holding, you may not get it from these companies. They are not best known for their customer TLC. They see their primary job as providing you with high-quality access technology, not a nurturing environment in which to learn. These

companies simply don't usually have the skill and resources to support things like 24-hour 800-numbers and such.

If you're looking for encyclopedias, stock quotes, and hard news, you will probably not find it on one of these providers' systems. They only give you access to the Internet. It's up to you to find what you want in cyberspace. This is only a disadvantage if you need or want services and features of this type.

As with almost everything connected with technology, you will have to make some trade-offs. You can get more for less if your main interest is in getting connected to the Internet. If, on the other hand, you want generous support and lots of prepackaged content, you may be better off with one of the Big Three. Many people find that they need both to fully meet their needs. The choice is yours.

Other options

If you don't have local access to any kind of service provider, there are nationwide providers who let you connect through an 800-number. It should come as no surprise that you will pay more for this service. Typically (if there is any such thing), you will pay the following fees: initial setup of \$35–\$50, flat monthly fee of \$15–\$35, and an hourly fee of \$5–\$10 depending on the service and time of day. Some of these providers have nonmetered 800-service at a cost of \$200–\$300 a month. In other words, it will cost you about ten times as much as the same service would if locally available.

UNIX shell and IP accounts

If you choose to go with an ISP, you will have one or both of the following types of accounts. There are fundamental differences between UNIX shell accounts and so-called IP accounts. When you connect to a host using a shell account, your computer becomes a "dumb" terminal on that system. In other words, it is as if you were sitting right there in the host's computer room at a terminal wired directly to their machine. This means, among other things, that the programs you use—e-mail readers, Telnet, and FTP, among others—are actually running on the host computer. Your computer is nothing more than a keyboard and a video monitor connected to the host system. The only software needed on your computer is a terminal program that teaches your computer how to pretend to be (called "emulation") a dumb terminal.

IP (Internet protocol) connections are quite different. Your computer dials the phone and establishes a connection, but that's where the similarity ends. An IP connection actually gives your computer its own presence on the Internet, coequal with your host and all the other millions of computers on the Net. The host computer simply provides you with a place to "plug in" to the Internet. Once that has been accomplished, the host acts as a simple (if anything like this can

be called simple) conduit through which your computer sends and receives data to and from the Internet.

There are great advantages to IP connections, and some disadvantages. First, because the host computer is there to serve as a conduit, its role is essentially passive. You must run the programs on your computer, instead of the host doing it. If you want to do e-mail, you need a mail program. To browse the Web, you need a Web browser. The same goes for FTP, Telnet, newsgroups, and all the other facilities available on the Internet. Since both IBM-compatibles and Macs are multitasking computers (they can run multiple programs simultaneously), you can run several of these programs at once. In other words, you can be composing an e-mail with one program, downloading a file with another, and waiting for an Internet phone call with yet another—all at the same time.

The same software that dials the phone for you usually takes care of managing the traffic shuttling between your computer and the host. All the programs are able to share this common resource at once. It is just another one of the modern miracles of technology. Amazingly, it works quite well.

The programs running on your computer are called client software. Their counterparts on the various system of the Internet are called servers. Clients use servers to do their bidding, which is actually your bidding. Many of the developers who have created such programs make them available on the Internet itself either as freeware or shareware. Your service provider should have everything you need available for downloading. Many even bundle several commonly used programs into a "starter kit" to make things simpler for you.

At the minimum you should have a Web browser and an e-mail program. Since browsers allow you to download files from FTP sites, navigate gopher menus, and read newsgroups, there is little need to have separate software for those purposes. Hopefully, it will soon become common for all Web browsers to fully support e-mail too. Most already allow you to jot off a quick note, but not receive and read messages.

Corporate accounts

Many corporations' internal computer networks are also connected to the Internet. If you are employed by one of these companies, you may have access to the Internet in that way.

You may or may not be authorized to use the Internet for personal purposes by calling in from home with your personal computer. If you are, you are fortunate indeed. Most employers, however, frown on personal use of company Internet access.

Government and nonprofit systems

Various governmental agencies provide some kind of public-access computer services. Many take the form of dial-up BBSs. These you must call directly by phone. Although a few have 800-numbers, most will be a long-distance call unless you happen to live in the same city. Most of these same services also are available on the Internet already. The rest will be soon.

Some communities offer free, or very inexpensive, access to the Internet. One of the first of these was the Cleveland Freenet in Cleveland, Ohio. Blacksburg, Virginia, has tried getting the whole town online with great success.

Below is a list of over 100 freenets in the USA. Some are sponsored by government agencies while others are operated by nonprofit organizations. Most allow free use by registered users. Registration is usually free also and can be done online or by picking up a form at a local library.

The services offered vary from one to another, but most have lots of local information, chat and discussion groups, and e-mail services, as well as other Internet facilities. You are typically limited to 60 minutes per session, but you may call as often as you wish. If you are lucky enough to live in an area with a freenet, it might be a good idea to try it out first, before you sign up with a service that will cost you money. At least you'll be a smarter shopper when the time comes.

If you don't see a freenet for your area on the list below, check with your local library. These nets usually work very closely with the libraries in the area. Chances are that if your librarian doesn't know about it, it's simply not there. Figure 2-4 shows Detroit Free-Net's home page.

- Akron Regional Free-Net (gopher)
- Alachua Freenet (telnet) login=visitor
- Alachua Freenet (WWW)
- Arizona Telecommunication Community (AzTeC) (telnet) login=guest,password=visitor
- Austin Free-Net (WWW)
- Big Sky Telegraph (telnet) login=bbs
- Blacksburg Electronic Village (Virginia) (WWW)
- Boulder Community Network (telnet) login=bcn
- Boulder Community Network (WWW)
- Buffalo Free-Net (telnet) login=freeport

Fig. 2-4 *Detroit Free-Net's home page*

- Buffalo Free-Net (WWW)
- Cambridge (MA) Civic Network (WWW)
- CapAccess : National Capital Area Public Access Network (telnet) login=guest password=visitor
- CapAccess : National Capital Area Public Access Network (WWW)
- CedarNet, Iowa
- Center for Civic Networking (gopher)
- Charlotte's Web (Charlotte, North Carolina) (WWW)
- Chesapeake Free-Net (telnet)
- Chesapeake Free-Net (WWW)
- Cleveland Free-Net (telnet) login=visitor
- COIN—Columbia Online Information Network (telnet) login=guest
- COIN—Columbia Online Information Network (WWW)
- Corvallis Metronet (gopher)
- CVaNet—Central Virginia's Free-Net (telnet) login=guest, password=visitor
- CVaNet—Central Virginia's Free-Net (WWW)

- DANEnet (Wisconsin) (telnet) login=guest
- DANEnet (Wisconsin) (WWW)
- Davis Community Network (WWW)
- Dayton Free-Net (telnet) login=visitor
- Denver Freenet (gopher)
- Denver Free-Net (telnet) login=guest
- EnviroFreenet (telnet) login=Press RETURN,password=Press RETURN
- EnviroFreenet (WWW)
- Eugene Free-Net (telnet) login=guest,password=Hit RETURN
- Eugene Free-Net (WWW)
- Fortnet: Fort Collins Community Computer Network (telnet) login=guest
- Fortnet: Fort Collins Community Computer Network (WWW)
- Genesee Free-Net (gopher)
- Genesee Free-Net (telnet) login=guest
- Genesee Free-Net (WWW)
- Grand Rapids Free-Net (telnet) login=visitor
- Grand Rapids Free-Net (WWW)
- Great Lakes Free-Net (telnet) login=visitor,password=visitor
- Greater Columbus Free-Net (gopher)
- Greater Columbus Free-Net (WWW)
- Greater Detroit FreeNet (telnet) login=visitor
- Greater Detroit FreeNet (WWW)
- Greater New Orleans Free-Net (telnet) login=visitor
- Greater New Orleans Free-Net (WWW)
- Heartland Regional Network, the community network for Central Illinois (telnet) login=bbguest, password=Press RETURN
- Huron Valley Community Network (WWW)
- IthacaNet, Ithaca, N.Y. (WWW)
- Jackson, TN Area Free-Net (telnet) login=visitor
- Jackson, TN Area Free-Net (WWW)
- La Plaza de Taos (Taos, NM) (gopher)
- Lebanon/Laclede Information Online Network (telnet) login=guest

- Lebanon/Laclede Information Online Network (LLION) (WWW)
- Lehigh Valley Free-Net (WWW)
- LibertyNet (telnet) login=liberty,password=liberty
- LibertyNet (WWW)
- Lorain County FREE-NET (telnet) login=guest
- Los Angeles Free-Net (telnet) login=Select (2) for visitor
- Macatawa Area Free-Net (WWW)
- Metropolitan Tucson Electronic Communications Network (METCOM) (gopher)
- Michiana Free-Net (WWW)
- MidNet: Community Access Network for Columbia & the Midlands of South Carolina (telnet) login=visitor
- Milwaukee Omnifest (telnet) login=visitor
- Mobile Area Free-Net (telnet) login=visitor
- Mobile Area Free-Net (WWW)
- Naples Free-Net (telnet) login=guest,password=guest
- Naples Free-Net (WWW)
- North Texas FreeNet (WWW)
- Ocean State Free-Net (gopher)
- Omaha Free-Net (telnet) login=visitor
- Omaha Free-Net (WWW)
- Ozarks Regional Information Online Network (ORION) (telnet) login=guest
- Ozarks Regional Information Online Network (ORION) (WWW)
- Prairienet: the Free-Net of East-Central Illinois (gopher)
- Prairienet, the Free-Net of East-Central Illinois (telnet) login=visitor
- Prairienet: the Free-Net of East-Central Illinois (WWW)
- RAIN, The Regional Alliance for Information Network (gopher)
- RAIN, The Regional Alliance for Information Network (WWW)
- R.A.I.N. (Rural Area Information Network) (telnet) login=VISITOR
- PSGnet/RAINet (gopher)
- Rio Grande FREE-NET (telnet) login=visitor
- Rio Grande FREE-NET (WWW)

- Rochester Free-Net (WWW)
- San Diego Freenet Initiative (gopher)
- Seattle Community Network Docs
- Seattle Community Network (telnet) login=visitor
- Seattle Community Network (WWW)
- SEFLIN Free-Net (telnet) login=visitor
- SENDIT North Dakota's K-12 Educational Telecommunications Network (telnet) login=bbs
- Silicon Valley Public Access Link (gopher)
- Silicon Valley Public Access Link (WWW)
- SouthEastern Ohio Regional Free-net (gopher)
- SouthEastern Ohio Regional Free-Net (telnet) login=guest
- Southeastern Virginia Regional Freenet (SEVAnet) (telnet) login=guest
- Southeastern Virginia Regional Freenet (SEVAnet) (WWW)
- Suncoast Free-Net (telnet) login=visitor
- Talawanda Learning Community Network (telnet) login=visitor
- Tallahassee Free-Net (telnet) login=visitor
- Tallahasee Free-Net (WWW)
- Texas Metronet (gopher)
- Texas Metronet (WWW)
- Three Rivers Free-Net (WWW)
- Toledo FREE-NET (telnet) login=visitor,password=visitor
- Traverse City Free-Net (telnet) login=visitor
- Triangle Free-Net (WWW)
- Tri-State Online (Cincinnati) (telnet) login=visitor
- Twin Cities Free-Net (telnet) login=guest
- Twin Cities Free-Net (WWW)
- Virgin Islands Paradise FreeNet (telnet)
- Virgin Islands Paradise FreeNet (WWW)
- Virginia's Public Education Network (telnet) login=guest,password=guest
- Westman Community Networks (WWW)
- Youngstown Free-Net (gopher)
- Youngstown Free-Net (telnet) login=visitor

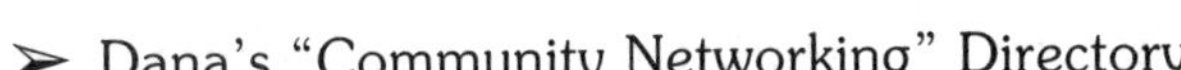

- Dana's "Community Networking" Directory
- ESUSDA's "Community-based Networks"
- Metronets—Metropolitan IP Network
- The WELL's "Community" Collection

Computer Bulletin Board Systems (BBSs)

A bulletin board service (BBS) can be thought of as a semi-private back road alongside the i-way. A BBS is usually run by a small company, a volunteer organization, or a single individual working at home in his or her basement. Naturally, there are exceptions to the rule. There are federal agencies that operate BBSs open to the general public. Many corporations also provide customer support and announce new product releases via a BBS.

BBSs are not new, and some have very large followings. One African American-run BBS in New York City became so popular, they opened a Los Angeles branch. In fact, there are a number of African-and African American-related BBSs. Art McGee (*amcgee@netcom.com*) manages some very comprehensive lists of African- and African American run-BBSs. The Black Data Processors Association (BDPA) is another excellent resource for information on AA (net shorthand for African American) bulletin boards. Using a modem, anyone can call up a BBS computer and acquire (download) any information that has been posted there. Many BBSs focus on a single topic, hobby, or group interest while others are more general.

Most BBSs are free. All you need is the BBS telephone number (which may be a long-distance toll call) and the appropriate communication settings or "protocols". You also may need to "register" before you can access the board. This usually involves giving your name, address, and other information. You then give yourself a password (or are assigned one). Many BBSs restrict your access to some features at first. You may only have to keep coming back to get upgraded to full access. In some cases, you may be required to send in a small amount of money to access certain features and areas. It's really up to the sysop (system operator).

There are a few limitations to most BBSs. Their telephone capacity is usually quite limited, often to a single incoming line. The number of simultaneous callers may be only a handful. Don't be surprised if you get busy signals and have to call back several times to get in. Don't expect a BBS to contain thousands of files (some do, but most don't). Another shortcoming with BBSs is their lack of full Internet access.

The upside of BBSs is that, due to their often specialized nature, they may have as much or more of what interests you than the larger services or even the Internet. Also, most BBSs cater to a local crowd and if you make new friends, it is more likely that they will be physically available to meet face-to-face.

There are listings for thousands of BBSs in computer publications and online. BBSs are popular and will remain so because they can be very private, and the price of setting one up is less than a Friday night date to the movies. If you already possess a home computer, all you need is a phone line and a BBS software package that you can obtain as shareware. Shareware is software that is distributed for free. You only pay for it after you're satisfied with its performance. Most shareware costs less than $25.

The bottom line for choosing a gateway

If you don't know what you will be wanting, or if you just want to shop around, any of the major commercial services provide a good starting point. America Online, Prodigy, and CompuServe currently offer at least five and as many as ten free hours the first month in which to test their services, so you may want to try all three. Just be sure to formally cancel any you don't choose to pay for once your free time has expired.

If you plan to use the Internet primarily or extensively, you should select a direct Internet access provider that allows generous or unlimited usage for a flat monthly rate. Many of these providers can be found in the classified section of newspapers and magazines.

If you can't find one, join one of the Big Three and use your free online time to locate a local provider. There are many extensive lists of service providers all over the world.

If you do opt for a local service provider, ask them what kind of connection they have between their system and the Internet "backbone." They should have what is called a "T1" or faster connection. This is a high-capacity communication line that is necessary to support a large number of users simultaneously. If they don't have a T1, you are likely to experience very slow response times.

Step three: Start cruising

Now you're ready to cruise cyberspace via your pumped-up 28.8 modem and Performa or 486 home computer. If you haven't done so

already, insert your America Online or Direct Internet Access Service Provider diskette(s) into the floppy diskette drive on the CPU. (Many new machines will have the appropriate Internet Software preinstalled. All you have to do is run the software to get started.)

The software will open up and ask you a series of simple questions about yourself and the specifications (specs) of your computer. A credit card or checking account number also may be required. (If you don't have a credit card or active bank account you may want to sign on to one of the public access Internet providers that requires no payment but have limited services.)

If all goes well, the software will dial up the service, transfer your information, and let you get on. Some services may require that you dial back using a local telephone number. Either way, you are now ready to cruise the Net.

With graphic interfaces, a colorful selection of things to do will be presented to you. But at this point you should pause, and take a brief moment for reflection.

Ask yourself these questions:

"Why am I taking time away from "Martin" to get on the i-way?"
"What real benefits can I expect to get?"
"Will this put food on my table?"
"What are my responsibilities as a citizen of cyberspace?"

The purpose of this exercise is to define your expectations and set the direction you want to go on the i-way. Many users travel the information superhighway for fun and entertainment. There are hundreds of free computer games, interactive role playing such as Dungeons & Dragons, as well as traditional entertainment involving casino, hobby, and sports activities available.

Other people may travel in search of employment or to conduct business. Advertising on the Net is growing rapidly, and major corporations and entrepreneurs are using the i-way to fill jobs or to reach potential customers and generate new sales.

In addition to their entertainment and business needs, many "cybernauts" simply choose to explore. They may randomly drift from site to site, just to go where "no one has gone before." This is the true spirit of "surfing the Net."

There is something for everyone on the Internet. All you have to do is get out there and find it. Pick a general direction and go for it. The following are Internet tools and activities you will find valuable after you have chosen the direction you want to go.

E-mail

E-mail is the heart of the Internet. It can be much more effective than voice messaging and can eliminate "telephone tag." Corporate employees are sending e-mail to coworkers across the hall as well as across the country. You can attach contracts, photographs, working drafts of documents, charts, authorizations, and other files to your e-mail.

Not all attachments are created equal

When you attach a file to an e-mail message, you should be sure that the recipient will be able to use it when it arrives. There are many methods of attaching files and they are by and large incompatible with one another. The most common (though not universal) method on the Internet is called MIME. Commercial systems, like Prodigy, have their own proprietary attachment methods that only work if you are sending the file to another member of the same service.

A simple test of compatibility is to send a test file to the person you want to send an attachment to. If it works, you're in business. If not, ask for some help from your provider. You are almost certainly not the first person to have this problem.

There is one method that always works when it is done right. It is an Internet technique that is so foolproof it should work on just about any system. The method is called uuencoding. The bad news is it requires that both the sender and receiver use some specialized software. The good news is that this software is commonly available for free. Virtually all the major commercial systems and most smaller ones can provide it to you.

Uuencoding converts binary computer files—whether documents, pictures, programs or anything else—to the kind of ordinary text that e-mail programs expect. It looks pretty weird, but everything is there. The first step is to use the software to convert your file to that form. Then you mail it as if it were a message itself. The recipient then converts the e-mail you sent them back into the original format using similar software. It is a bit of a pain, but once you get used to it, it's not bad at all. If it is the only way you can get the job done, it's well worth the effort of acquiring the software and learning how to use it.

If you have friends, relatives, or associates locally or around the world, you can e-mail them for much less than the cost of a postage stamp. It doesn't matter which online service you use—CompuServe, Prodigy, MCI Mail, AT&T Mail, Applelink, or any of the others—your e-mail will get through. E-mail is common and accessible to all i-way activity around the world.

After you sign on with a service you will immediately receive an e-mail address. The following are the author's e-mail addresses: Stafford L. Battle can be reached at *sbattle@aol.com* or

sbattle@cityofnewelam.com. Rey O. Harris can be reached at *cityofnewelam.com*.

When using e-mail it is important to remember that, unlike a sealed first-class postal letter, it is at least theoretically possible that the eyes of strangers may have access to it. This is particularly important if you are using e-mail facilities from your place of employment. Many employers frown upon workers using the company's Internet connection for personal e-mail and have been known to eavesdrop.

Needless to say, you are held accountable for your e-mail content. It is very easy to copy and forward e-mail. Your personal correspondence intended as a private joke or snide remark can inadvertently go to thousands of readers.

E-mail addresses

At first glance, e-mail addresses look like so much symbol salad. Once you understand how they are put together, however, they are really quite simple.

All Internet e-mail addresses are composed of two parts: the e-mail name (their user ID) of the party you are sending the message to and the name of the computer system where their e-mail box is located. These two names are separated by the "at" symbol, @. Here's an example:

joebloe@aol.com

*Sometimes the person's user ID resembles their name. Other times, it is completely arbitrary. On the Prodigy service, for example, all user IDs are composed of four letters, a two-digit number and a letter from A to F (*ABCD09A@prodigy.com*). On CompuServe, user names are two multi-digit numbers separated by a period (*1234.999@compuserve.com*). Both CompuServe and Prodigy have announced that they will be allowing users to choose alternate IDs that are less cryptic.*

*Most full-service Internet providers allow you to choose your own ID provided no one else has already reserved it. Most people find it convenient to use their first name and last initial or the opposite. Some prefer to use a nickname of some kind (*homeboy@somewhere.com*).*

So, all you need to know about someone to send them e-mail is their user ID and the name of the computer system where they have their e-mail account. See how easy that is?

Web browsing

Without question, the World Wide Web offers the best possible connection to the information superhighway. By using Web hypertext

links, anyone can zoom up and down the i-way and around the world to find text, graphics, video, sound, and other data related to any topic imaginable.

Hypertext

The basis of the World Wide Web is hypertext. To understand what hypertext is you need look no further than the dictionary. How often have you looked up a word, only to find it defined using other words you didn't understand? So you put a bookmark on the original word and look up the words used to define it. These words may also have new words in their definitions. It can get very confusing quickly. Wouldn't it be nice if you could bring the definitions of words to you instead of you having to chase after them? You've just invented hypertext.

With hypertext, references are "alive." That is to say that you can click your mouse button on them and go right to the referred-to document. What's more, the document may include, in addition to text, pictures, sound, or even a video clip. To make it perfect, the reference can be to anything in the world that is accessible through the World Wide Web. Sure beats the old-fashioned bookmark.

On the Web, text that is "linked" in this fashion to other information is highlighted (usually in blue). It will also probably be underlined too.

A Web page as seen on your computer can be composed of text, graphics, color photographs, video clips, or sound. A Web site consists of a series of Web pages connected together through a "home" page. The home page serves as the starting point. For instance, America Online and Prodigy have impressive home pages that contain all the tools you need to browse the Web. When you browse the Web, you travel from one Web page to another via hypertext links. These links can be to anything on the Internet worldwide. You never see a UNIX road sign and never have to key in complex line commands.

However, you will need to be familiar with Web directories and search engines. Directories are usually similar to the telephone Yellow Pages. They list major categories on one page and the contents of those categories on other pages. You just keep selecting from these lists until you have found what you want.

Figure 2-5 shows the main screen for the Yahoo service. As you can see, you can either type in words to search for, or just click on a category and see a more detailed list of topics. Figure 2-6 shows what happens if you click on Education on the main list. Don't you wish the telephone Yellow Pages worked this easily?

Search engines are fairly easy tools to use. You simply type in one or more words you are interested in finding, and a list of Web sites containing those words is displayed for you. This is called a keyword

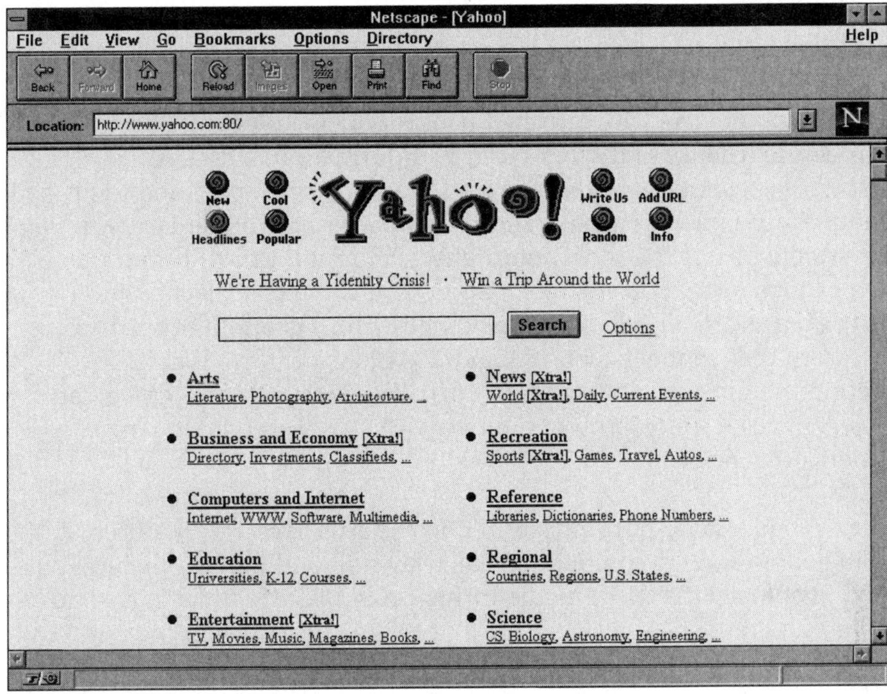

Fig. 2-5 *Yahoo's opening screen and subject list*

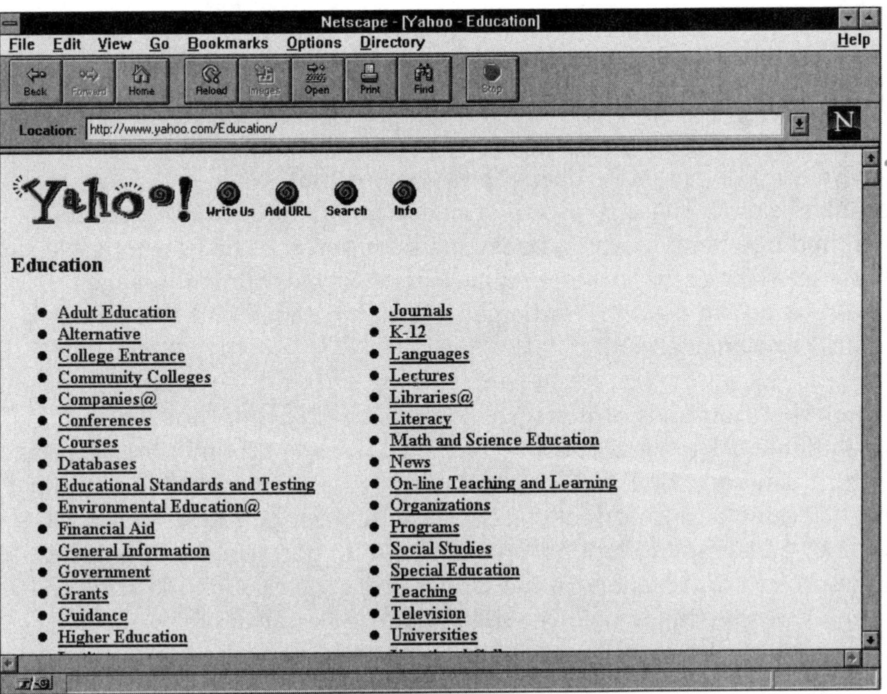

Fig. 2-6 *Yahoo's list of educational topics*

search. All you have to do to look at the material is click on a selection and a desired document will be found and displayed. Short of mind reading, it couldn't get much simpler.

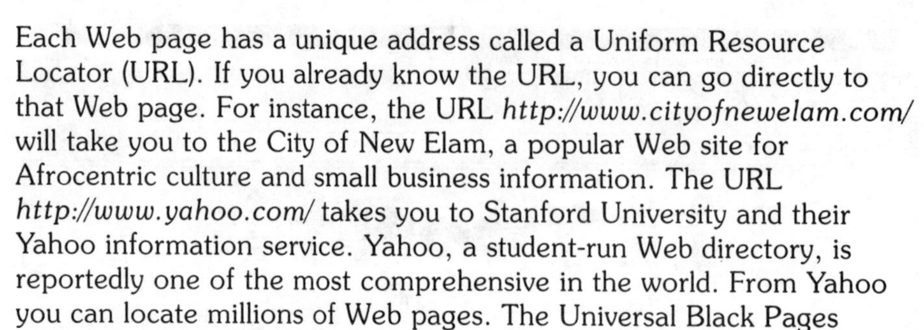

Each Web page has a unique address called a Uniform Resource Locator (URL). If you already know the URL, you can go directly to that Web page. For instance, the URL *http://www.cityofnewelam.com/* will take you to the City of New Elam, a popular Web site for Afrocentric culture and small business information. The URL *http://www.yahoo.com/* takes you to Stanford University and their Yahoo information service. Yahoo, a student-run Web directory, is reportedly one of the most comprehensive in the world. From Yahoo you can locate millions of Web pages. The Universal Black Pages *(http://www.gatech.edu/bgsa/blackpages.html)* is another outstanding directory that connects you to hundreds of Afrocentric Web sites around the Internet. Likewise, the *http://drum.ncat.edu/)* can be an excellent resource to browse the i-way for African and African American activities.

The Web is a fairly new innovation on the Net. But as it matures, it will become serious competition for television and motion pictures. In fact, eventually the three media forms could become indistinguishable from one another.

"Martin" may not be on the Net yet, but some TV programming has started the migration to the digital medium. The Sci-Fi Channel, CNN, TBS, and MTV, among others, have lead the way with very innovative Internet presentations. Others are not far behind.

Newsgroups

There are things said in Usenet newsgroups that would shock a drunken sailor. There is also informative and helpful advice that you can find nowhere else on a public medium. Internet newsgroups are lively exchanges that are the equivalent of an electronic message board or gossip column. Participants post messages that enlighten, shock, and amaze.

There are thousands of newsgroups on virtually every topic imaginable. As a newbie, you may want to "lurk" around a newsgroup before joining in on the dialogue. Lurking just means reading without participating and is perfectly acceptable Internet behavior. In fact, it is to your advantage to lurk as long as possible, because if you enter a newsgroup conversation on the wrong foot, you may get flamed! A flame is a sometimes vicious e-mail attack. Flame wars may occur when two rival newsgroups take a dislike to one another.

To join a newsgroup you must first subscribe to it. Then you can post original comments or respond to existing messages. Newsgroups may have a file called Frequently Asked Questions (FAQ) that will give you important background on discussions that have previously occurred. It is always a good idea to read the FAQ for a newsgroup with which

you are not familiar. It will often keep you from unknowingly embarrassing yourself.

The number of participants in a newsgroup varies from day to day. Some groups may have only 10 or 15 posted messages, but others may have hundreds or thousands.

One of the most popular newsgroups on the Net of special interest to AAs is *soc.culture.african.american*. On an average day, you may find as many as 10,000 postings. There are several other newsgroups with African or African American subject matter. Use the keyword search function found in your news "reader" program to find discussions that interest you.

Other Net tools

The Internet has other tools that could be of help to you. Each Internet access provider or online service, however, may have a different selection of tools available. As the Net matures and changes, the need for specific tools will change. Here are descriptions of some of the traditional core services.

File Transfer Protocol (FTP)

You will use FTP to download files from remote computers. FTP will likely require the use of some UNIX commands if you are using a shell account. There are tens of thousands of FTP sites around the world that allow you to log on, browse through the file library, and download the specific files that interest you. Use "anonymous" as your name when logging on. Use your own e-mail address as your password if it is requested. Virtually all Web browsers can be used to access FTP sites so you may never need to know any more about it than how to click your mouse.

Telnet

Telnet is another Net tool that allows you to sign on to a remote computer and use it as if you are on premises. This tool can be useful when you are out of town and wish to check your e-mail on your host system without incurring long-distance charges.

Gopher

There are a number of tools for searching the Internet. Gopher has been one of the more popular ones. When you search using Gopher, you actually sign on to a remote computer that maintains a huge database of Internet sites. The University of Minnesota is a favorite "gopher hole." Once in the database, you can travel from menu to menu to locate and download information. Gopher was created to simplify the Internet by replacing complicated commands with a system of menus. The World Wide Web has taken the simplification process one notch higher by replacing the menus with hypertext documents. Most Web browsers are equipped to deal with Gopher menus automatically.

Bottom line for cruising!

Use the World Wide Web for all your Internet activities. Go directly to Web Crawler or to Yahoo (*http://www.yahoo.com*) to start your browsing. The Web offers a glimpse of what all future Internet content will look like. Also, at least for now, the great majority of Web sites are free. But there may be surcharges to visit popular or corporate-sponsored Web pages at some point.

Also if you have a small business, advertising on the Web is definitely the direction to go. Online shopping malls are very hot items right now and excellent places in which to be seen. But more important, by placing your company on the Web, you can establish a business presence around the globe. You'll learn more about business on the Net in Chapter 6.

3

Black America Online

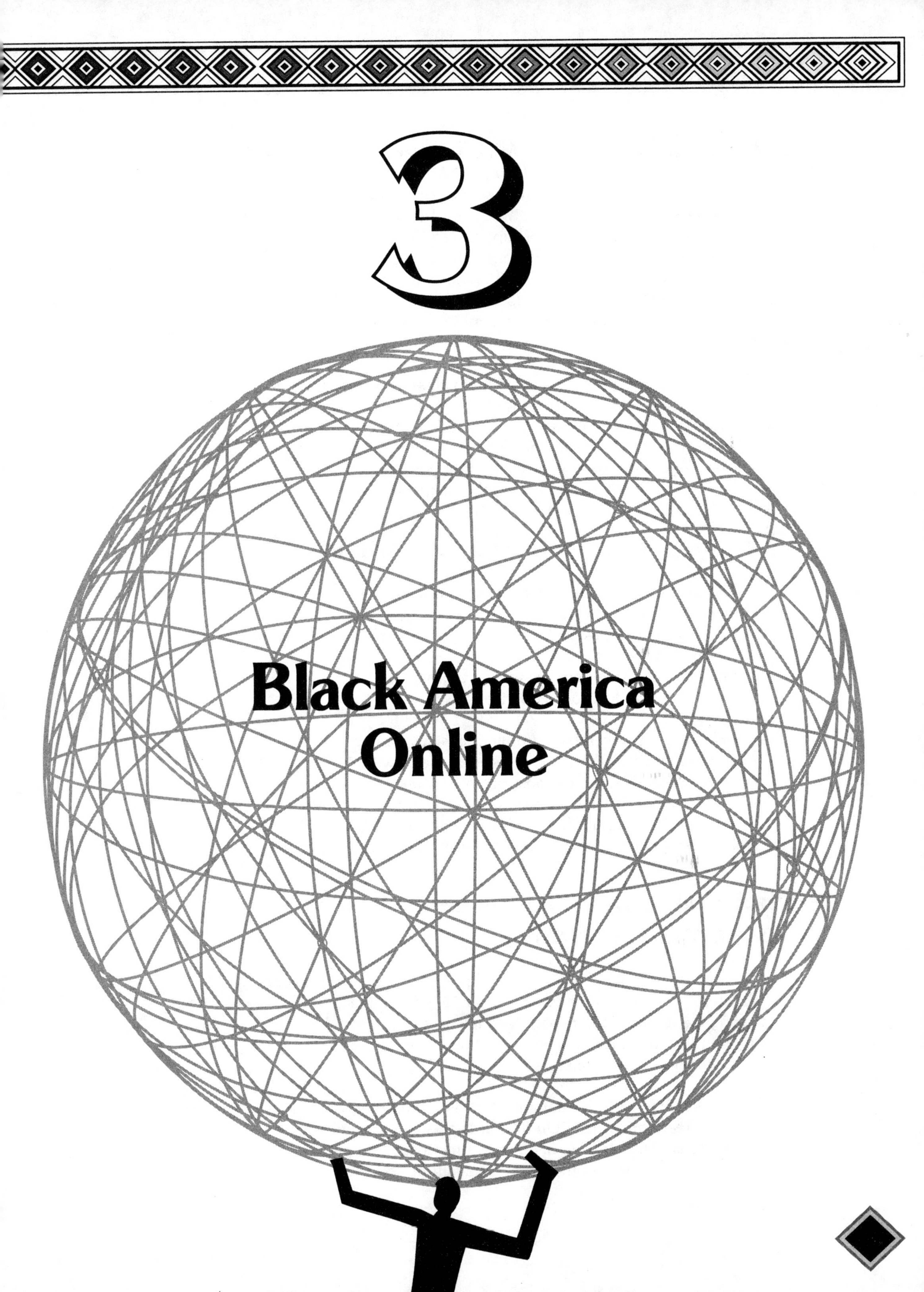

MAKE no mistake about it; African Americans are alive and well on the information superhighway. AAs—slang for Net citizens of African descent—are doing all the things that millions of people from other cultures are doing. Essentially, on the super i-way, AAs are offering personal advice, technical support, and vital business services, as well as opportunities for education, employment, and entertainment, all with a dash of "soul." There are individuals, educational facilities, political and social institutions, churches, government agencies, and commercial entities that cater to Afrocentric interests.

There are several good starting points that will assist you in your trip along the super i-way. Using the following services, pointers, and home pages, anyone, regardless of race or cultural background, will be rewarded with valuable information and resources about black people around the world. Your biggest problem, if any, will be narrowing down the possible sites for exploration to a manageable list.

Organizations from the real world

African American organizations have started a mass migration to the World Wide Web. Membership organizations particularly have benefited from tremendous cost savings on postage and advertising to stay in touch with the rank and file. Also, more than ever, the public at large can get an inside peek, as well as a grasp on the facts and issues that are critical for black Americans.

The Internet has the potential not only to destroy damaging stereotypes about Black America, it also has the power to heal social and civil inequities. Two of the most prominent black organizations online, the National African American Leadership Summit and the National Urban League, are featured here. Others can be found on the Web by using the search phrase African American.

National African American Leadership Summit

The National African American Leadership Summit (NAALS), under the direction of Dr. Benjamin F. Chavis, Jr., is committed to employing the Internet and related technologies as tools for information dissemination, planning, and development for NAALS and its member organizations.

NAALS, in keeping with this commitment, is establishing the online publication *Freedom Journal On-line*. It is a weekly commentary on critical issues affecting the life of African Americans and people of African descent throughout the world. In addition, the *Freedom*

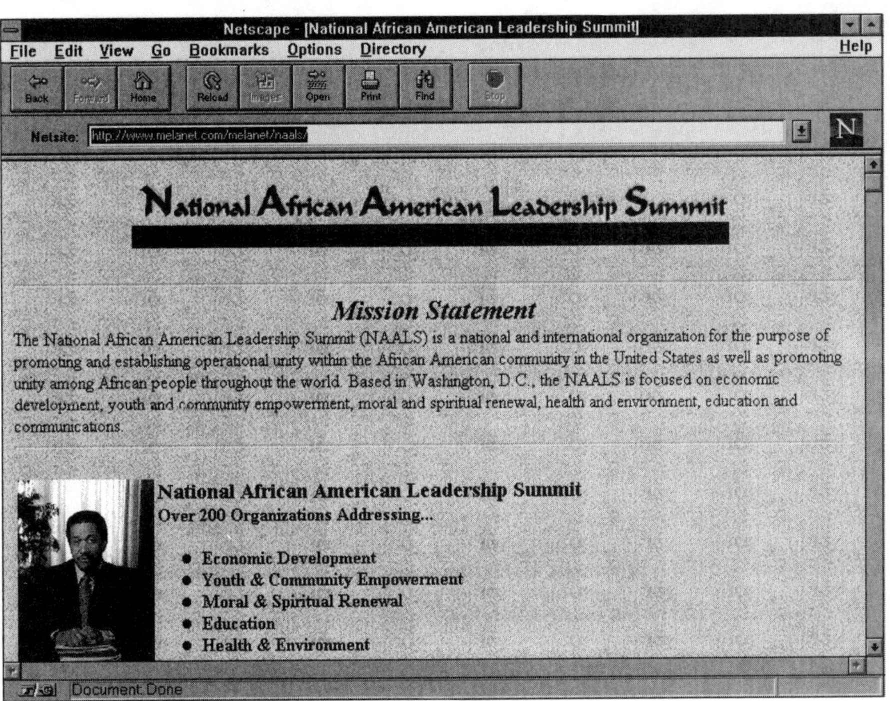

Fig. 3-1 *National African American Leadership Summit's home page*

Journal On-line provides timely analysis and preparation of an agenda toward reaching the goals of social, economic, and political empowerment for African Americans.

Dr. Chavis is a 35-year veteran of the civil rights movement in both the United States and the international community. The *Freedom Journal* is the official voice of the National African American Leadership Summit and the The Million Man March, Inc. NAALS was founded in 1994 to promote operational unity among African American organizations. The Web page is located at *http://www.melanet./naals/*.

The National Urban League

The National Urban League is sponsoring a Web site crammed full of relevant information about black activities in America. There is also an Internet mailing list (listserv) that anyone can join to receive periodic updates from the organization as well as to participate in discussions of black issues.

Each year, Urban League affiliates serve more than two million African Americans and others in need. Urban League affiliates operate programs in education, job training and placement, housing, business development, crime prevention, and many other important categories. Local Urban League staff and volunteers are committed to building communities through service.

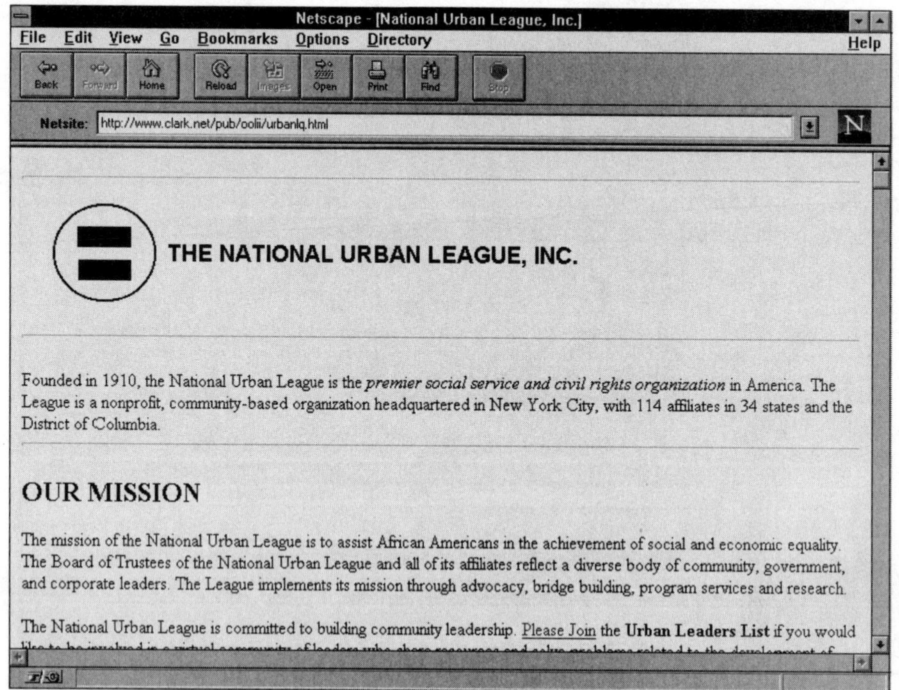

Fig. 3-2 *The National Urban League's home page*

The mission of the National Urban League is to assist African Americans in the achievement of social and economic equality. The board of trustees of the National Urban League and all of its affiliates reflect a diverse body of community, government, and corporate leaders. The League implements its mission through advocacy, bridge building, program services, and research.

The National Urban League has sought to emphasize greater reliance on the unique resources and strengths of the African-American community to find solutions to its own problems. To accomplish this, the League's approach has been to utilize fully the tools of advocacy, research, program service, and bridge building.

Founded in 1910, the National Urban League is considered by many AAs and others to be the premier social service and civil rights organization in America. The League is a nonprofit, community-based organization headquartered in New York City, with 114 affiliates in 34 states and the District of Columbia.

You can send e-mail to the Urban League at *bkfulton@pipeline.com*. Or, if you would like to participate in Urban Leaders Internet discussions, send a message stating *subscribe urbanleaders-L@nyo.com* and your name.

Online resources

The Universal Black Pages

The Universal Black Pages (UBP) has been called the Black Yahoo (Yahoo is a very popular Internet directory at Stanford University). The main purpose of the UBP, however, is to have a complete and comprehensive listing of African diaspora-related Web pages at a central site. Currently, the World Wide Web consists of many islands, each page addressing the particular interests of the sponsoring institution (or individual). A particular page may have links to other pages that are related, however, those links are far from being exhaustive or organized. The UBP maintains numerous links to the different sites.

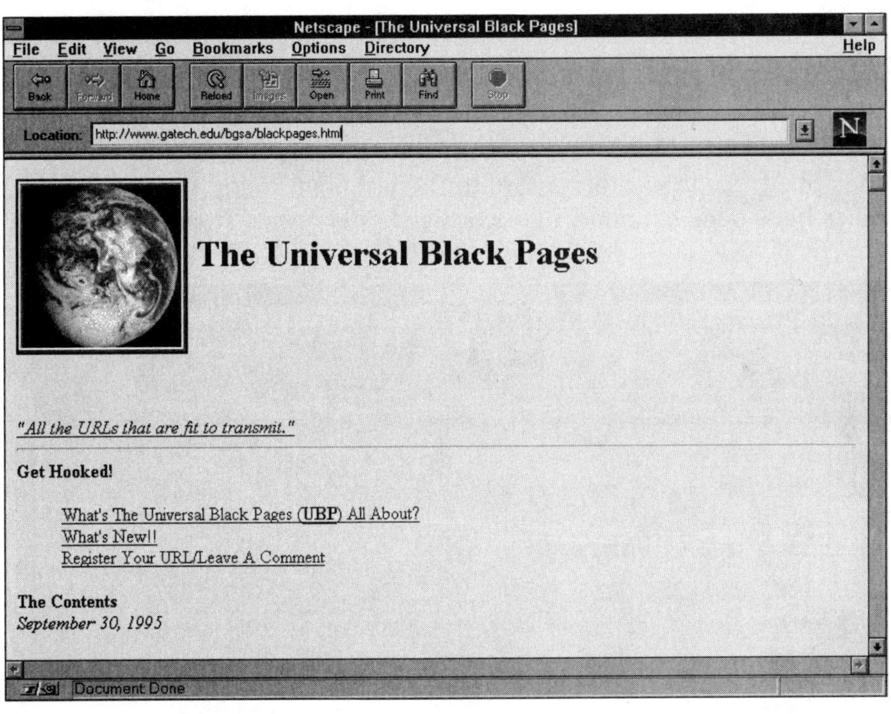

Fig. 3-3 *The Universal Black Pages Online*

Another purpose of the UBP is to encourage development of categories and topics that are not currently available via existing Web pages. The UBP hopes to facilitate this development, and it exists as a reference resource by which to avoid duplication of effort.

Some possible benefits of such a framework:

- It will serve as a means of networking people with interests in the African diaspora.
- It may offer a more global perspective of the African diaspora and of its peoples and cultures.

- ➢ It could be used as an educational resource (in conjunction with traditional media such as books) by students and teachers in high schools and colleges.
- ➢ It will be a tool for getting new (and old) users quickly accustomed to the World Wide Web and the Internet.
- ➢ People may see where it could be improved and offer suggestions that may be readily incorporated.

Though some areas are still under construction at the time of this writing, there are more than enough "connections," otherwise known as hypertext links, to satisfy the heartiest of appetites for knowledge. The UBP was created (and is developed) by members of the Black Graduate Students Association at the Georgia Institute of Technology. Their e-mail address is *bgsa@www.gatech.edu*. Their Web URL is *http://www.gatech.edu/bgsa/blackpages.html*.

WWW Virtual Library: African Studies

The WWW Virtual Library is another fast-growing resource for all kinds of Afrocentric information. In the last year, many specialized topics have been expanded; African studies is one of them.

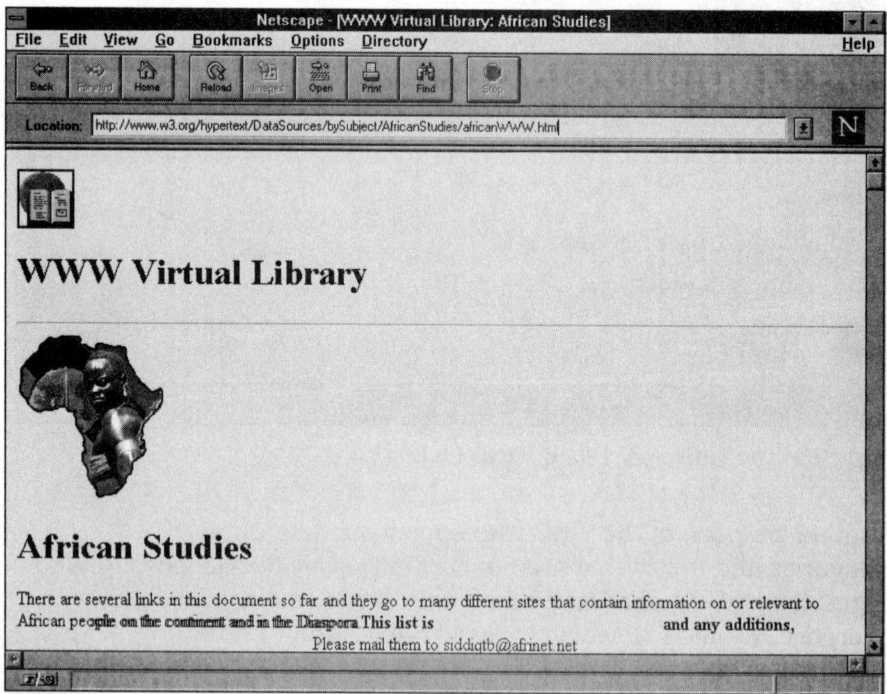

Fig. 3-4 *WWW Virtual Library: African Studies*

There are many, many links that go to many different areas on the Net that contain information relevant to African people on the U.S. continent and in the diaspora. Like most popular Web sites, the pages

are continually under construction and revisions. Additions, corrections or suggestions are welcome. Please mail them to *siddiqtb@afrinet.net*.

Resources located at this site include:

- Southern African WWW servers.
- AERN, the African Educational Research Network. This is a gopher hole.
- The Western Historical Manuscripts Black Studies Area offers a selection of works by well-known African Americans.
- ANC Newswire.
- The Library of Congress Resource Guide for the Study of Black Culture.
- Afro American Newspaper Home Page.
- AfroNet is a network of students who are interested in distributing information among schools about issues pertaining to race relations.
- Isis: An Urban Black Women's Cultural Salon.
- 'Blacklife is an IRC channel which has developed a home page.
- African Students Union at Temple University.
- Internet Living Swahili Dictionary Project.
- BANI (*Base d'Anthropologie physique du Niger*) offers info in French about Niger.
- Women and Minorities in Science and Engineering from MIT.
- Abwenzi African Studies is a private project promoting friendship between Africans and Americans.
- Rasta Language guide is available online, and is an amalgamation of American and Caribbean Ebonics terms.
- Aboriginal Studies information.
- The World Bank offers an information bank on African Development Studies.
- The Fourth World Documentation Project provides a great deal of information for African people.

WWW Virtual Library: African Studies is located at *http://www.w3.org/hypertext/DataSources/bySubject/AfricanStudies/africanWWW.htlm*.

KPOO-FM radio

KPOO-FM in San Francisco is, reportedly, the only independent African American-owned and -operated noncommercial radio station west of the Mississippi. According to some sources, it also has the distinction of being considered the first black radio station in the country to go online. KPOO features jazz, reggae, salsa, blues, gospel, and hip hop music, as well as prime-time news and public affairs programs highlighting the concerns of San Francisco's African American, Asian, gay, and poor communities.

KPOO serves the Bay Area's Latin community with four bilingual programs a week, and also produces programs concerning Irish American, women's, and Native American issues. KPOO broadcasts live the weekly meeting of the San Francisco Board of Supervisors and provides nonstop election night coverage.

The station plans to use the Internet to communicate with its listeners and encourage other African American- and Latin-owned stations around the country to get online. On their Web page is a listing of selected musical, cultural, and social events featuring African Americans in the San Francisco Bay Area.

KPOO is supported by listener donations. Anyone wishing to support their efforts can send e-mail to *KPOO@SFBayguardian.com*. On the Web, KPOO can be found at *http://www.microweb.com/kpoo*.

AfriNET

AfriNET IRS (Information Retrieval System) is a service designed to allow the retrieval of any information that is publicly available within the AfriNET online community. It allows users to find documents and to query the AfriNET database for searchable items. You may also submit documents into the database, thereby contributing information to the community.

This is a good place to find information on upcoming events such as expos, conferences, meetings, lectures, or social gatherings. You may also register an event that you'd like everyone to know about.

AfriNET Pages contain a long listing of businesses and organizations. For a detailed query, fill out a form online and a listing will be returned to your screen. You may also register your business or organization, so you can be included in the database. From then on, Internet users can find information about you and your organization.

The AfriNET community consists of individual members, businesses, and organizations in which every entity within this electronic

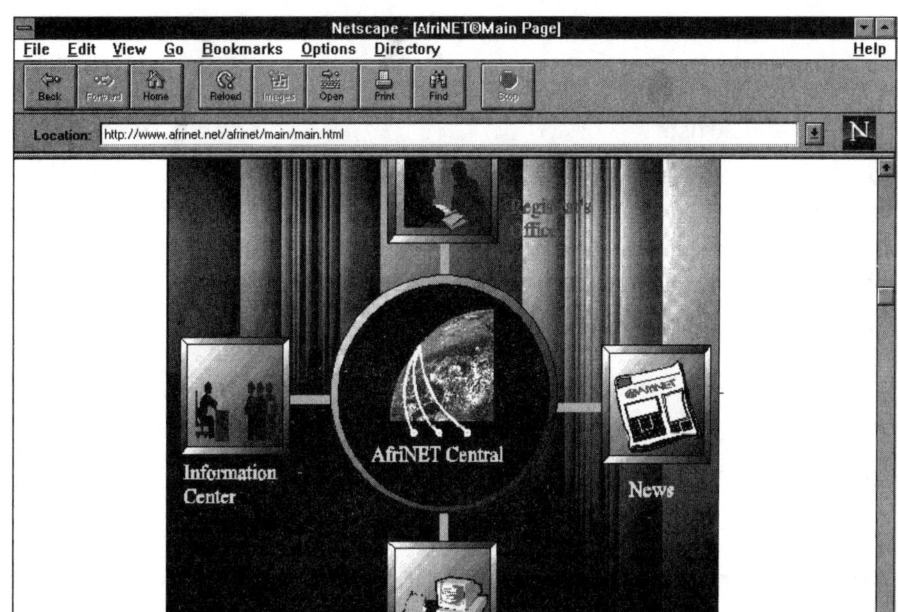

Fig. 3-5 *AfriNet's home page on the World Wide Web*

community is not only able to communicate with each other, but can also use AfriNET to serve their business, personal, political, recreational, religious, and social needs.

The AfriNET Announcements Center provides information on the continuing AfriNET projects, including new products and services, as well as updates to existing applications. This newsletter allows users to be connected with the providers of AfriNET.

For more information about AfriNET send e-mail to: *afrinetinfo@afrinet.net*. To subscribe to their mailing list, please send mail to *majordomo@afrinet.net* and the body of your message should read *subscribe afrinet-fyi*.

African-American Culture and Arts Forum

On CompuServe, you can find the African-American Forum (keyword GO AFRO). This forum gives you the opportunity to experience the culture and art of African Americans. You can discuss current events, cultural issues, politics, and other matters pertaining to African-American society. Anyone can visit libraries to download graphic images of African-American art, excerpts from books by important African-American authors, and articles from favorite Afrocentric journals. The forum is sponsored by *American Visions* magazine.

The following sections and libraries are available:

- ➢ Calendar of Events
- ➢ Art and Artists
- ➢ History & Biography
- ➢ Books & Writers
- ➢ Cuisine
- ➢ Film—Theater—Dance
- ➢ Music and Musicians
- ➢ Genealogy
- ➢ Travel
- ➢ The Salon
- ➢ Education
- ➢ Information Highway
- ➢ SW Development
- ➢ Culture of Trade
- ➢ Talk to *American Visions*

NSBE TSIG Entrepreneurship and Economic Development Team

Members of the National Society of Black Engineers (NSBE) Telecommunications Special Interest Group have established the Entreprenuership and Economic Development Team. This team, formed at the 1995 NSBE National Conference under the umbrella of the TSIG, has accepted the mission to foster an environment of viable opportunities for African American entrepreneurs on the Internet. Using telecommunications and computer information systems as the vehicle for empowerment, the EEDTs strategic objectives are to:

- ➢ increase African American access to the telecommunications industries.
- ➢ cultivate entrepreneurship.
- ➢ facilitate the development and operations of consortiums.
- ➢ establish black entrepreneurs, consultants, and companies as a global resource.

The key 1996 activity is to establish a resource database of the top revenue-generating AA telecommunications and information technology companies. This database is intended to be used as a

networking and communications vehicle to encourage new business opportunities.

Member communications, meetings, and activities are regularly conducted through the Internet. For additional information or to get involved with their activities contact: Vince Mansel (*wvmansel @mediasphere.com*), Gerald Charles, Jr. (*gcharles@lan.mcl.bdm.com*), or David Daniel (*gddaniel@pacbell.com*).

National Council of Black Engineers and Scientists (NCBES)

NCBES is a nonprofit 501(c)-3 corporation dedicated to the advancement of blacks in science and engineering careers. They are one of more than 30 black technical organizations (BTOs) on the Internet across the United States dedicated to similar ideals. For more information on NCBES, subscribe to their mail listing at: *listserv@arizvml.ccit.arizona.edu*.

Science, Engineering, Business and Science Education (SEBSEL)

SEBSEL's purpose is to provide an international, interactive communication network among black technical professionals. Information provided includes: calls for papers, conference announcements, social gathering announcements, job announcements (a very successful vehicle for employment), calls for assistance, short (five pages maximum) newsletters, technical information, grants, Requests For Proposal (RFPs), and more. SEBSEL also has the NCBES SEBSEL Library. Their e-mail address is *sebsel@arizvm1 .ccit.arizona.edu*.

To access the library, send e-mail to *listserv@arizvm1.ccit.arizona.edu*.

The NubianNetwork

The NubianNetwork is an "Internet Electronic Communication Infrastructure" focusing on Internet and World Wide Web research, management, and service by academic discipline. They are a student-run organization that was founded at Syracuse University. In addition to a Web page, the Network has a gopher site under the Syracuse University gopher. Their objectives include:

- Prepare potential students for 21st-century education.
- Create an interdisciplinary network of students.

- ➢ Support campus organizations.
- ➢ Develop real and virtual world links with national organizations.
- ➢ Design innovative communications within the World Wide Web.

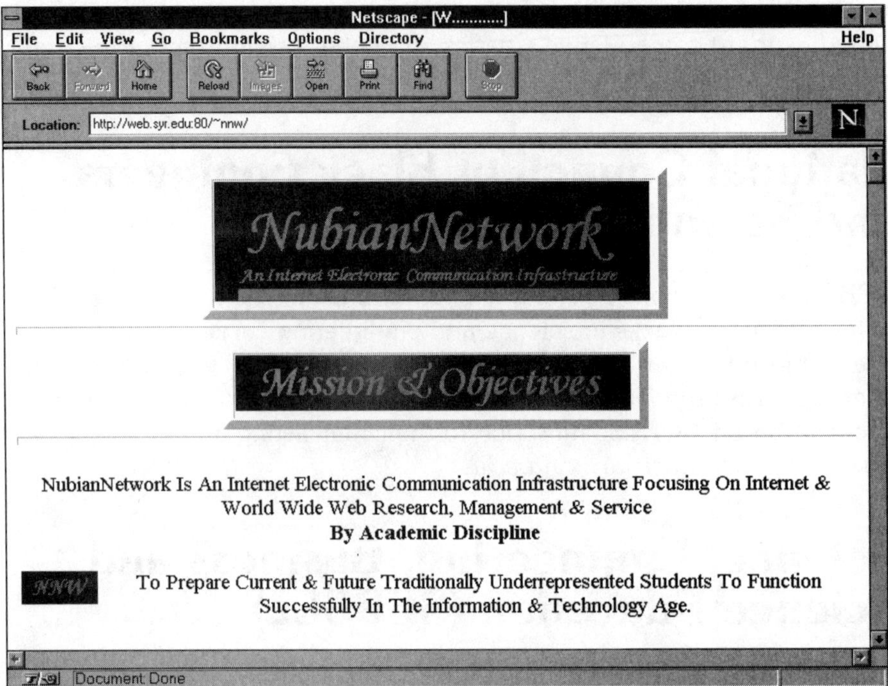

Fig. 3-6 *The NubianNetwork's home page*

For more information about the NubianNetwork, send e-mail to *delliott@mailbox.syr.edu*.

Computers and You

Computers and You is located in San Francisco's Tenderloin District. They provide computer access and training to the economically "impoverished" in the community. They also are a part of Glide Memorial Church, which provides crack recovery, AIDS services, and many other services, including about 2 million meals a year. Computers and You was founded in 1989 and has trained more than 5000 adults and children in Mac and IBM PC use.

Computers and You has an Internet site to provide people (many of whom are homeless) with e-mail accounts and access to Internet resources for use on computers donated to shelters. Many students (and volunteers) are African. Their Web address is http://www.glide.org/.

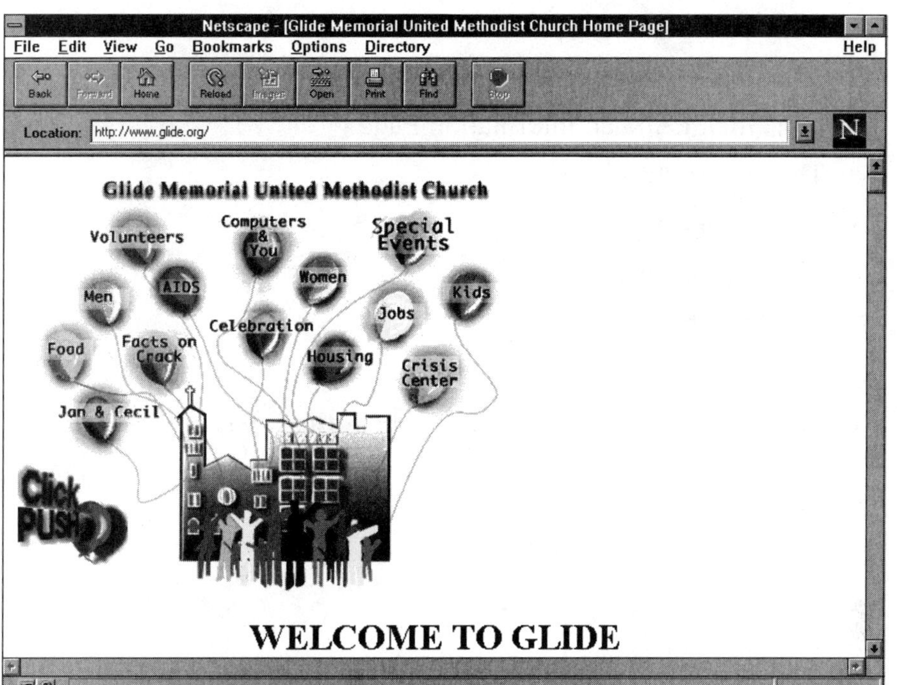

Fig. 3-7 *Computers and You at the Glide Web site*

The ebony room

The ebony room is a place in the People Connection section of America Online (AOL) in which AAs have carved out a little niche for themselves. There is an online newsletter that is published bimonthly and distributed to all those who register as members of the room. Of course, there is no charge for membership; just an interest in AA networking online is needed. In addition, there are local gatherings in each part of the country at which ebony members become acquainted with each other offline. Once a year, there is a national get-together at a site voted on by the membership. Send e-mail to *fremen@access.digex.net*.

The Drum

The Drum's mission is to provide access to the information superhighway (Internet) and various other state information highways for the African and African American community. It started out as an informal group in September 1988. They were a list of 10 users then, and have grown to a group of more than 600 throughout the United States, South Africa, England, and Canada.

The Drum welcomes comments and suggestions. Contact Carter Bing at *carter@drum.ncsc.org* for information about the Drum or Charles Isbell at *isbell@ai.mit.edu* for information or comments about the Drum Web Server.

The services that the Drum offers include:

- ➢ The DRUM African American Universities Page
- ➢ The DRUM African Information Page
- ➢ The DRUM Arts Page
- ➢ The DRUM Articles Page
- ➢ The DRUM Civil Rights Page
- ➢ The DRUM FTP Service
- ➢ The DRUM Ourstory Page
- ➢ Important dates, events, and people in Black History Page maintained by Charles Isbell
- ➢ The DRUM Members Page
- ➢ The DRUM Organizations Page
- ➢ The DRUM Speeches Page
- ➢ The DRUM Ujamaa Page
- ➢ The DRUM Holistic Page maintained by Eddie Reed and Okolo

Africa World Press

The catalogue of Africa World Press is available on the Net. It has offerings from Africa World Press, Red Sea Press, Black Classic Press, and other black book publishers. It also contains selected offerings relating to African people and other people of color from Harry N. Abrams, African American Images, Afro Visions Inc., Carol Publishing Group, Braziller Publishers, Blacklight Fellowship Press, Black Think Tank, Fourth Dynasty Publishing Company, Heinemann Educational Books, and many others.

Books featured are: *Yurugu*, *Afrocentricity*, *Black Priest/White Church*, *Black Messiah*, *Black Man in the Old Testament*, *Orisha's: The Living Gods of Africa*, *Voices from the Battlefront: Achieving Cultural Equity*, *Book of African Names*, and *Marxism and African Literature*. These books also will appear on the World Wide Web (WWW). The e-mail address is *africawpress@nyo.com*.

Vibe Online

This Web site is a good example of the future of the Internet and of AA electronic publishing. The material offered here ranges from your basic hip-hop to cool sophisticated jazz. The graphics are excellent. The content can be hard-hitting, political, humorous, engaging, and definitely 21st-century black.

Expect to see many more electronic magazines of this type in the near future. Traditional "dead tree publishing" is losing ground to electronic publishing. It's relatively inexpensive to put a quality four-color magazine on the Net that has the potential to reach more than 30 million people. For anyone who has aspirations of publishing a newsletter, magazine, or newspaper, check out Vibe Online (Fig. 3-8) and similar publications. (Just use your Web Browser.) Vibe Online can be accessed at *http://www.pathfinder.com/*.

Fig. 3-8 *Vibe Online Magazine's home page*

African-American–owned Internet service providers

Not only are African Americans creating Web pages, they are creating Internet service providers. As of this writing, there are a number of new AA Internet providers that are coming into existence that cater to African Americans. It's been said that "black folks take to the Net, like a duck takes to water!" According to the National Urban League (which supplies information to the U.S. Census Bureau), African American consumers spend more than four billion on consumer electronics. The Internet may soon be a valuable part of every black home in America.

The following is a very brief overview of some AA Internet service companies. To get a more up-to-date list, use your favorite Web browser.

United States Black On-Line (US/BOL)

United States Black On-Line is a commercial online information service and nationwide Internet access provider. US/BOL offers a variety of online services for individuals and organizations, such as a research database of statistics and facts about African Americans, World Wide Web (WWW) browsing, home page listings, electronic commerce (shopping), electronic mail, an electronic newsstand, Internet newsfeeds, software downloading, and online interactive discussion rooms/forums pertaining to topics and events of vital interest to African Americans and the Africans throughout the diaspora. US/BOL can be accessed using a local telephone call throughout the United States or throughout the world via the Internet. All of the dial-up connections to US/BOL are via 28.8K modems.

Their Virtual Office Access provides business and individual users with the capability to access information critical to their daily operations from anywhere in the United States using a cellular or standard telephone and a modem. The Virtual Office Access account provides users with the capability to easily store and retrieve files from our secure information server.

US/BOL believes that by putting people in touch with each other and providing timely access to information with intuitive and user-friendly computer interfaces, African Americans will be empowered in their educational, business, and interpersonal endeavors utilizing the power of the Net.

US/BOL is 100 percent African-American owned.

For the latest information on their growing list of services please send mail to their auto-mailer *info@usbol.com* or visit their home page at *http://www.usbol.com*.

Black News Network

BNN, Inc., is an information technology consulting firm headquartered in Southwestern Virginia, with offices in Salem, Virginia; Washington, DC; Richmond, Virginia; Pittsburgh, Pennsylvania; and Baltimore, Maryland. They specialize in Internet consulting.

Their first product was the Black News Network forum hosted on Delphi Internet Services. This was one of the first national Black online forums concentrating solely on providing black news on the Net. Due to the success of that product, they decided to name their consulting firm "BNN, Inc." For more information, send e-mail to

Ghee@roanoke.infi.net or Mr. S. Shabaka at *bnn_sshabaka@usbol.com*.

Cybertech

Cybertech is an African-American, full-service Internet company. The company has a number of services that covers a wide range of digital production work, including CD-ROM production, video presentation, Web hosting, and desktop publishing. Some of the highlights of its Web site include a page dedicated to natural healing and voodoo, a page for the National Council of Negro Women, and a directory of lawyers. Work is also being completed for a virtual-reality American Slave Museum. In September 1995, Cybertech broadcast the Congressional Black Caucus Fund Annual Conference live on the Internet each day of the event. The Cybertech Mall also features the International Embassies Web site. This site lists all embassies in the USA, some with home pages and tourist information, and also features links to foreign countries.

Cybertech has begun production on three new CD-ROM games—a new learning game for children, titled "Children of the World" an adventure game similar to the popular game "Myst," and a new digital video game. All special effects, animation, and programming will be completed at the Cybertech Game Development Center. The Cybertech Game Development Center offers full multimedia production, digital video, mpeg and QuickTime recording, as well as custom application development and authoring in Macromedia, Director, Authorware, Visual Basic, and C++. Cybertech's Web site can be located at *http://www.cybertech-mall.com*.

CyberExel, Inc.

CyberExel, Inc., was incorporated in early 1995 with the sole purpose of providing Internet connection, Web page design, development, and housing, and Internet seminars and training. CyberExel is owned and operated by Sharon H. Kent and is one of but a handful of African-American women-owned Internet businesses today. Sharon Kent has more than 15 years experience in the information technology industry and attributes the success of CyberExel to her committment to excellence and her goal of making the Internet an integral part of the African-American experience.

CyberExel can be reached by phone at (301) 297-7773, e-mail at *skent@nvi.nvi.net*, or visit its Web page at *http://www.nvi.net/cygnus/cyberexel*.

The City of New Elam

The City Of New Elam (CONE) is located in cyberspace on Exit 1A of the Information Superhighway. City founders are encouraging tourists to move in, businesses to set up shop, and national associations to construct a headquarters on the newly constructed "digital" city streets. Each establishment will be represented by a colorful digital image of a storefront, doorway, interior, or other illustration. The city "interface" to online information retrieval has several benefits, most important, that for individuals who are not computer literate, it is an easy concept for locating information.

As a resident of the City of New Elam, you can send electronic mail to anyone who is connected to the Internet—whether they are a resident of New Elam City or not. If you have friends or associates who use any of the popular online networks— CompuServe, AOL, Prodigy, MCI Mail, AT&T Mail, AppleLink, and many others—you can send them e-mail. You can reach thousands of individuals for less than the cost of one stamp.

In City of New Elam, every office suite, storefront, skyscraper, and "pool hall" can be used as an e-mail center for discussion and social exchange. Residents can stay on-line as long as they like to read and write messages without incurring additional on-line fees.

The the City Of New Elam offers full Internet service, ease of use, no service charge to tourists, low competitive pricing for registered residents, and most important of all, an exciting interface (buildings, stores, and pavilions instead of electronic boards or databases) filled with relevant and timely information and entertainment. It is the computer equivalent of all the best events that can occur in places such as New York City, Las Vegas, Washington, D.C, or Los Angeles—without the travel, bad weather, or time constraints.

Use your favorite Web browser to reach the City of New Elam or connect via *http://www.cityofnewelam.com*.

MelaNet

MelaNet is a centralized communication and information system serving the needs of commerce, business, and information-sharing. MelaNet provides a location where businesspersons may market their goods and services to one another as well as to the rapidly growing African American online consumer market. MelaNet also houses demographic data relevant to the black community. In addition, MelaNet has "links" to other online data available for the empowerment of Blacks located throughout the world.

Utilizing the World Wide Web, MelaNet integrates full color images, sound, and text. Services currently offered on MelaNet include:

- The MelaNet Marketplace: an online Afrocentric mall
- The MelaNet Electronic Business Center: a meeting place for businesses
- MelaPages: a worldwide online black business directory
- The MelaNet Ida B. Wells Media Center: contains article submissions and subscription advertisements for African-based media.

To reach MelaNet send e-mail to *raj@melanet.com* (voice (800) 757-5499) or see their Web site at *http://www.melanet.com/*.

Black Bulletin Boards

African Americans have been online for many years prior to the recent glory of the World Wide Web and the Internet. Computer bulletin board services (BBSs) were the first computerized, widespread means to connect people with similar interests. Granted, today, many people consider BBS use to be ancient technology, but BBSs remain popular among a number of groups who prefer a quieter and more private means to connect with each other via computer. (If you have questions, reread chapter 2.)

A BBS system can operate on a single PC or Mac and typcially may have only one phone line. They are usually operated as a hobby. Unlike the Internet, to reach your favorite BBS you may have to dial in and pay long distance toll rates.

So, why are BBS still useful?

Again, BBS systems are close, personal, and intimate. They often focus on topics of local interest or concerns. And, although far from state-of-the-art in computer telecommunications, a BBS can be very, very useful.

For instance, it is very easy to connect with a BBS. You don't need an Internet connection or an account with a commercial online service. Most BBSs are free (except for long distance telephone charges). Simply follow the instructions that accompany your communications software. Adjust your modem's settings (telephone number and other protocols) to conform with the BBS you select and dial in. You may have to dial in several times to get a connection but don't get discouraged. After a few tries, you will discover the best times to call in.

Arthur R. McGee & Associates

The following is a North American list of Black/African-run or Black/African-oriented Bulletin Board Systems (BBSs) put together by Art McGee. McGee is an important "icon" of AA participation on the Net. His collection of AA lists is more than likely the most comprehensive on the Net.

Be warned that telephone numbers and access change frequently. Please send updates, additions, corrections, or suggestions to Arthur McGee. Use your favorite browser to find Art McGee on the World Wide Web, or you can send e-mail to *72377.1351@compuserve.com* or *amcgee@netcom.com*. ("The revolution will not be televised, but the proceedings will be available online.")

Name	Number	Speed
A.E.A.O.N.M.S.	(510) 644-9307	2400
Afra-Span	(404) 270-5522	9600
African American	(215) 844-8145	2400
African Civilization	(510) 623-8744	2400
African Studies (U of WI)	(608) 262-9689	2400
Alex's Place	(213) 937-8734	2400
Ashanti Connection	(718) 634-4175	2400
VirtualNet@7180 Baoba	(202) 296-9790	14400
BatCave	(904) 384-2112	14400
BDPA BAC (BDPA)	(707) 552-3314	9600
BDPANet BDPA Cleveland (BDPA)	(216) 663-6020	2400
BDPA Online (BDPA)	(313) 864-2372	2400
Philadelphia (BDPA)	(215) 365-8858	2400
BDPA Wash., D.C. (BDPA)	(202) 986-4219	14400
BlackBoard Int'l	(416) 599-1707	2400
Blacklands	(410) 254-9069	2400
The BlackNet	(718) 692-0943	14400
Boardroom (IABPFF)	(201) 923-3967	2400
Capital Area Network	(301) 499-4671	14400
Caribbean Connection[1]	(809) 779-4066	14400
Caribbean Connection[2]	(809) 693-8711	14400
CIDA	(819) 953-8207	9600
CPTime Online	(213) 732-7923	2400
Voice Data Bits Online (BDPA)	(213) 295-6094	2400
Ebony Shack[1]	(419) 241-4600	2400
IMHOTEP	(718) 297-4829	2400

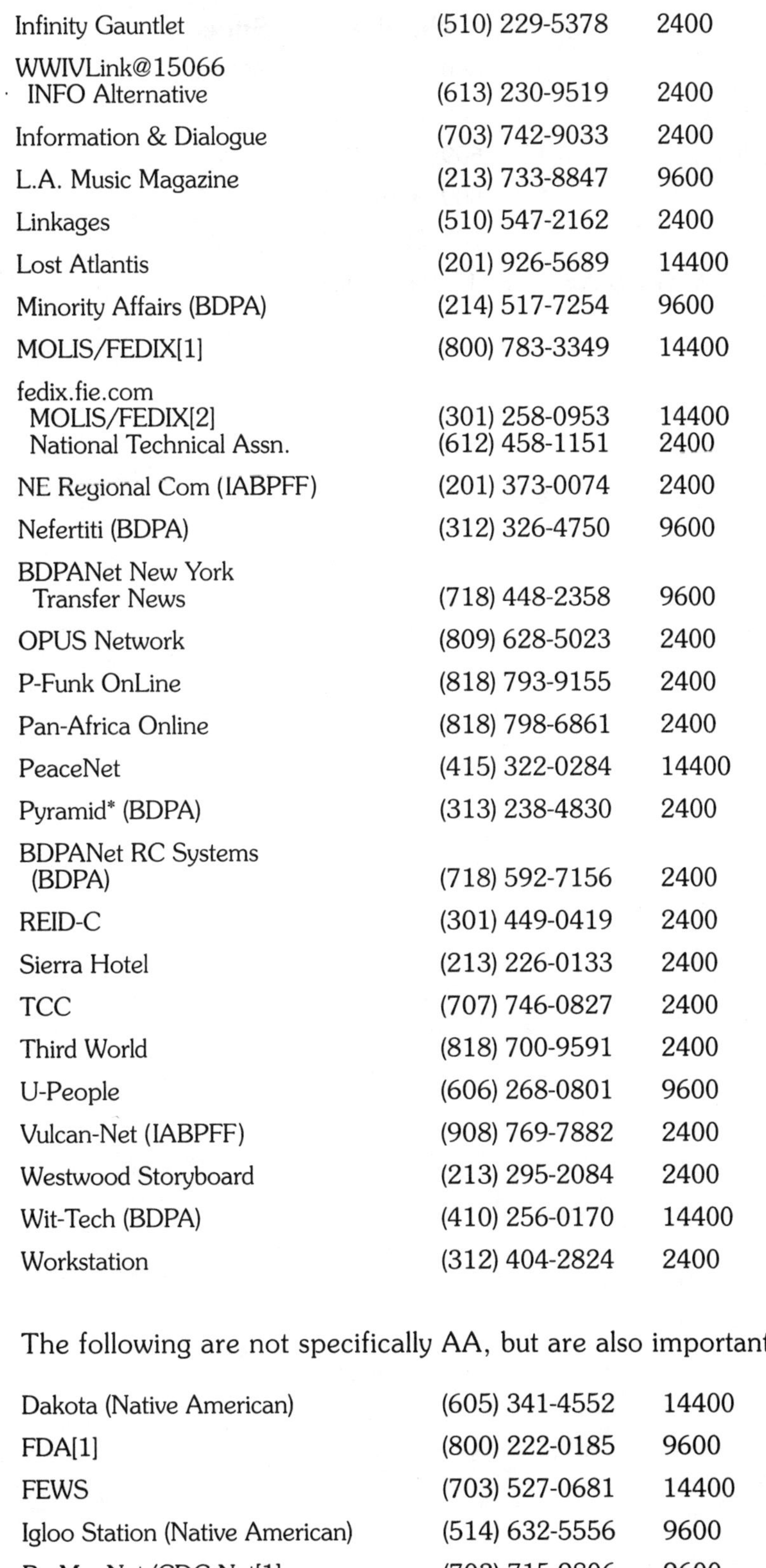

Infinity Gauntlet	(510) 229-5378	2400
WWIVLink@15066		
INFO Alternative	(613) 230-9519	2400
Information & Dialogue	(703) 742-9033	2400
L.A. Music Magazine	(213) 733-8847	9600
Linkages	(510) 547-2162	2400
Lost Atlantis	(201) 926-5689	14400
Minority Affairs (BDPA)	(214) 517-7254	9600
MOLIS/FEDIX[1]	(800) 783-3349	14400
fedix.fie.com		
MOLIS/FEDIX[2]	(301) 258-0953	14400
National Technical Assn.	(612) 458-1151	2400
NE Regional Com (IABPFF)	(201) 373-0074	2400
Nefertiti (BDPA)	(312) 326-4750	9600
BDPANet New York		
Transfer News	(718) 448-2358	9600
OPUS Network	(809) 628-5023	2400
P-Funk OnLine	(818) 793-9155	2400
Pan-Africa Online	(818) 798-6861	2400
PeaceNet	(415) 322-0284	14400
Pyramid* (BDPA)	(313) 238-4830	2400
BDPANet RC Systems		
(BDPA)	(718) 592-7156	2400
REID-C	(301) 449-0419	2400
Sierra Hotel	(213) 226-0133	2400
TCC	(707) 746-0827	2400
Third World	(818) 700-9591	2400
U-People	(606) 268-0801	9600
Vulcan-Net (IABPFF)	(908) 769-7882	2400
Westwood Storyboard	(213) 295-2084	2400
Wit-Tech (BDPA)	(410) 256-0170	14400
Workstation	(312) 404-2824	2400

The following are not specifically AA, but are also important:

Dakota (Native American)	(605) 341-4552	14400
FDA[1]	(800) 222-0185	9600
FEWS	(703) 527-0681	14400
Igloo Station (Native American)	(514) 632-5556	9600
PerManNet/CDC-Net[1]	(703) 715-9806	9600
PerManNet/CDC-Net[2]	(703) 715-9832	14400
SBA[1]	(800) 859-4636	2400

Name	Number	Speed
SBA[2]	(800) 697-4636	9600
Towers Int'l (NA) [1]	(609) 327-9133	14400
Towers Int'l (NA) [2]	(609) 825-5717	2400
Tropical Island	(809) 849-5921	14400
VITANet	(703) 527-1086	14400

4

Black Chat

IN cyberspace, interaction between individuals is a mainstay. People just can't wait to reach out and touch someone, anyone, everyone. There are a variety of ways in which to do this on the Net. Some involve the worldwide resources of the Internet, while others are local to a particular service or community.

On the Internet, there are newsgroups, bulletin boards, listservs (e-mail lists), IRC (Internet Relay Chat), and now, even voice chatting. Most of these have counterparts on individual systems like Prodigy, CompuServe, and America Online. This all amounts to one thing: You have a lot of choices.

In this chapter, you will be introduced to not only the media available, but to samples of what you are likely to find in some of these forums, just to give you a taste of the real thing.

All the various types of electronic interaction are one of two types: delayed or real time. Delayed forums work much like e-mail; in fact some of them are based entirely on e-mail. You write a message which is then posted so that others can read and respond to it. Real-time interaction, usually called chat, is more interactive. The participants "talk" just as they would if they were sitting together across the kitchen table. Traditionally this is done by typing your thoughts into the computer's keyboard, but in recent times programs have evolved that actually let you speak to others almost anywhere in the world.

You can find these interactive environments on the Internet itself, on thousands of local BBSs and on the larger commercial services. For our purposes, it seems most appropriate to take these facilities category by category and look at some of the variations.

The Internet

Discussion topics on the Internet number in the tens of thousands and change constantly. The vehicles provided are also numerous and still growing. Here we will discuss several of the most popular; the delayed forums first, followed by the real-time, interactive ones.

Delayed forums

This group includes the Internet's USENET newsgroups, listservs, BBS conferences, BBSs and conferences on commercial services, and even some sites on the World Wide Web.

USENET newsgroups

USENET is a collection of messages organized by topics and subtopics. Individuals post "articles" to a particular topic (called a

newsgroup) where they can be read and responded to by others. Responses can be either public—posted right back to the public message list—or they can be nothing more than private e-mail.

The topics of newsgroups are extremely varied. Though there is no firm count available, there are at least 15,000 different newsgroups around, each devoted to a different topic. Each message within a newsgroup has its own subject. A series of messages with the same subject is called a thread.

These topics are arranged in a hierarchy. For example, rec.sports.baseball is a newsgroup devoted to recreation (rec), specifically the sport (.sports) of baseball (.baseball). As you can see in this example, the name of the newsgroup is composed of a series of terms separated by periods (called "dots"). These terms become more specific as you read from left to right. There are hundreds of rec newsgroups and dozens of rec.sports topics, one of which is .baseball.

Traditionally, there have been seven major subject areas within the USENET hierarchy:

sci	scientifically oriented newsgroups (sci.anthropology)
comp	computer related newsgroups (comp.multimedia)
rec	recreational topics (rec.parks.theme)
soc	social/cultural issues (soc.culture.african.american)
news	announcements and Net news (news.announce.newusers)
talk	topical talk groups (talk.environment)
misc	miscellaneous topics (misc.transport.urban-transit)

There was, and still is, a fairly rigorous process through which new newsgroups must pass before they are added to any of the above categories. To relax these requirements, another major topic was later added: the alt (alternative) group. The requirements for creating a new alt group are far more casual.

In more recent times, a large number of other categories have been introduced. Some are focused on topics of general interest, but many are of special interest to people at a certain college, or in a certain city or country. These types of newsgroups usually bear names that relate to the main topic. For example bay for San Francisco Bay Area, pnw for Pacific Northwest and uk for United Kingdom. Many of these specialized newsgroups are only carried by systems within their geographical area.

Mailing lists

Many Internet users, perhaps the majority worldwide, are limited to e-mail. They don't have access to the more sophisticated features like USENET, Telnet, FTP, and the World Wide Web. However, they

can still participate in round-robin discussions via e-mail. This is accomplished through the use of automated mailing lists. An automated mailing list is a program that manages lists of people who are interested in a particular topic. Participants submit "articles" by sending them via e-mail to the mailing list program. The program then distributes copies to all the people on the list for that topic. Anyone can then respond by e-mail to any of the posted messages.

This can happen surprisingly quickly. For example, if you open your e-mail box one morning and see a recent posting from someone and respond to it, you may already have a response while your are composing your next note. This would require that the user involved just happened to be online at the same time, but it does happen.

In order to participate in such a mailing list, you must first subscribe. This is done by sending an e-mail message to the computer that manages that particular list with the text. Not all lists are managed by the same program, but there are two programs (each with subtle variants) that are most common. These are "listserv" and "majordomo". Though both programs have a variety of commands you can use to query and control them, the two most important ones at first are HELP and SUBSCRIBE.

Sending an e-mail message to a listserv or majordomo server program with the text HELP as the entire text will cause it to send you a short list of commands and instructions by return e-mail. Both listserv and majordomo use the command SUBSCRIBE, but there is a subtle difference in what they expect to follow it. Both need the name of the mailing list you want to subscribe to immediately follow the word SUBSCRIBE. Listserv then wants your full name, whereas majordomo wants your e-mail address.

Here are a couple of hypothetical examples.

Address the message to *listserv@whatsamatau.edu* and place the following text in the body of the message: subscribe hiphop My Full Name.

If the list is managed by majordomo, you would send something like this:

majordomo@whatsamatau.edu

with the following text in the body of the message:

subscribe hiphop *me@here.com*

In any case, you can always get information on how a particular list manager works by sending an e-mail message to it with the word HELP

as the entire message. In most cases, replacing HELP with INFO or MANUAL will bring you even more information.

Often listserv is used in a generic sense to refer to any and all list managers, regardless of the program actually used. It's sort of like calling any old tissue Kleenex. In addition to their technical differences, there are more subtle differences in the ways listservs and newsgroups are used. Because newsgroups are more visible due to their messages being generally available to all, they tend to be more public. Listservs, on the other hand, tend to be a bit more private because you have to take the initiative by subscribing to them. As a result, they also tend to be somewhat more intimate and personal.

Because anyone can just drop in and post a message to a newsgroup, they are more prone to off-topic intrusions and other "noise." Listservs, while not immune to such things, seem to provide much smaller targets for the casual or disruptive user.

Another key difference between listservs and newsgroups is that it is much easier to start your own listserv. If you have an account on a system that offers such services, all you have to do is ask for it. You may or may not have to pay an additional fee to cover the increased e-mail traffic an active list produces. This traffic may not be trivial.

For example, if you have a list of 100 people, each of whom posts just one message a day to 100 people, that means 100 times 100, or 10,000 messages a day (don't forget, every posting must go to everyone on the list separately). Over the course of a month, that adds up to around 300,000 e-mail messages.

As with newsgroups, some listservs are moderated and others are not. In the case of a moderated list, the moderator (usually called the list owner) actually receives all posted messages and must pass judgment on them before they are distributed to the members of the list. In some cases, incoming messages are never posted. This permits the automatic distribution of newsletters and other periodicals.

You will see several examples of listservs in the material quoted later in this chapter.

The World Wide Web

Some sites on the World Wide Web include discussion groups in one form or another. These often take a form that is a cross between newsgroups and listservs. You make your submission right at the Web site and it is added to a list of responses already posted by others. The

result is a single Web document containing all the submissions over a period of time.

This approach has advantages and disadvantages over listservs and newsgroups. It is harder to follow because the messages are generally posted in the order they were received. This is in contrast to newsgroups where you can elect to follow the "thread" of a discussion, skipping over other comments on different topics.

The advantage is that it is highly spontaneous. Anyone visiting the Web site can drop in their two bits' worth at any time. *Vibeonline Magazine* has an arrangement like this on their site *http://www.pathfinder.com/@@@3Te6kDkBwMAQJ4v/vibe/*.

E-mail

Most e-mail systems support mail forwarding and distribution lists. This allows you to create something like a listserv, but it takes more effort. It can be done in either of two ways. You can send all the messages manually to one person who then forwards them to the others on the list. Alternatively, each list member can send all of their postings to the entire list themselves. This makes it harder to add new members because everyone on the list must add their address to their copy of the list. It may, however, be the only way available to get the job done. The effect, if properly implemented, is almost identical to a simple listserv.

Real-time forums

The Internet provides a medium in which anyone with the needed software can interact with anyone else in real time. Many people have taken their best shot at creating the ideal software to enable such interactions. The first and still most popular of these is IRC (Internet Relay Chat).

IRC

IRC was originated at the University of Oulu, Finland, in 1988. It provides for user-created "channels" in which individuals interact in real-time conversations. A channel is roughly similar to a newsgroup. It has a stated topic and is "owned" by whomever enters first. Users then simply join the created channel.

A few channels are almost perpetually active, but most come and go. In order for a channel to remain open, someone must be online and joined to that channel. The channel #hottub (all channel names begin with #) is open 24 hours a day, 7 days a week. The channel #black is only open when someone is there to join it. When you look at a list of

open channels, you will notice that many, if not most, are populated by only one person. It is not unusual to see two or three thousand different channels open with only a few hundred populated by more than one person.

IRC channels can be made private (no one can join without the permission of the owner) or even invisible (they won't even show up on a listing). Obviously, you can have any degree of privacy or public visibility you want if you own the list.

There are two ways to access IRC. If you have an IP account, you can download an IRC client program. Most are freeware or shareware. If you are limited to UNIX shell access, your host system probably has an IRC client you can use.

The typical IP account is much easier to use than the standard UNIX IRC account. You can join multiple channels and keep each one in a separate window. Whereas with the UNIX program, they are all interspersed with one another and can be difficult to read. There are numerous other "creature comforts" that you won't have access to. On the other hand, all IRC clients basically do the same things. The differences are largely a matter of convenience and ease of use.

All you have to do to start your own channel is to log on to IRC and join an empty channel. For example, if you wanted to start a channel about jazz, you would type:

/join #jazz

If that channel already existed, you would be "enrolled" (assuming it was not private). If there was no such channel at that moment, one would be created and you would be its owner and only occupant. Others could then join you by typing the same thing you did to enroll.

Two channels you might want to try on your first outing are #black and #blaklife. These are ongoing channels with their own "regulars" and "drop-ins."

Once you own a channel, you can supply some descriptive information that will be available to others who are shopping for a channel to join. To learn how to do this and many other things, just type /help after you log on to IRC. You will get a list of commands and other useful information.

Iphone

One of the newest and most appealing uses for the basic IRC technology is voice communication. Yes, that's right, you can now actually speak to people over the Internet. Programs like Iphone (for

IBM compatibles) and Webphone (for Macs) are starting to appear on the Net.

These programs may or may not use the facilities of IRC to connect people to one another. Whether they use IRC or some other means to achieve connection does not matter to the user, so don't be concerned.

The first thing Iphone does when you log on is to "call home." This registers you as a user who is online. Once you have logged on with Iphone, you can look at a list of all the other people who are presently logged on. You can call any one of them right off the list and talk to them.

You will need a multimedia board if you have an IBM compatible. You will also need a microphone and speakers to go with it. The other essential is the Iphone software. You can download a demo version from any of several sites on the Web. The demo version works just like the real thing but is limited to 60 seconds of speech. You can listen all you want, but every time you open your mouth, the meter starts running. If you like it, you can register your copy on the Net for $69. Here is where you can get the demo: *http://vocaltec.com:80/dnload.htm*.

The quality of sound is not what you're used to on a regular telephone, but when you consider that you can talk to people all over the world for free, it begins to sound a lot better.

PowWow

Another new and highly innovative product was created by a small band of Native Americans in Colorado. Not surprisingly, they call it PowWow. This clever program allows up to seven people to engage in private or semi-private chats together. However, its capabilities don't stop there.

The newest version also supports voice communication similar to, though not quite as slick as, Iphone. With the voice ability comes the ability to send sounds to others. The program comes with a modest list of sound effects and messages, such as "Coooool," "Boooooh," "Are you still there," and some pretty weird laughter.

Probably the most innovative feature of PowWow is the Cruise Mode. This allows two or more people to surf the Web together automatically. Whoever initiates Cruise Mode becomes the leader. Whenever they access a new Web page, all their fellow cruisers see it too—automatically! This does require that everyone use the Netscape Web browser, but since almost everyone does (and it's free), why not?

The other excellent feature of PowWow is its ability to send files from one person directly to another. You just click on a Send button and tell it which file you want to send. That's it. Best of all, you can keep chatting while the file is being transferred, and the best news is that it isn't even shareware, it's absolutely free.

Commercial online services

All the commercial online services offer large numbers of topical forums for group discussion. Each of the Big Three has one or more areas that cater to AAs. Some of these forums are message-oriented while others are for chatting in real time. Following is a brief description of the most populated of these. Hopefully, there will be more as the number of cybernauts of African descent increases.

All the commercial online services offer Internet connections, so most of what is available on the Internet is also available through these services, in addition to their own private offerings.

Delayed forums

The mainstay of the delayed forums is the topical bulletin board (BB). On these, users read messages posted by others with similar interests and post their own thoughts in reply. The topics are as varied as the people who participate. As with newsgroups and listservs, it is usually a good idea to "lurk" for a while before jumping in. If there is an FAQ or other document describing the group, read it even before examining the current postings. Here are some of the BBSs on the Big Three that are of special interest to AAs.

Bulletin boards

CompuServe's Afro-American Culture (AAC) group The AAC forum is sponsored by *American Visions* magazine. *American Visions* is the official publication of the African American Museums Association. To get to the AAC forum, GO AFRO. It provides a lively and well populated forum in which to discuss topics of interest. The sponsors see it as "a celebration of Afro-American culture and art." Figure 4-1 shows the opening screen you see when you enter the forum for the first time.

America Online's African-American Board America Online offers the African-American Board as part of "The Exchange," a collection of special interest groups. It is a popular and active forum for discussion and debate. Expect a wide variety of topics and thousands of messages. Figure 4-2 shows less than half of the available topics.

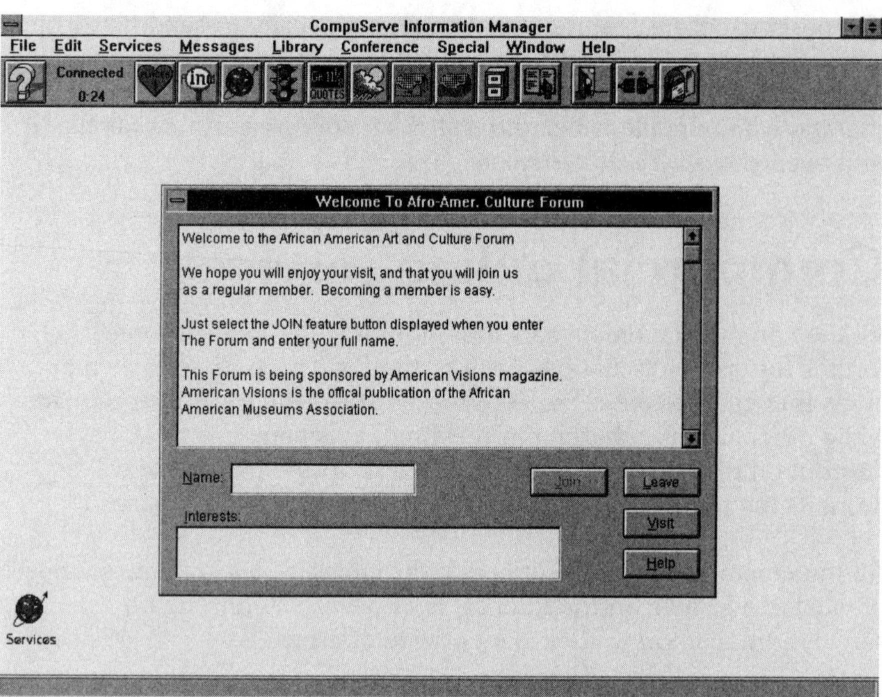

Fig. 4-1 *CompuServe's Afro-American Culture (AAC) group*

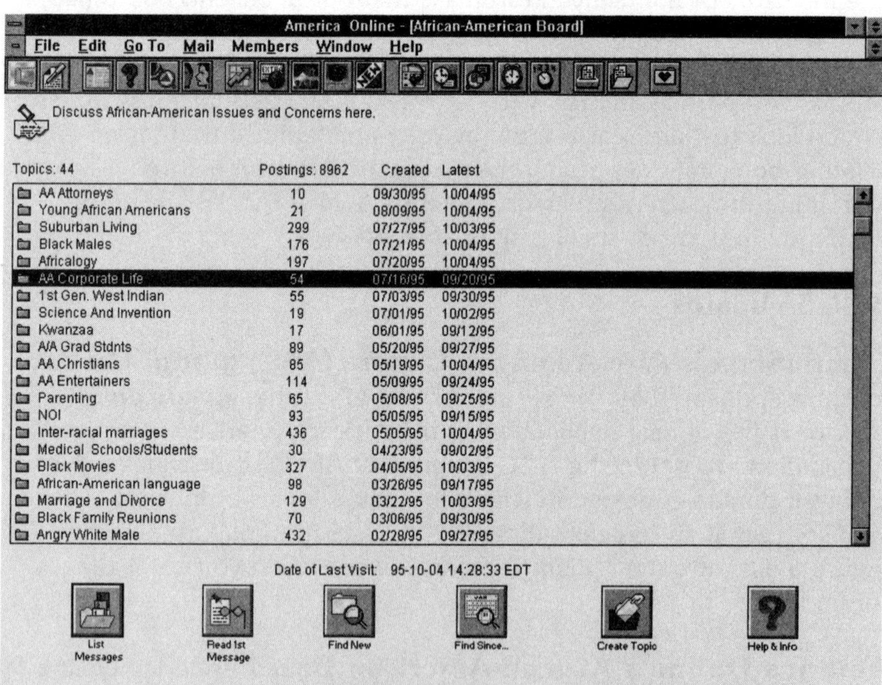

Fig. 4-2 *America Online's African-American board*

To get to the African-American Board, go to the keyword EXCHANGE and select Communities Center. The boards are listed there alphabetically.

Prodigy's Black Experience BB The Prodigy service's counterpart to the forums already mentioned is called the Black Experience Bulletin Board. As with the others already mentioned, you will find dozens of subjects, each with numerous sub-topics and thousands of messages. Figure 4-3 shows the opening screen of the Black Experience BB. If you look carefully, you can see a button sticking out under the topics window that says "Chat." On Prodigy, you can enter directly into a live chat session right from the BB screen. Which is our cue to move on to the subject of real-time forums. But first, here is the Black Experience BB screen.

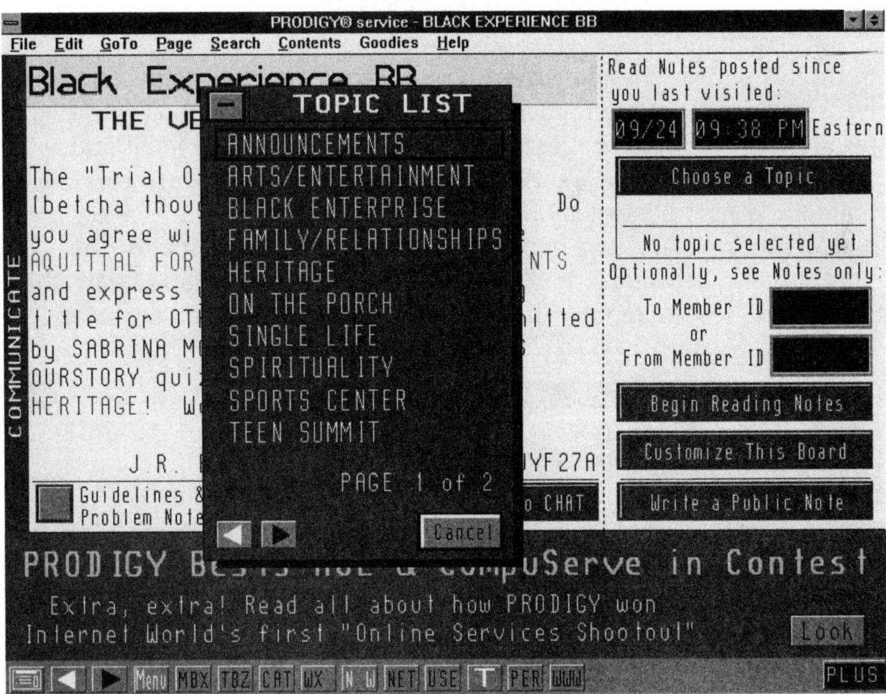

Fig. 4-3 *Prodigy's Black Experience bulletin board*

Real-time forums

For many people, chatting live is more exciting and interesting than reading and writing notes. Interacting, whether with one other person or dozens, is a much more intense experience. For these and other reasons, live chat is very popular in cyberspace. In fact, next to e-mail, it may be the most popular online pastime around.

The Internet has IRC and the commercial online services have their own chat areas. Here are some examples.

Chat

One of the chief differences between chatting and BBSs is that the topics of chat areas are much more fluid. Anyone can at any time open a new room with a new topic and see who drops in. The lifetime

of a chat topic may be from a few minutes to a few hours. Some topics are created by the service, others by users. Most are not permanent. In the case of user-created rooms, the last one to leave "turns out the lights." This does not mean that someone else might not start the same topic again five minutes later, but for the present, the room is closed.

Prodigy's Black Experience chat rooms Chat topics are often similar to those on any related BB. Since they are so fluid, they tend to come and go fairly quickly. One of the nice things about Prodigy's facilities is that private chat rooms are supported. These are areas to which you must be invited unless you yourself initiate it.

Figure 4-4 shows Prodigy's Black Experience board's display. You can choose from any of the numerous areas, and within each area are specific topics. Some of these are created by the service itself and others are created by users. A few, called "auditoriums," are service-created and hold hundreds of people. These are intended to allow speakers to address the group on their chosen topic, much as one might in a public lecture. In most cases, you can also interact with the speaker and the audience. The rules are different for each situation.

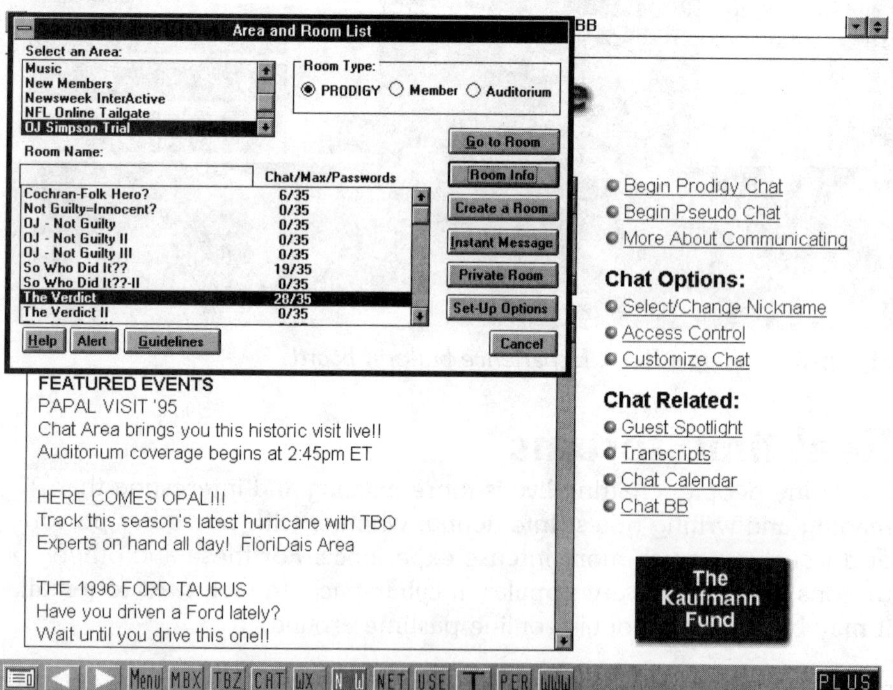

Fig. 4-4 *Prodigy's Black Experience chat rooms*

CompuServe's Afro-American Culture chat rooms

CompuServe also offers topical chat rooms that are closely associated with their BBSs. As with the other services, users can create their own rooms and invite others to join them. There are also scheduled chats

with notable personalities. You may have seen CNN's coverage of such an event with the cast of *Apollo 13*. It was considered quite an event at the time. For a snapshot of the AAC chat screen, see Fig. 4-5.

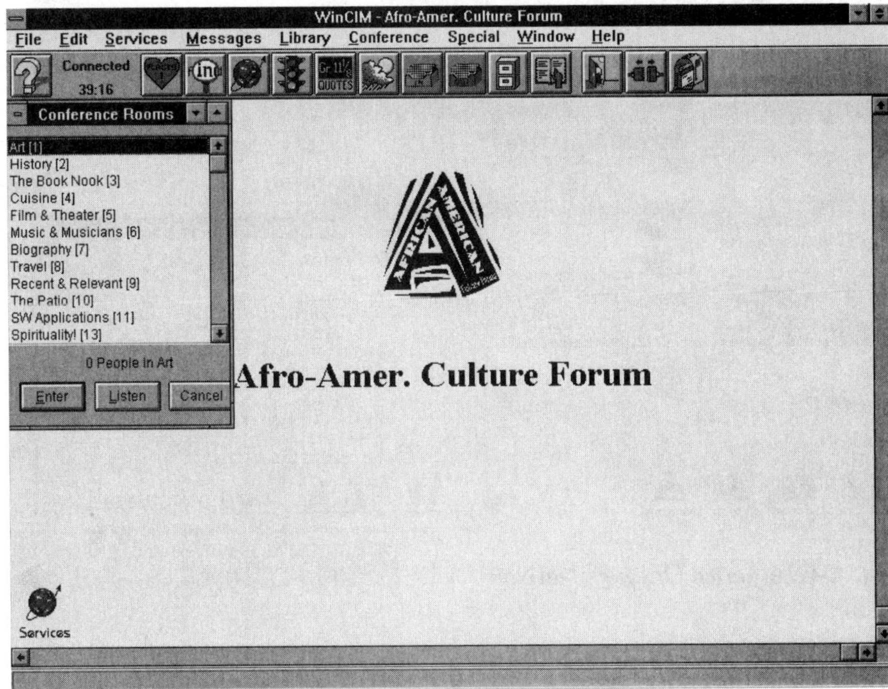

Fig. 4-5 *CompuServe's Afro-American Culture chat rooms*

America Online's NetNoir Here's what NetNoir's sponsors have to say about their mission.

> NetNoir, Inc. ("NN"), a California corporation, is a new media company based in San Francisco. It's mission is to digitize, archive, and distribute Afrocentric culture in cyberspace.

In line with these purposes, they provide online chat capabilities along with many other features and services. In addition to topical chats between individuals, they also offer chats with celebrities like Herbie Hancock, Carl Lewis, and President Aristide. Take a look at Fig. 4-6 for a sample screen.

BBS systems

Direct dial-in BBSs provide an alternative to the Internet and commercial services. Their offerings are of necessity less elaborate in most cases, but they nevertheless fill needs at a community level. One of the great things about local BBSs is that if you meet someone online whom you like, they are usually accessible in the real world as

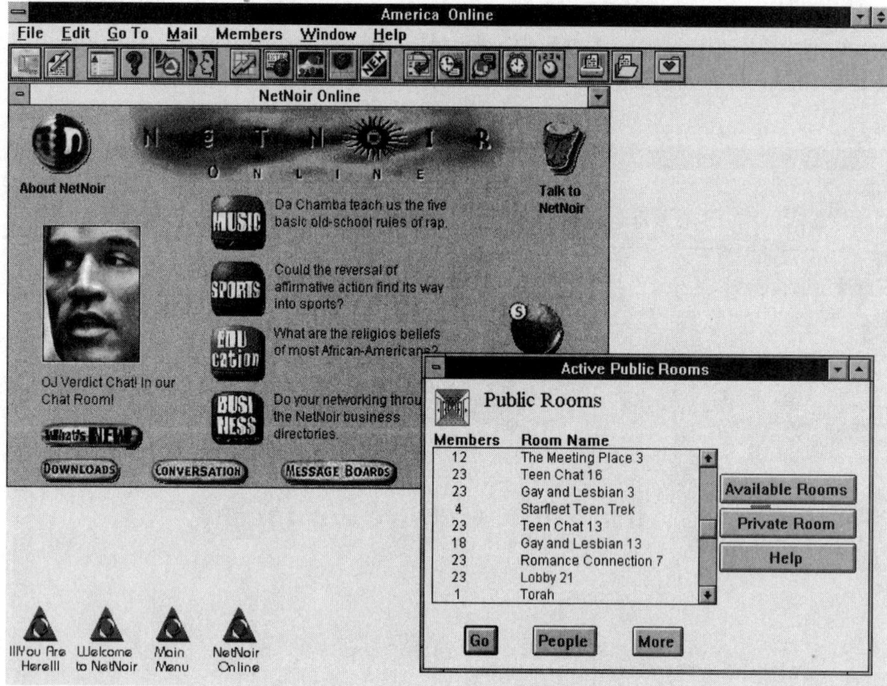

Fig. 4-6 *America Online's NetNoir*

well. That isn't often true in the larger reaches of cyberspace. Here are some of the things you can expect to find.

Delayed forums

Local BBSs were the first electronic forums for public discussion that were available to everyone. You didn't have to be a student or defense contractor to play then, and you still don't. Before there was the Internet (as we now know it), there was Fidonet.

Fidonet Fidonet was created years before the term *information superhighway* was first spoken. Though it developed around the same time as the Internet, they were essentially separate. While the Internet was growing in the rarefied atmosphere of higher education and the defense industry, Fidonet was spawned and nurtured by hobbyists around the world on a shoestring.

It is still one of the most clever and workable schemes ever invented to bring information and people together electronically. Fidonet, much like the Internet, was a semi-formal and completely voluntary collection of BBS systems who agreed to exchange information from point to point electronically.

Not having access to hi-tech fiber optic cables and mainframe computers, these people managed to accomplish many of the same things using only their personal computers and conventional phone

lines. In order to move information any distance at all, they had to pay for long distance calls out of their own pockets.

They created an ingenious method for moving information called Echo Mail. It was part Pony Express, and part Internet, but it worked for many years and served millions of people while the Internet was still in diapers.

Moving Echo Mail required that all the systems in Fidonet shut down in the middle of the night for an hour or two. During this downtime, they passed the day's collection of e-mail and other information to the next station down the line. Eventually, it arrived at its destination. Sometimes it might take several days for a message to arrive on another continent—and sometimes it didn't arrive at all—but it was a remarkably efficient and useful system.

Keep in mind, this was for the most part done by volunteers with equipment and phone lines bought with their own hard-earned money. Some charged a modest fee to their subscribers (seldom more than $25 a year), but many asked only for a small "donation" to help with maintenance.

Fidonet was very popular on the African continent from the beginning. Many of the first systems outside North America were established in Africa. There are still thousands of Fidonet BBSs alive and functioning. In many parts of the world, they are still the only electronic communications medium in existence and will probably remain so for some time to come.

Echos One of the first uses for Fido Mail was to support the precursor of USENET's newsgroups. In the Fido world, these are variously called "conferences," "discussion groups," or "topics." In the end, they are the same as newsgroups or listservs: a vehicle by which people can discuss topics which interest them.

With the rise of the commercial services and the Internet, these small BBSs are assuming the role of local information collection and distribution centers. Many have narrowed their focus to specific interest areas, though few are completely limited to one topic. If your community has such a system, you may want to check it out. You could be in for a pleasant surprise.

There is also a newer type of BBS that is much bigger than most traditional boards, yet much smaller than the Big Three. These often allow for limited access to the facilities of the Internet, most often e-mail and USENET. They also tend to charge at least minimal fees for all access. Often too, they are heavily involved with helping local people to meet one another.

Real-time forums

Since most BBSs are limited to one or two phone lines, there really isn't any way for users to interact in real time. The exceptions are the mid-sized boards just mentioned. These can have hundreds of incoming phone lines (but not the thousands available to the Big Three). This allows users to interact in real time.

Chat boards As the i-way wends its way into the hinterlands, these systems will either get connected or die from lack of interest. Time does, after all, march on. Meanwhile, if you live in an area where they are the only game in town, or if you happen to have an active, vital BBS of this type operating nearby, take a look. I know lots of people who have had a great deal of fun with them.

One of the strongest appeals these boards have is local chat. In this context, local may mean anything from a neighborhood to a major metropolitan area. To find out what's going on in your area, check local BBSs or call a few computer stores and libraries. If all else fails, pick up a copy of *Computer Shopper* magazine, which has a lengthy list of BBSs nationally. Find one in your area and give it a call. Once you get plugged in to the local scene, it won't be much trouble to find what you're looking for if it exists.

Inside Black Chat

What follows here are actual messages posted to various forums devoted to AA topics and issues. They are offered to give you an idea of the type and variety of postings to these public forums.

So take a peek at an AA online discussion. Some of the comments are funny, some serious, some downright nasty, but all of them are important in their own way.

Subject: afro-centric T-shirt slogans

I'm writing a "piece" based on afro-centric T-shirt slogans.
Anyone care to share some slogans they've seen on T-shirts?

Subject: afro-centric T-shirt slogans

"No, White lady, I DON'T want your
purse!"

Subject: afro-centric T-shirt slogans

Front: Imported From Africa U.S. Inspected

Back: And I Didn't Ask To Come

Subject: afro-centric T-shirt slogans

1. Black Is A Force To Be Reckoned With
2. Africa-Land of Heroes and Warriors
3. Black, Proud, and Dangerous
4. We Are A Nation
5. I Ain't No Slave
6. I'll Be Back (Mike Tyson)
7. African in America
8. No Justice No Peace
9. Know Our History
10. We Was Here First

Subject: afro-centric-shirt slogans

My favorite is the one with the Black Bart Simpson and the words:

I didn't do it.
Nobody saw me.
You can't prove anything.

Also rather memorable is "We don't die, we multiply!"

Subject: afro-centric T-shirt slogans

I have a shirt that says: The Blacker the College, the Sweeter the Knowledge.

On the back, it lists all 100+ of the nation's historically black colleges. I used to have one that said: Black to the Future. Also, Bring plenty of guns, money, and lawyers, the s*** is about to hit the fan!!

Subject: afro-centric T-shirt slogans

I own these: Black is Beautiful, Green is Necessary; Support Black Businesses & Know Real Black Power; Before There Was Any History, There Was Black History

Finally, on a souvenir shirt from the 63rd Annual Conference of The National Technical Association (NTA):
Renaissance: Accelerating the Movement Through Science and Technology

Subject: Waiting to Exhale

In my humble opinion, Waiting To Exhale (WtE) was not meant to be a vehicle for positive Black male role models. In fact, the existence of one might have spoiled the story. Now *before* you fly off the handle, let me explain. The point of WtE was that many Black women—and women in general—are waiting for their Prince Charming to appear, to sweep them off their feet and to make their lives complete.

They are in a sense "holding their breath" waiting for this Man to enter their lives. (Thus the title of the book) Now if one of the characters had met their Prince Charming halfway through the book, the moral would be lost—that moral being that Black women should feel complete in themselves without a man. Now perhaps all the men needn't have been quite so unsavory, but often, in fiction, authors exaggerate to make a point.

What I am saying basically is this. WtE is not a book about bad Black men. It is a story about women learning to be comfortable alone and with female friends. And as such, I enjoyed the book immensely.

I think about the idea the book tried to convey often, as I look around my world and am tempted to think how much more complete my life would be if only I had a boyfriend. Women do that a lot; we tend to place romantic relationships with men above our female friendships. Perhaps if you think of this meaning of WtE you will see why it was written the way it was.

Board: Cultures BB (Prodigy)
Subject: AA Quote for Today

Attention all "Newbies"!! (Those of you new to the net). This is your captain speaking. . . . Thank you for choosing AA Airways for this leg of your cyberspace journey. My co-captains and I want to make your trip as comfortable and enjoyable as possible. Please direct your attention to the front of your screen. On it you will see a list of abbreviations used here in cyberspace:
<g> = grin
<eg> = evil grin
<sg> = sly grin
<LOL> = Laugh Out Loud
ROTFL = Rolling On The Floor Laughing
BTW = By The Way
IMHO = In My Humble Opinion (sometimes just IMO)
TTYL = Talk To You Later
WBS = Write Back Soon
May I introduce you to our mascot "Smiley" :) (Tilt your head to the left) Smiley is a very emotional person
:((frown)
;) (wink)
>:((anger)

In order to not annoy the other passengers, may I suggest that you turn your caps light OFF? Using ALL CAPITAL letters in cyberspace equates to SHOUTING <g>,

Also, to make your ride smoother you may want to take a gander at the GUIDELINES posted on the wall at the door. The gist being that you should treat your conversations as in any social setting and behave accordingly. (No profanity or EXPLICIT details of your <ahem> "personal affairs") <LOL>

If you have need of any further assistance, might I also direct you to ask J.R., Lee, or Liz. There, you will also find information that will assist you in getting into the "fast lane" (i.e., reading and writing notes OFFLINE) which will greatly reduce your fare. Once again, thank you for choosing this route on the Info Highway!

We now return you to your regularly scheduled program. . . .

Subject: Re: Black Conservative

Can a Black person still be down with his people, while espousing conservative philosophy and beliefs. Being conservative doesn't necessarily mean you are a member of the Republican party or want to be white. Why do all Blacks have to be in the same boat, politically speaking? Hasn't the strategy of placing all our eggs in the Democratic basket been a dismal failure?

If you are asking if a Black person can be "down" (whatever that means) and conservative, I think the answer is yes. But, perhaps a better description of what you mean by conservative is needed.

If you are asking if a Black person can be "down" and Republican, my personal response is why bother. Sure the Democrats are full of it, but that doesn't automatically mean that the Republicans are not (full of it, that is).

I personally can't see currently how placing our "eggs" in either party's basket can be a success. The Democrats take us for granted and the Republicans just take us.

Rather than just rewarding the Republican party with our support despite their obvious nonsupport of AA issues, I would suggest that AAs stay home en mass during the primaries. Or better yet, let us have our own "primary" and invite donkeys and elephants both to try and impress us.

The last presidential election gave us a great opportunity to see the wisdom of this option. Despite their obvious discontent with both parties, Perot's supporters got considerably more interest from both parties than Blacks. Especially after Perot dropped out of the race and there was the specter of all those votes and no one knowing which way they would vote. Hmm. . . .

The following comments were in response to the posted question:
"What do you think of Dr. Frances Cress Welsing's writings?"

Subject: Re: Dr. Frances Cress Welsing

I am a young white man who has had a brief introduction to Dr. Cress Welsing's theory, and I must say that I find the assignation of particular psychological traits to an entire geographical group of ethnicities to be reminiscent of similar pronouncements upon the psychology of *all* Black people. Although it cannot be denied that Europeans have been the invaders and despoilers of late, this has not always been the case. Furthermore, there have been many Euros who have consistently opposed colonialism and racism. It is important for those people that they not be lumped in with those who they vehemently oppose (many communists, socialists, anarchists, and pacifists were iced by the nazis, as well as many Jews and Roma [Gypsies]).

After 400+ years of wacked-out theories justifying white racism, it is understandable that Blacks should find "mirror" arguments such as those of Jeffries and Cress Welsing appealing, but it just seems like a rehash of the same racist nonsense that white supremacists have been dishing out for years. Just thought I'd let you know. . . . Peace

Subject: Re: Dr. Frances Cress Welsing

I think they are "cute." However, I also think they are methodologically unsound. Her understanding of physiology for example is exceedingly weak. White people are not albinos, they DO have melanin, just not a lot of it. As for the claims made about melanin, Welsing confuses melanin which is simply a skin pigment, with melatonin which is something a lot different.

Now with all that said, I think her conclusions are not far off the mark at all. This is why I said that her works were "cute" rather than total BS. But does employing Jungian symbolism to look at Europeans really get us anywhere? I have seen her a couple of times, and all I get from her is entertainment, something to trip on. We have far too many problems in our community for this type of presentation to be as prevalent in our community as it is.
—Peace

Subject: Futility of Focusing on Skin Color

A few weeks ago I heard or read somewhere that race was an artificial concept and that it was commonly used to make one set of persons inferior/superior to another and that there was no practical application of the concept. So, I decided to check it out. My first stop was going to be a library and some heavy research. But I first checked out the CD-ROM encyclopedia that came with my computer. It is from Software Toolworks. Under the subject of Race or some related subject I found the following (paraphrased):

Humans are classified as Caucasian, Negroid, or Mongoloid. Caucasian and Negroid blood groups are similar, more so than Mongoloid, thus giving rise to two major groups rather than three where blood factors are concerned. The entry for Caucasian was really lame. They claim to have given their name to the great white race. More work to do here.

Many dark-skinned Africans are considered Caucasian. Surprising since this is the opposite of the practice in the New World (coincidence?).

I then did a search on names by which Africans have been known and came up with Cushites, Thebians(sp?), Nubians, and others. Some of the descendants of these people exist today in Africa. Some were described as having Caucasian features, others as non

Negroid and others yet as having Caucasian and Negroid features. Confusing at first look, but not really when factoring the numerous conquests of Africa by Eurasians and Europeans over the last 6500 years (+/- a few hundred years). Mixing of Africans and Arabs and Europeans has been going on for hundreds of years.

I found the passages on migration very interesting and will share it in another post.

What race is pure today?

But this I do believe: there is but one people on this planet.

[soapbox mode] There is a reason why we (Blacks) believe the things we believe and I think it's because someone else has written and is teaching us their version of history, anthropology, and other fields of study. We can buy in, or learn it from our perspective. [soapbox off)

—Peace

Subject: Opinion on NAACP/Chavis?

As a white Jewish male whose family has actively supported the NAACP since the 1930s, I could not be more delighted with Chavis getting the sack. I am 46 years old, and was raised in the civil rights movement. I had the honor of meeting Dr. King (I could not EVER call him Martin!) when I was 19; not a day passes that I do not think about that meeting and the message of his life.

But Benjamin Chavis was one of the great disappointments of my life.

Since the United Church of Christ is headquartered here, I was familiar with Rev. Chavis, and was delighted with his having been chosen to head an organization that has been so important in this country's struggle to achieve racial and ethnic equality for each and every American.

But Chavis turned out to be something less than what is needed to head such an important organization.

First, he sucked up to Louis Farrakhan, a man whose racism and ethnic hatred flies in the face of everything that both the NAACP and my family has fought for together for more than four generations.

Then, it was revealed that he used a third of a million dollars to pay off a woman who insists that she was sexually harassed, by him. His lame defense was that he broke no NAACP regulations. I find that justification pathetic.

There are many things that are not illegal, but clearly wrong. And his use of the NAACP's money for such a matter is wrong.

He should be ashamed of himself for what he did. But he seems to lack the personal integrity to understand that what he did was wrong.

Regarding his courting of Farrakhan, that was also wrong.
Every positive thing that Farrakhan has done "is erased by his bigotry" just as anything positive David Duke may have said or done (anything is possible) is undone by his racism.

I am saddened for such a fine organization. I am disappointed by a man who I supported wholeheartedly when he was selected to head the NAACP. I only hope that the NAACP can get back on track and find some man or woman of inner moral strength sufficient to lead the group back to its rightful place as an organization whose rightness and sense of purpose is self-evident to all Americans of good will.

Subject: Opinion on NAACP/Chavis?

Ben Chavis was tried and convicted by the media without ever being given the opportunity to tell his side. As for the facts of the case, we still have very few. Did the national press really care that much about the charges of misconduct or were they really after Chavis for reaching out to other AA leaders Including Min. Farrakhan? It didn't matter enough to keep President Clinton or Clarence Thomas out of office!

I believe Chavis was canned for his work to create a unified AA leadership council!! I hope he continues to work for this. We must not ever allow anyone to tell us who we are as a people.

Subject: Opinion on NAACP/Chavis?

Let's just say if Chavis had been a good little Negro, none of this would have happened. I am sorry that the board sold out so fast to appease certain peoples, especially because most of the fervor was coming from non-African Americans.

Subject: Opinion on NAACP/Chavis?

My ideas are many, because this is not a simple issue.

On the organizational level, it seems as if the inertia of an organization with a 64-member board of directors pulled Chavis down, because his agenda was not the traditional agenda of the NAACP. We have to remember that this is the same NAACP that went against Du Bois when he called for economic rather than political empowerment, the same NAACP that went against Dr. King when he took a MORAL, PRINCIPLED stance against the Vietnam War.

Another factor in the organizational analysis is undoubtedly the financial one. The NAACP is an organization created BY and to a certain extent FOR the interests of institutions outside of the African American community. Hence the "image" thing, because their image is tied to their money (at least they THINK it is). So when Chavis seeks to make fundamental changes in the image of the NAACP, changes that go against its nature, an organizational response almost HAD to occur.

What I wish I could see is the "inside scoop." Because it appears to me that much of what we've read has been tainted.

For example, there is at least one similar sexual harassment complaint being leveled against an NAACP Board member, and it is being handled in a similar fashion, without fanfare.

The person who leveled the sexual harassment complaint against Chavis wanted to go back to work for him, even though she stood to make more money if she didn't, through the suit. Something else related to this is the fact that Chavis has only paid her $64,000 rather than the third of a million figure alluded to. Most of this came from the NAACP; however, a significant portion came from Chavis supporters.

There are other concerns also, but in conclusion I think that the agenda that Chavis pushed for was the NAACP's undoing. Notice that in this case I didn't say Chavis' undoing because I think that he'll be straight, and I think that we as a community will be OK too. The NAACP though, unless they pull a rabbit out of a hat, will become more and more irrelevant.

Given that the legal barriers to integration have been removed, that might not be a bad thing.

Subject: Black Media

My prediction is that the Black media will have to come into the 20th Century (at least) or become obsolete. You'd be surprised (maybe you wouldn't) at how many of these

operations don't have computers at this late date. Also, a major mistake, in my judgment, is that often the Black press tries to duplicate news that readers already have, making the Black press dated indeed.

I suspect some Black magazines will do extremely well; I hope Emerge is among them. But others will fall by the wayside. I feel that some magazines (I'm not going to call names, at least not on Prodigy) take their audience for granted and their circulation numbers will eventually reflect that.

I think in some ways the Black media will be segmented like White publications. We already have it: Essence is for women; Ebony is a general interest magazine; and Emerge is an issues-oriented publication for the serious-minded reader. Considering that there are more than 3,000 white publications I think there's room for all of us.

Of course, it would help a whole lot more if our people subscribed to our publications rather than buy so many off the newsstands.

Well, there you have it—the Black Chat sampler. It should be abundantly obvious by now that the gloves are off and that diversity of people and opinion reigns supreme. How sweet it is.

5

Historically Black Colleges and Universities and Minority Institutions

ON April 29, 1854, the Ashmun Institute (now Lincoln University of Pennsylvania) was chartered. It was the first institution founded anywhere in the new world to provide a higher education in the arts and sciences for youth of African descent. Since that day, over 100 more colleges and universities have come into existence whose mission is to confer upon students of African heritage the blessings of higher education.

In this chapter you will find current information on those institutions of higher learning and profiles of a representative sampling. These examples were selected largely because each has established a presence on the World Wide Web through which to inform the world of their aims, facilities, people, and programs. Who could have imagined in the spring of 1854, at the signing of the charter of the Ashmun Institute, that a century and a half later there would be over 100 times as many such schools and that they would be accessible in such an amazing fashion.

As the United Negro College Fund is so fond of reminding us, a mind is indeed a terrible thing to waste. These institutions exist for the sole purpose of preventing that terrible thing from happening. The power of knowledge is immeasurable and the fundamental limitation to that power is the ability of those with the knowledge to share it with those who want and need it. The Internet and its related technologies are the ultimate means to that end.

Many colleges and universities are already offering degree-granting programs which include online participation. In the coming years, it seems inevitable that we will all have the opportunity to complete a higher education without ever leaving home. What's more, imagine the effect that such methods will have on the cost of such an education. No additional expenses for a campus, classrooms, professor, heating, lighting, or dormitories will be required. A teacher can "lecture" to a million students as easily as to one. The only real time required will be to create the curricula and guide students individually by grading papers and counseling them as they progress. Can this be anything but good news for those who have traditionally had the hardest time gaining the advantages of higher education? Can't you just feel the playing field tilting back toward neutrality even now?

So read on here and see what is already happening. Then take heart in the clear and certain outcome: The mountain is finally coming to Mohammed—via the Internet. Let's begin our tour at the beginning, with the letter A for Alabama State University. The text cited below was taken from the Web pages of these institutions or, where needed, from the Federal Information Exchange at *http://web.fie.com/web/mol/allhbcu.htm* on the World Wide Web.

Alabama State University

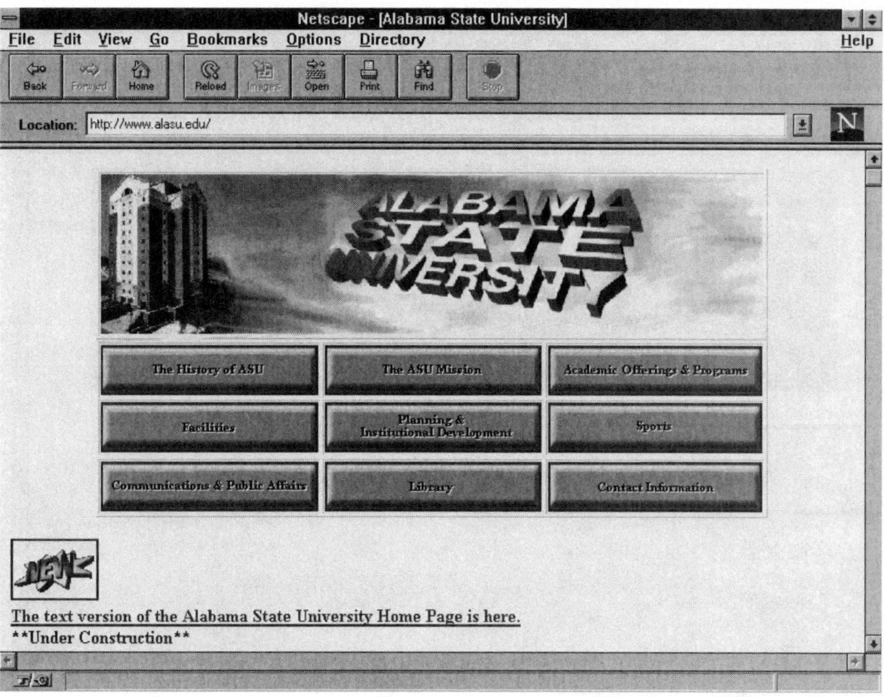

Fig. 5-1 *Alabama State University:* http://www.alasu.edu

Alabama State University is a publicly supported, coeducational institution with a statewide mission. Its major commitments are quality programs of undergraduate and graduate instruction, residential life, continuing education, public service, and research provided at the most reasonable cost to individual students and taxpayers.

The University's programs are particularly responsive to the needs of individual citizens, public groups, and agencies in the Montgomery community.

The University aims to develop and pursue these programs in a manner to ensure that eligible students who desire to develop and expand their scholastic skills for personal, occupational, or professional growth have the opportunity to do so, regardless of socioeconomic status. Respect for the intellectual potential and dignity of students as individual human beings, without regard for racial, ethnic, or cultural background, shall be paramount.

Elizabeth City State University

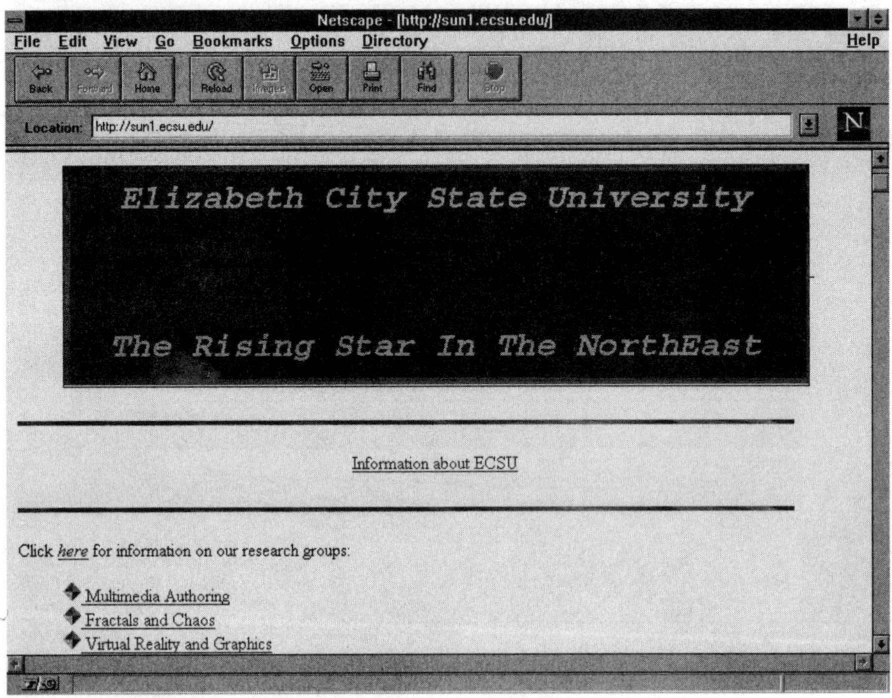

Fig. 5-2 *Elizabeth City State University:* http://sun1.ecsu.edu

What is now Elizabeth City State University was chartered and established in 1891 through the efforts of Hugh Cale, a black representative from Pasquotank County, who introduced the idea to the North Carolina General Assembly. Initially, the institution was created, by law, as a normal school for the specific purpose of "teaching and training teachers" of the "colored race" to "teach in the common schools" of North Carolina. It was named Elizabeth City State Colored Normal School and began operation on January 4, 1892, with a budget of $900, a faculty of two members, and a student enrollment of 23. Under the leadership of John Henry Bias, second president, the institution was elevated from a two-year normal to a four-year teacher's college in 1937. Its name was officially changed to Elizabeth City State Teacher's College on March 30, 1939. The college was again elevated from the "approved" list of colleges to full membership in the Southern Association of Colleges and Schools in December, 1961. The school's name was then changed again in 1963 to Elizabeth City State College. Then on July 1, 1972, the university was made one of the 16 senior institutions of the University of North Carolina, and its final name change occurred when it became Elizabeth City State University.

The University's position at the mouth of the Pasquotank River in Elizabeth City, N.C. (a short distance from the outer banks of North Carolina) provides it with a mild climate all year round. And its approximately 839-acre campus is located in a very historic area. It is one of the oldest historically black colleges in the U.S. Enrollment is approximately 3,500 students of many nationalities and religions.

Fayetteville State University

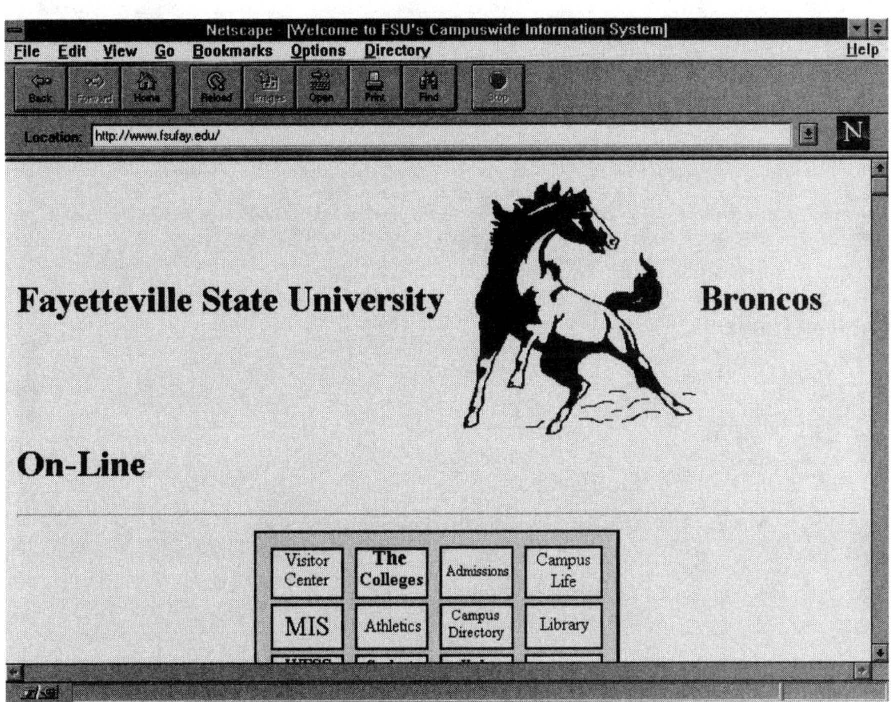

Fig. 5-3 *Fayetteville State University:* http://www.fsufay.edu

A comprehensive institution. Instructional programs at the undergraduate level are organized under two schools (School of Business and Economics; School of Education) and one college (College of Arts and Sciences). Provides undergraduate and graduate instruction in the educational center at nearby Fort Bragg. Offers graduate degrees in elementary education, middle grade education, special education, educational leadership and secondary education, business administration, English, history, biology, mathematics, psychology, and master of arts in teaching. Fayetteville State University is committed to equality of opportunity. To further racial integration, the University actively seeks to recruit and enroll a greater number of non-Black students.

Established as Howard School in 1867. Became state-supported State Colored Normal School in 1877, and Normal State School in

1926. First four-year class graduated and institution renamed Fayetteville State Teachers College in 1939. Merged into the University of North Carolina in 1972.

Fisk University

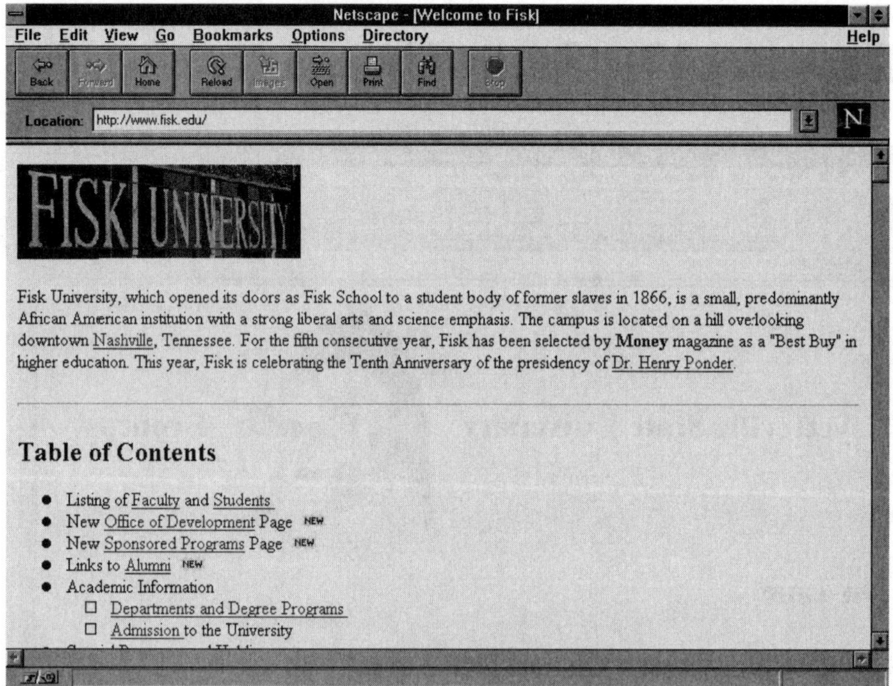
Netscape - [Welcome to Fisk]
File Edit View Go Bookmarks Options Directory Help
Back Forward Home Reload Images Open Print Find Stop
Location: http://www.fisk.edu/
FISK UNIVERSITY
Fisk University, which opened its doors as Fisk School to a student body of former slaves in 1866, is a small, predominantly African American institution with a strong liberal arts and science emphasis. The campus is located on a hill overlooking downtown Nashville, Tennessee. For the fifth consecutive year, Fisk has been selected by Money magazine as a "Best Buy" in higher education. This year, Fisk is celebrating the Tenth Anniversary of the presidency of Dr. Henry Ponder.
Table of Contents
Listing of Faculty and Students
New Office of Development Page NEW
New Sponsored Programs Page NEW
Links to Alumni NEW
Academic Information
Departments and Degree Programs
Admission to the University

Fig. 5-4 *Fisk University:* http://www.fisk.edu

Fisk University, which opened its doors as Fisk School to a student body of former slaves in 1866, is a small, predominantly African-American institution with a strong liberal arts and science emphasis. The campus is located on a hill overlooking downtown Nashville, Tennessee. For the fifth consecutive year, Fisk has been selected by *Money* magazine as a "Best Buy" in higher education. In 1995, Fisk celebrated the tenth anniversary of the presidency of Dr. Henry Ponder.

The origins of Fisk University may be traced to the days immediately following the abolition of slavery in the United States. Historians have richly documented the zeal with which the freed slaves of those days took to the books which had been forbidden them in their time of bondage. Learning was to be the bridge that would carry them from emancipation onward to real freedom and dignity.

Barely six months after the end of the Civil War, and just two years after the Emancipation Proclamation, three men—John Ogden, the

Reverend Erastus Milo Cravath, and the Reverend Edward P. Smith—established the Fisk School in Nashville, named in honor of General Clinton B. Fisk of the Tennessee Freedmen's Bureau, who provided the new institution with facilities in former Union army barracks near the present site of Nashville's Union Station. In these facilities Fisk convened its first classes on January 9, 1866. The first students ranged in age from seven to seventy, but shared common experiences of slavery and poverty—and an extraordinary thirst for learning.

Hampton University

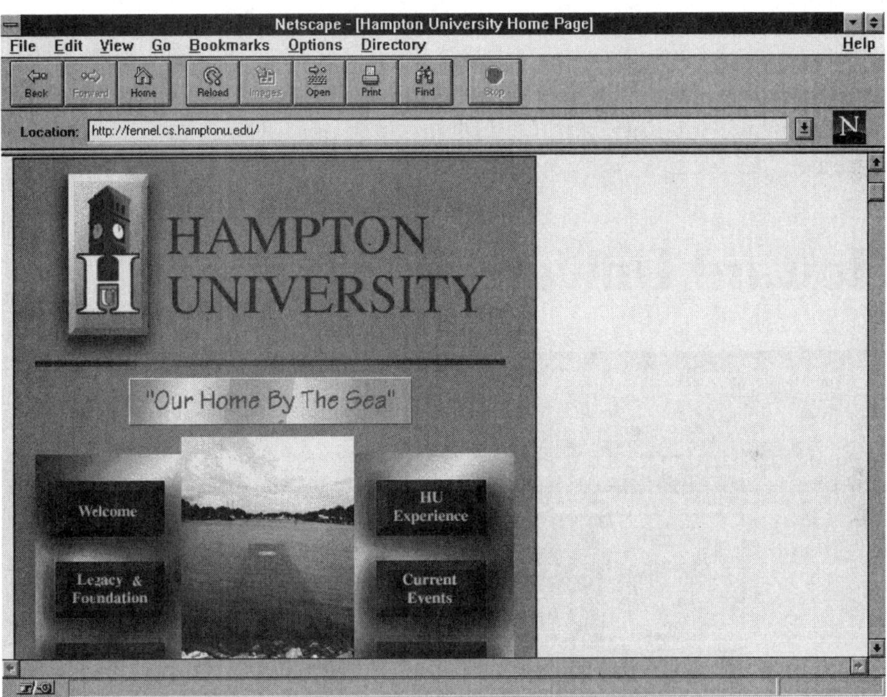

Fig. 5-5 *Hampton University:* http://fennel.cs.hamptonu.edu

Hampton University is a comprehensive institution of higher education, dedicated to the promotion of learning, building of character, and preparation of promising students for positions of leadership and service. Its curricular emphasis is scientific and professional with a strong liberal arts undergirding. In carrying out its objective, everything that the University does must be of the highest quality.

An historically black institution, the University is committed to multiculturalism. Hampton University serves students from diverse national, cultural, educational, and economic backgrounds. From its beginning, the institution has enrolled students from Africa, Japan, China, Cuba, Hawaii, Gabon, Russia, Armenia, and the

United States of America and many of the Native American nations. Placing its students at the center of its planning, the University provides a holistic educational environment. Learning is facilitated by a range of educational offerings, including a rigorous curriculum, good teaching, professional experiences, multiple leadership, and service opportunities, along with the development of character which values respect, dignity, integrity, and decency.

Research and public service are integral parts of the University's mission. Faculty members are encouraged to engage in research, grantsmanship, and writing to enhance discovery, understanding, and scholarship. It is expected that faculty, staff, and students will provide leadership and service to the Hampton University and wider communities.

In achieving its mission, the University provides exemplary opportunities and programs which enable students, faculty, and staff to grow, develop, and contribute in a useful and productive manner.

Howard University

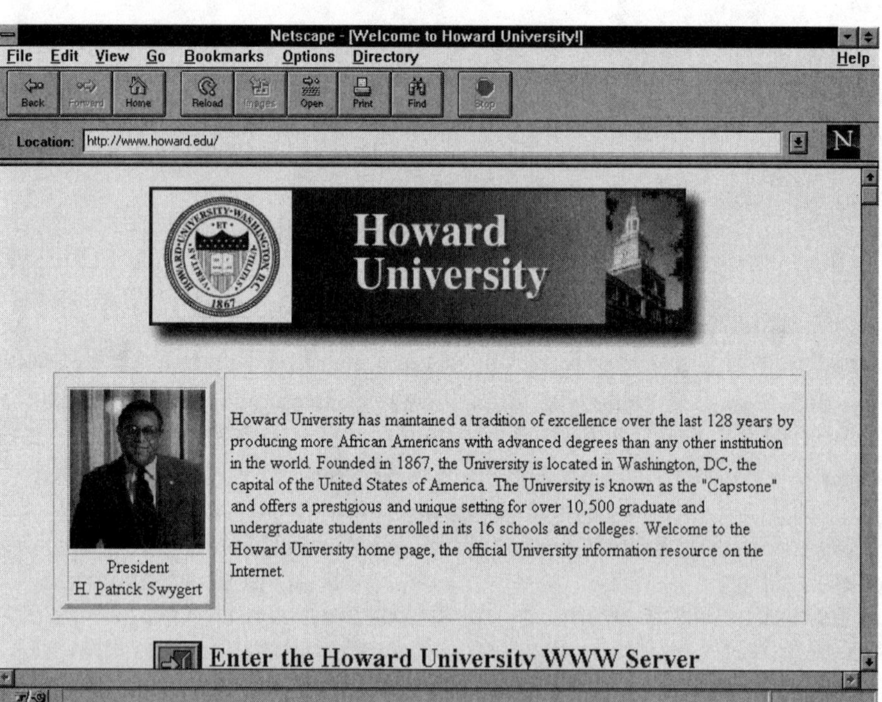

Fig. 5-6 *Howard University:* http://www.howard.edu

The mission of Howard University as a comprehensive, research-oriented, predominantly African-American university is to provide an educational experience of exceptional quality at

reasonable cost to students of high academic potential. Particular emphasis is placed upon providing educational opportunities for African-American men and women and for other historically disenfranchised groups. Furthermore, Howard University is dedicated to attracting, sustaining, and developing a cadre of faculty who, through their teaching and research, are committed to producing distinguished and compassionate graduates who seek solutions to human and social problems in the United States and throughout the world.

The Howard University charter, as enacted by Congress and subsequently approved by President Andrew Johnson on March 2, 1867, designated Howard University as "a university for the education of youth in the liberal arts and sciences." The new institution was named for General Oliver O. Howard, one of the founders and, at the time, Commissioner of the Freedmen's Bureau.

Most of the University's early financial support came from the Freedmen's Bureau. In 1879, Congress approved a special appropriation for the University. The charter was amended in 1928 to authorize an annual federal appropriation for construction, development, improvement, and maintenance of the University.

Jackson State University

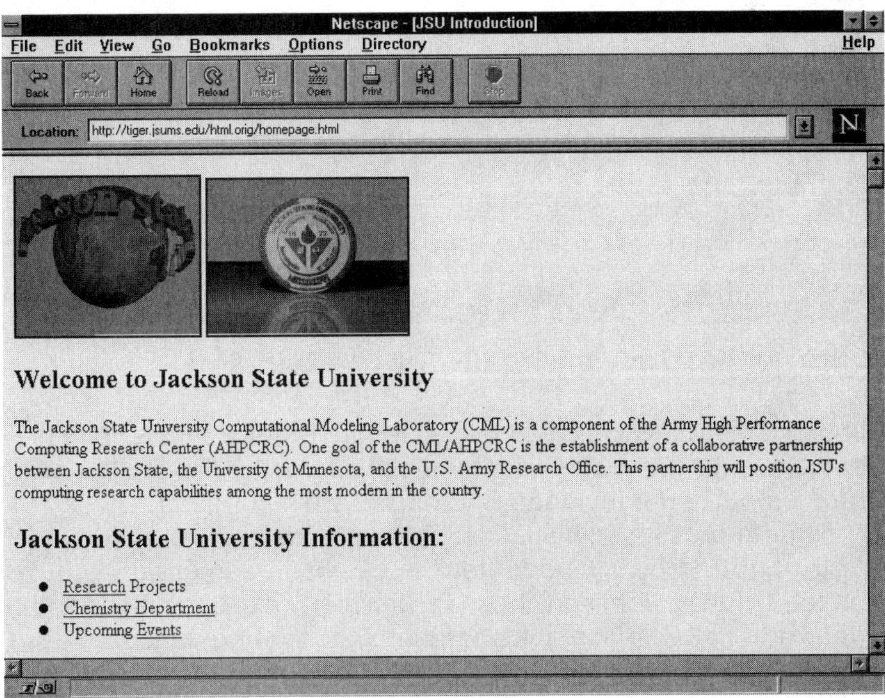

Fig. 5-7 *Jackson State University:* http://tiger.jsums.edu/html.orig/homepage.html

Jackson State is Mississippi's only urban university. It offers the energy and excitement of a major university in a bustling capital city. Internships at top-notch companies and graduate school opportunities are available.

JSU has been guiding students to new futures since 1877. It offers a proud heritage as one of America's leading historically black universities. It is also a dynamic, comprehensive, educational institution where you'll discover myriad opportunities for personal growth. It offers programs and experiences that address the needs and reflect the broad diversity of a cosmopolitan community.

Johnson C. Smith University

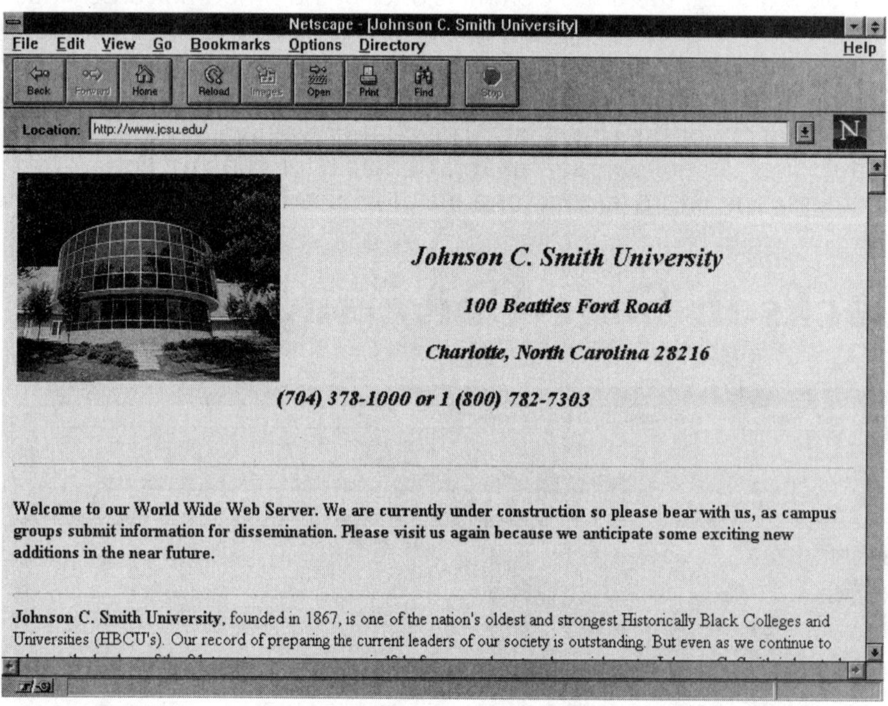

Fig. 5-8 *Johnson C. Smith University:* http://www.jcsu.edu

Johnson C. Smith University, an independent, private college of liberal arts, was founded under the auspices of the Committee on Freedmen of the Presbyterian Church, USA. The original purpose—to provide an institution of training of men "for the ministry, for catechists, and for teachers"—has been greatly expanded. Today, Johnson C. Smith University exists as a coed undergraduate institution of higher learning, offering varied fields of study in the context of the small liberal arts college, open to all qualified persons regardless of race.

Langston University

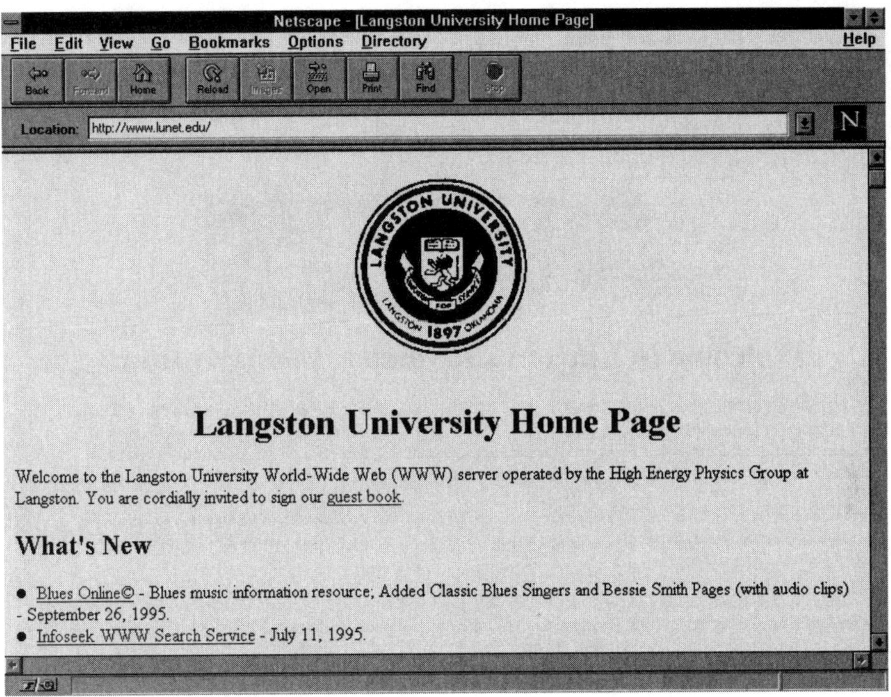

Fig. 5-9 *Langston University:* http://www.lunet.edu

Langston University, a land-grant institution with an urban mission, is an integral part of the Oklahoma State system for higher education. Designated as a special purpose university by the State Regents for Higher Education, Langston University is charged with the responsibility to provide both lower-division and upper-division undergraduate study in several fields leading to a bachelor's degree. In this construct, Langston University has moved to curricular changes that will embrace new career opportunities for its students with positive educational outcomes.

A goal of Langston University is to place its graduates in a highly favorable position to assume careers that meet the changing demands in the urban society today and in the future. This is to be achieved by demanding a high degree of excellence in its instruction, research, and community services as a land-grant institution with an urban mission. Flexibility in academic offerings to keep stride with changes in the world of work for the advantage of Langston University students is implied in the University's mission statement. The dynamics of a free society predict the evolution of new challenges and new opportunities; thus a significant part of Langston University's thrust is to keep abreast of programs and community services using human resources and new technologies emerging on the horizon.

Lincoln University, PA

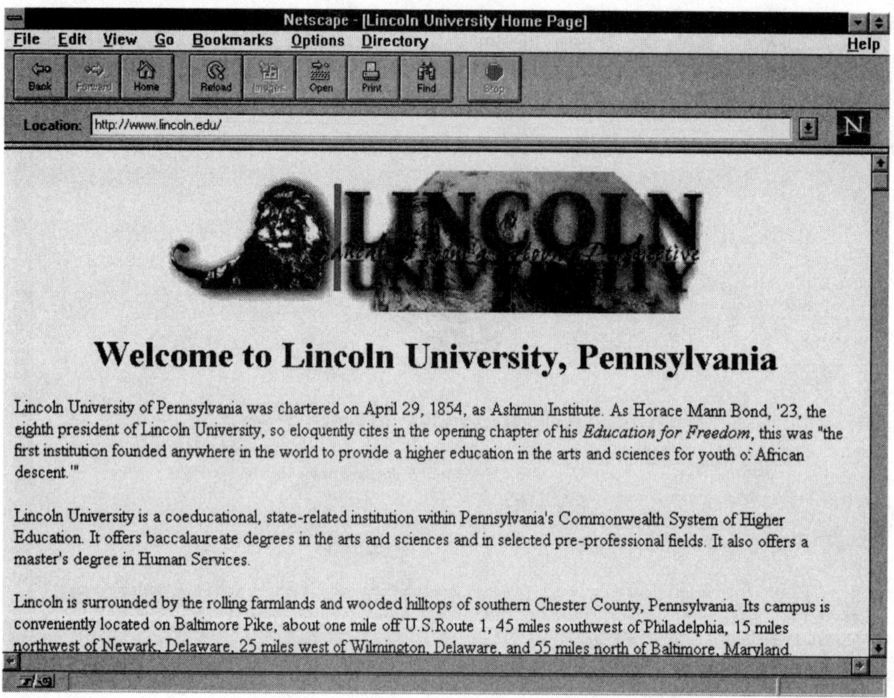

Fig. 5-10 *Lincoln University (Pennsylvania):* http://www.lincoln.edu

Lincoln University of Pennsylvania was chartered on April 29, 1854, as Ashmun Institute. As Horace Mann Bond, '23, the eighth president of Lincoln University, so eloquently cites in the opening chapter of his Education for Freedom, this was "the first institution founded anywhere in the world to provide a higher education in the arts and sciences for youth of African descent."

Lincoln University is a coeducational, state-related institution within Pennsylvania's Commonwealth System of Higher Education. It offers baccalaureate degrees in the arts and sciences and in selected pre-professional fields. It also offers a master's degree in Human Services.

Lincoln is surrounded by the rolling farmlands and wooded hilltops of southern Chester County, Pennsylvania. Its campus is conveniently located on Baltimore Pike, about one mile off U.S. Route 1, 45 miles southwest of Philadelphia, 15 miles northwest of Newark, Delaware, 25 miles west of Wilmington, Delaware, and 55 miles north of Baltimore, Maryland.

From its inception, Lincoln has attracted an interracial and international enrollment from the surrounding community and around the world. First admitting women in 1952, and formally

associating with the Commonwealth in 1971, Lincoln exists today as a coeducational, state-related university. Lincoln is proud of its faculty for the high quality of their teaching, research, and service, and of its notable alumni.

Norfolk State University

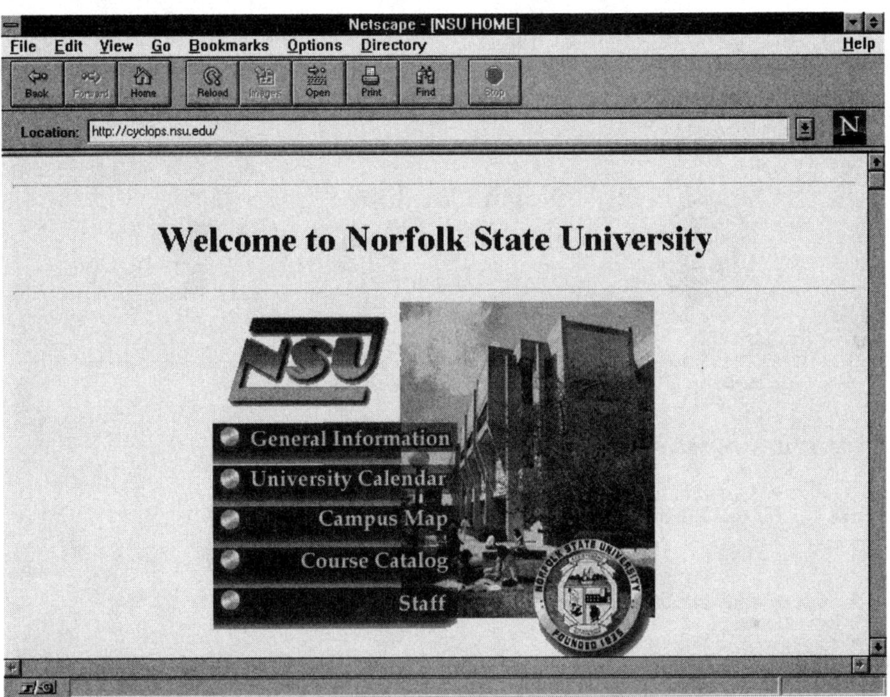

Fig. 5-11 *Norfolk State University:* http://cyclops.nsu.edu

Norfolk State College was founded in 1935. The College, brought to life in the midst of the Great Depression, provided a setting in which the youth of the region could give expression to their hopes and aspirations. At this founding, it was named the Norfolk Unit of Virginia Union University. In 1942, the College became the independent Norfolk Polytechnic College, and two years later an Act of the Virginia Legislature mandated that it become a part of Virginia State College.

The College was able to pursue an expanded mission with even greater emphasis in 1956 when another Act of the Legislature enabled the Institution to offer its first bachelor's degree. The College was separated from Virginia State College and became fully independent in 1969. Subsequent legislative acts designated the institution as a University and authorized the granting of graduate degrees. In 1979, University status was attained.

Today, the University is proud to be one of the largest predominantly black institutions in the nation. Furthermore, it is committed to pursuing its vital role of serving the people of the Hampton Roads area.

North Carolina A&T University

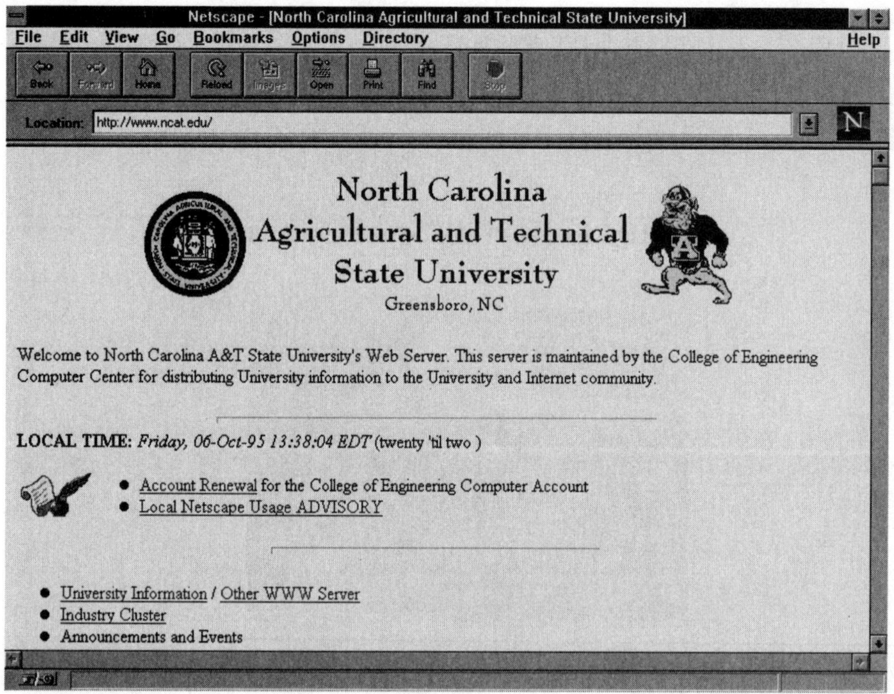

Fig. 5-12 *North Carolina A&T University:* http://www.ncat.edu

North Carolina Agricultural and Technical State University is a public, comprehensive, land-grant university committed to fulfilling its fundamental purposes through exemplary undergraduate and graduate instruction, scholarly and creative research, and effective public service. The university offers degree programs at the baccalaureate, master's, and doctoral levels with emphasis on engineering, science, technology, literature, and other selected areas.

As one of North Carolina's three engineering schools, the university offers Ph.D. programs in engineering. Basic and applied research is conducted by faculty in university centers of excellence, in interinstitutional relationships, and through significant involvement with several public and private agencies. The university also conducts major research through engineering and its extension programs in agriculture.

For the present planning period (1992–1997), the University will continue to place emphasis on strengthening its programs in engineering, the sciences, and technology. The University is also authorized to plan, in conjunction with the University of North Carolina at Greensboro, a joint master's degree program in social work.

The purpose of the University is to provide an intellectual setting where students in higher education may find a sense of identification, belonging, responsibility, and achievement that will prepare them for roles of leadership and service in the communities where they will live and work. In this sense, the University serves as a laboratory for the development of excellence in teaching, research, and public service.

Prairie View A&M University

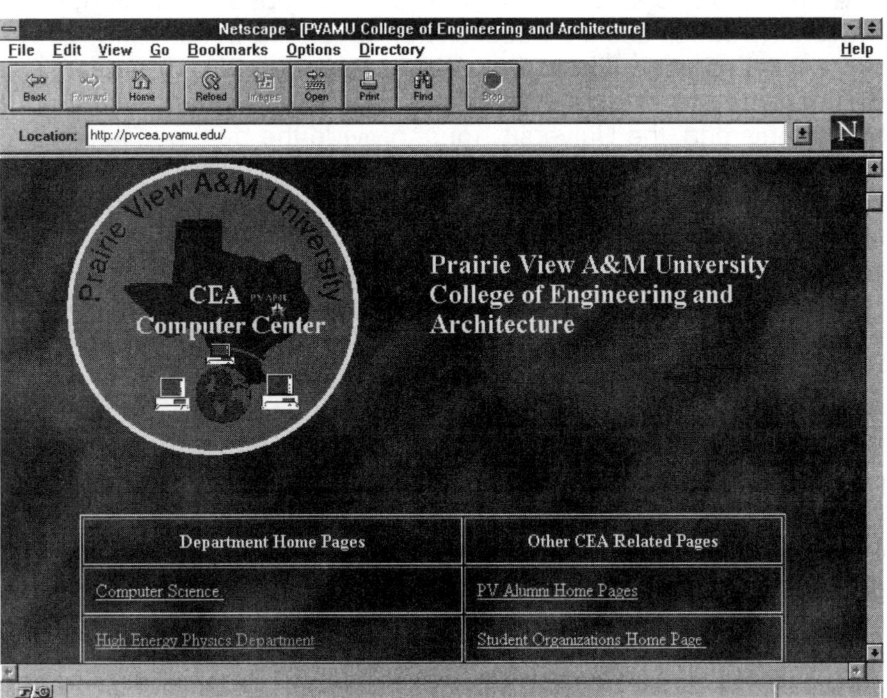

Fig. 5-13 *Prairie View A&M University:* http://hp73.pvamu.edu

The mission of Prairie View A&M University was redefined by the people through an amendment to the constitution in 1984. Through that amendment, Prairie View A&M University joined the University of Texas at Austin and Texas A&M University as the only constitutionally designated "institutions of the first class."

In support of that designation, in January, 1985, the Board of Regents of The Texas A&M University System stated its intention

that Prairie View A&M University become "an institution nationally recognized in its areas of education and research." Prairie View A&M University is a land-grant institution by federal statute. It is also a "statewide special purpose institution" providing special services to students of "diverse ethnic and socioeconomic backgrounds."

Prairie View A&M University is dedicated to fulfilling these missions by achieving excellence in education, research, and service. The University is committed to offering the highest quality programs and instruction for courses or degrees in agriculture, arts and sciences, business, education, engineering, engineering technology, architecture, home economics, and nursing.

While striving to maintain excellent instruction and a strong curriculum, the University understands its role to include the nurture of students' academic development and intellectual curiosity by providing stimulating and healthy physical and cultural environments and services. As a "special purpose" institution, the University recognizes the necessity to develop unique programming to identify and assist talented students. The University is committed to the total development of the person, and, to this end, the University must provide the best possible support services in academic and nonacademic areas. The University is committed to fostering research on campus. Quality research is the critical thread that weaves together a strong faculty, state-of-the-art facilities, learning opportunities for students, and relevant service to the community beyond the campus.

Spelman College

Spelman College, an outstanding historically black college for women, is recognized for excellence in liberal education. This predominately residential college is a member of the Atlanta University Center(AUC). AUC membership benefits students by giving them access to the resources of the six participating institutions while allowing them to retain all the advantages of a small college. The intimate nature of Spelman provides women with an academic climate conducive to the full development of their academic and leadership potential.

Spelman's educational program is designed to give students a comprehensive liberal arts background through study in the fine arts, humanities, social sciences, and natural sciences. At Spelman, students are encouraged to think critically, logically, and creatively; to develop competence in decision-making and problem-solving; and to improve their use of communicative and quantitative skills.

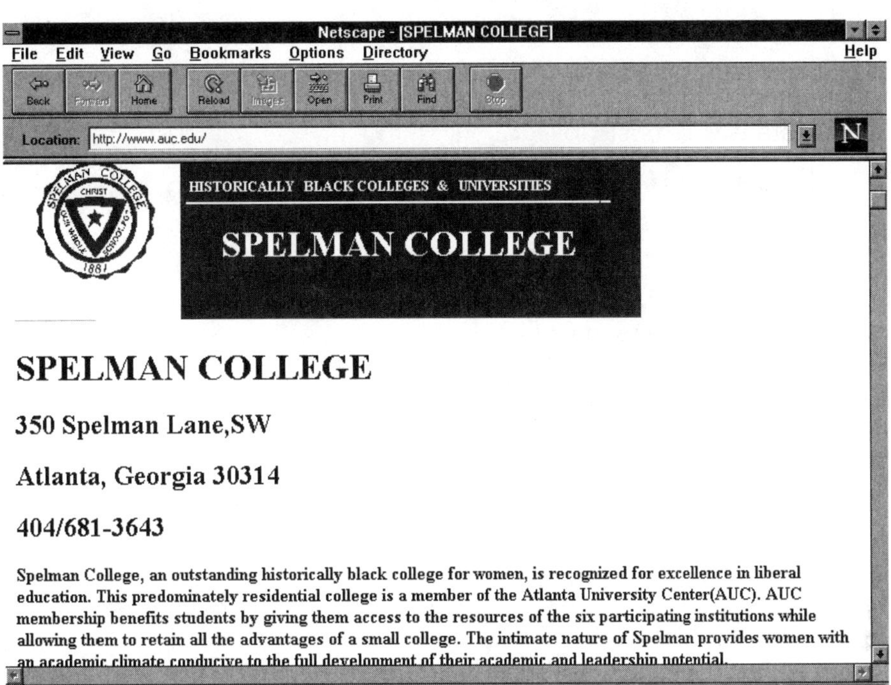

Fig. 5-14 *Spelman College:* http://www.auc.edu

The Spelman experience, however, extends beyond intellectual development and professional career preparation of students. It develops the whole person. The College provides an academic and social environment that enables women to be self-confident as well as culturally and spiritually enriched. Spelman women are encouraged to develop an appreciation for the multicultural communities of the world in which they live, and a sense of responsibility for affecting positive change in those communities. Spelman has been and expects to continue to be a major resource for educating black women leaders.

The historically black colleges and universities and minority institutions in America

Below is a list of the historically black colleges and universities and minority institutions in America. Most, if not all, have some kind of presence on the Internet. For more information on each of them, see the Federal Information Exchange Web page at *http://web.fie.com/web/mol/allhbcu.htm.*

- Alabama A&M University
- Alabama State University
- Albany State College

- Alcorn State University
- Allen University
- Arkansas Baptist College
- Barber-Scotia College
- Benedict College
- Bennett College
- Bethune-Cookman College
- Bishop State Community College, Main Campus
- Bishop State Community College, Carver Campus
- Bluefield State College
- Bowie State University
- Central State University
- Cheyney State University
- Claflin College
- Clark Atlanta University
- Clinton Junior College
- Coahoma Community College
- Concordia College
- Coppin State College
- Delaware State University
- Denmark Technical College
- Dillard University
- Edward Waters College
- Elizabeth City State University
- Fayetteville State University
- Fisk University
- Florida A&M University
- Florida Memorial College
- Fort Valley State College
- Fredd State Technical College
- Grambling State University
- Hampton University
- Harris-Stowe State College
- Hinds Community College

- Howard University
- Huston-Tillotson College
- Interdenominational Theological Center
- J.F. Drake State Technical College
- Jackson State University
- Jarvis Christian College
- Johnson C. Smith University
- Kentucky State University
- Knoxville College
- Lane College
- Langston University
- Lawson State Community College
- LeMoyne-Owen College
- Lewis College of Business
- Lincoln University (Pennsylvania)
- Livingstone College
- Mary Holmes College
- Meharry Medical College
- Miles College
- Mississippi Valley State University
- Morehouse College
- Morehouse School of Medicine
- Morgan State University
- Morris Brown College
- Morris College
- Norfolk State University
- North Carolina A&T University
- North Carolina Central University
- Oakwood College
- Paine College
- Paul Quinn College
- Philander Smith College
- Prairie View A&M University
- Rust College

- Savannah State College
- Selma University
- Shaw University
- Shorter College
- South Carolina State University
- Southern University A&M College
- Southern University at New Orleans
- Southern University at Shreveport
- Southwestern Christian College
- Spelman College
- St. Augustine's College
- St. Paul's College
- St. Philip's College
- Stillman College
- Talladega College
- Tennessee State University
- Texas College
- Texas Southern University
- Tougaloo College
- Trenholm State Technical College
- Tuskegee University
- University of Arkansas at Pine Bluff
- University of Maryland Eastern Shore
- University of the District of Columbia
- University of the Virgin Islands
- Virginia State University
- Virginia Union University
- Voorhees College
- West Virginia State College
- Wilberforce University
- Wiley College
- Winston-Salem State University
- Xavier University

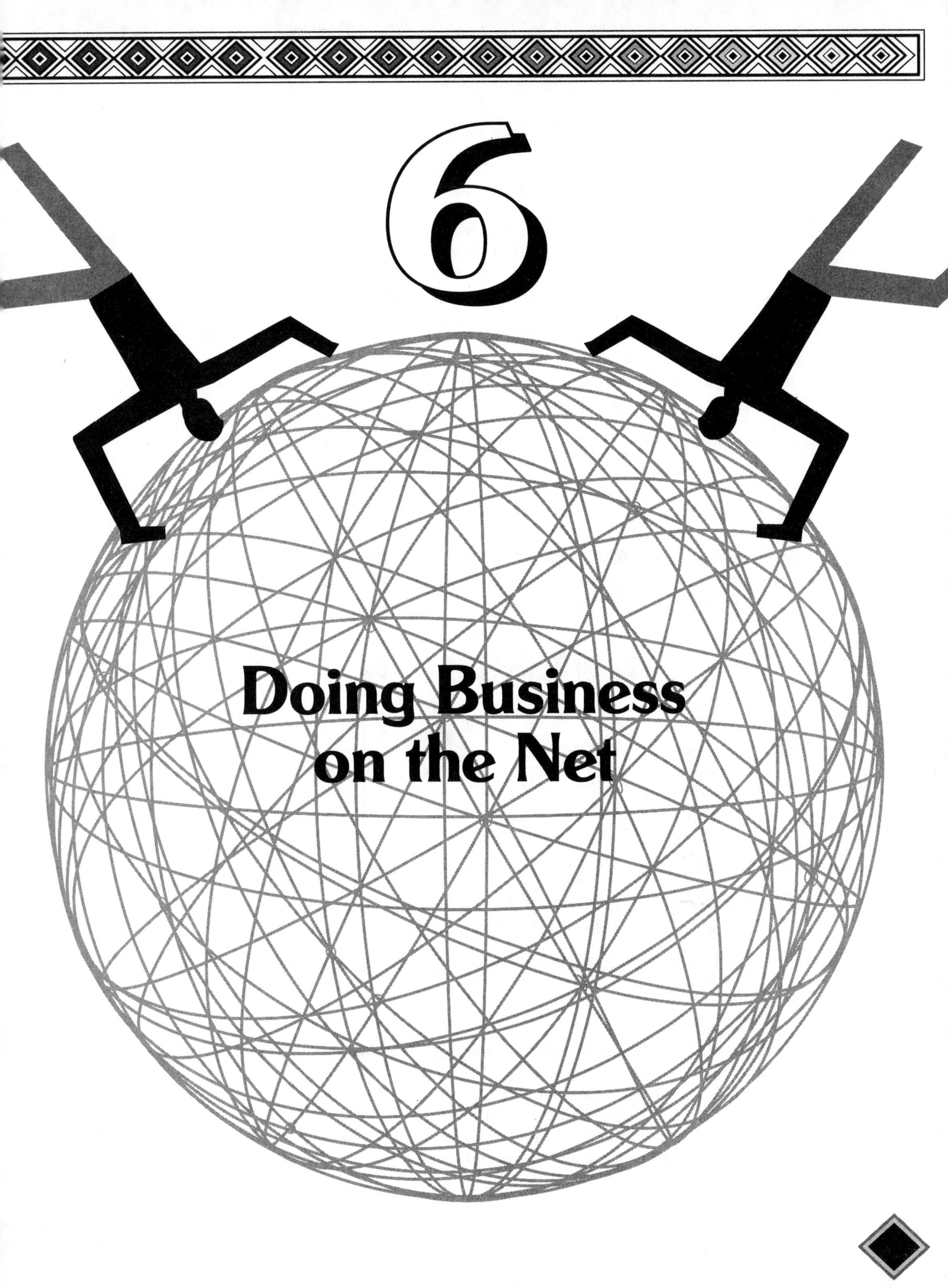

6

Doing Business on the Net

CONTRARY to popular conception, anyone can conduct business on the Internet. Every major U.S. corporation has an Internet presence. Some have elaborate sites on the World Wide Web and others a simple e-mail address. Every major university and historically black college and university (HBCU) can be found online. Thousands of nonprofit organizations and tens of thousands of entrepreneurs are online. Having an Internet address is fast becoming as important as having a telephone, business card, or product.

Small businesses and corporations that want to stay in business must use the Internet to promote and sell their products and services. African American-owned businesses are certainly no exception. Many black businesses and entrepreneurs have already discovered the immense benefits of using the information superhighway. MelaNet, created by William and Rodney Jordan, has a site on the World Wide Web at *http://www.melanet.com/*. There you will find an online shopping mall and other activities. MelaNet's home page is shown in Fig. 6-1.

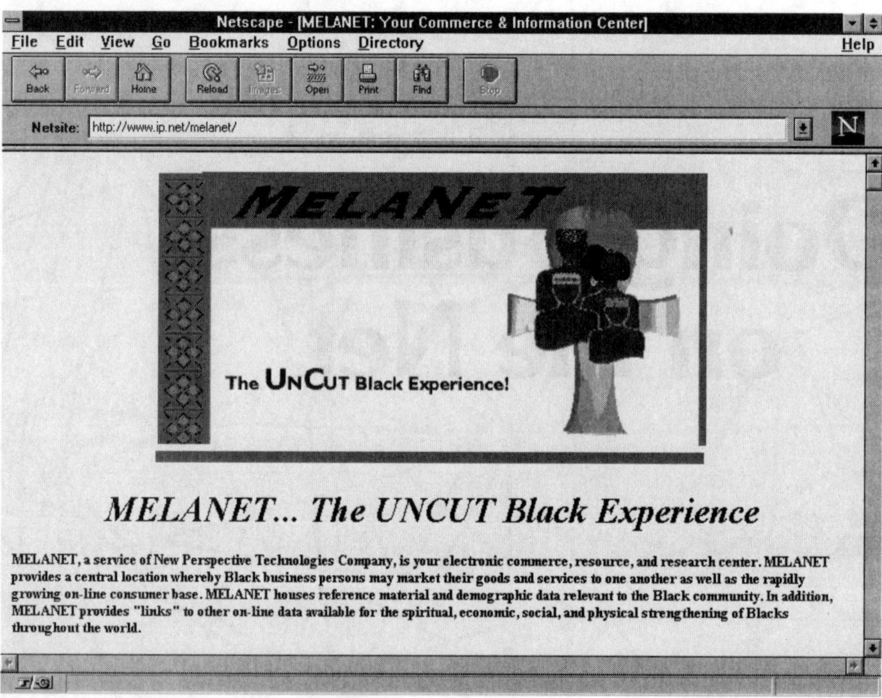

Fig. 6-1 *MelaNet's home page*

The Universal Black Pages, one of the most important AA sites on the Web, may be found at *http://www.gatech.edu/bgsa/blackpages/info.html*. See the information page in Fig. 6-2. The City of New Elam, found at *http://cityofnewelam.com* offers virtual storefronts and real estate for companies and entrepreneurs on the information superhighway. The home page is shown in Fig. 6-3.

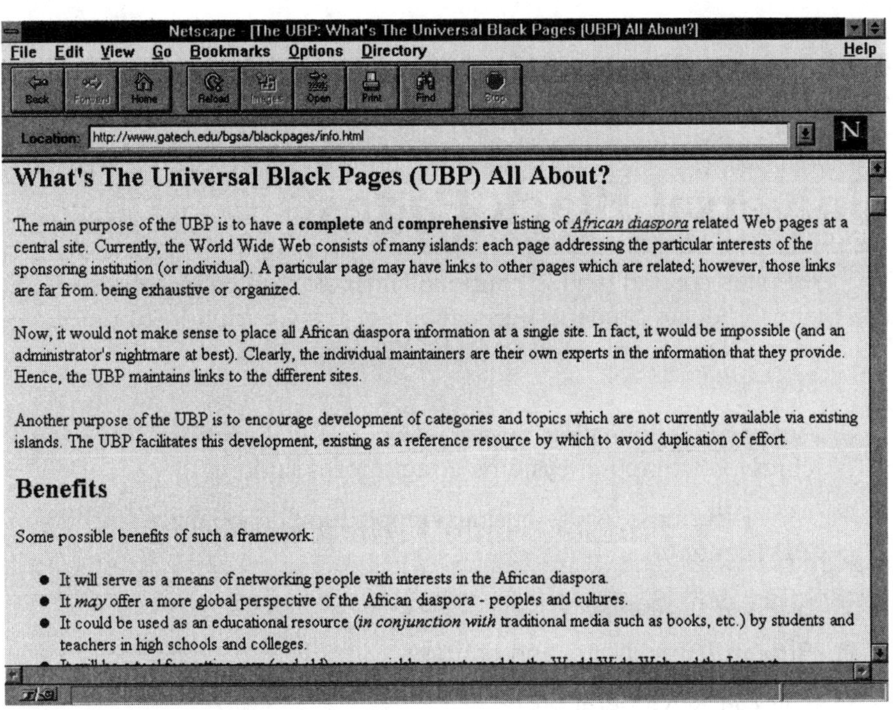

Netscape - [The UBP: What's The Universal Black Pages (UBP) All About?]

Location: http://www.gatech.edu/bgsa/blackpages/info.html

What's The Universal Black Pages (UBP) All About?

The main purpose of the UBP is to have a **complete** and **comprehensive** listing of *African diaspora* related Web pages at a central site. Currently, the World Wide Web consists of many islands: each page addressing the particular interests of the sponsoring institution (or individual). A particular page may have links to other pages which are related; however, those links are far from. being exhaustive or organized.

Now, it would not make sense to place all African diaspora information at a single site. In fact, it would be impossible (and an administrator's nightmare at best). Clearly, the individual maintainers are their own experts in the information that they provide. Hence, the UBP maintains links to the different sites.

Another purpose of the UBP is to encourage development of categories and topics which are not currently available via existing islands. The UBP facilitates this development, existing as a reference resource by which to avoid duplication of effort.

Benefits

Some possible benefits of such a framework:

- It will serve as a means of networking people with interests in the African diaspora.
- It *may* offer a more global perspective of the African diaspora - peoples and cultures.
- It could be used as an educational resource (*in conjunction with* traditional media such as books, etc.) by students and teachers in high schools and colleges.

Fig. 6-2 *Universal Black Pages information page*

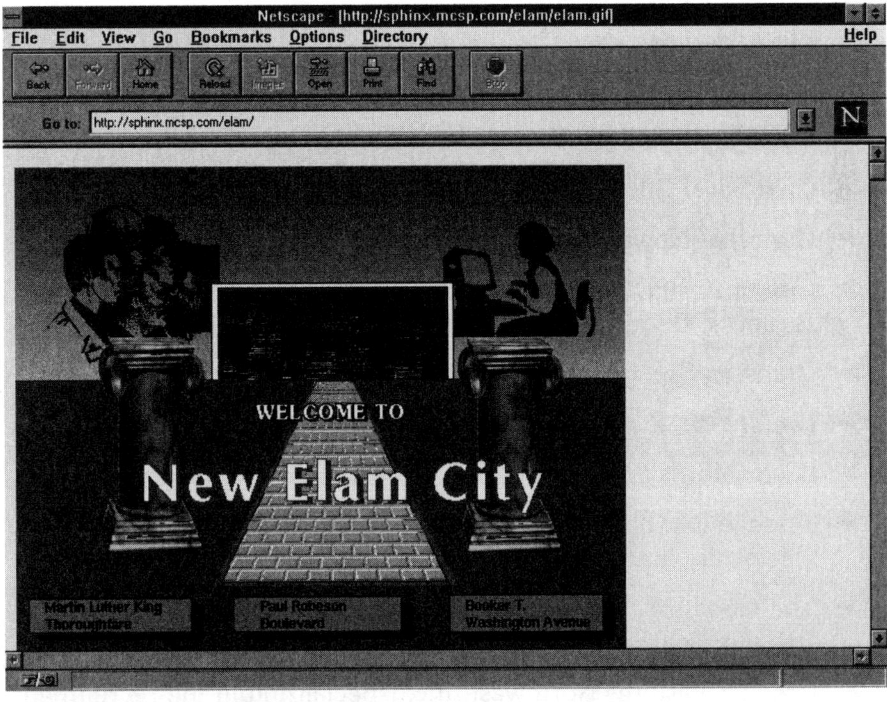

Fig. 6-3 *The City of New Elam home page*

Once you get on the Net, you will find many, many other examples of African-American electronic stores, directories, and online entrepreneurship. What follows is a small sample of African American-

related businesses that can be found in the Universal Black Pages (UBP) Web site. The variety of activities hints at activities some operators find useful as well as profitable.

Universal Black Pages

The UBP was created (and is continually developed) by members of the Black Graduate Students Association at the Georgia Institute of Technology. Once connected to their Web page, the user can reach the following:

- Advanced Information Systems Group, Inc. (a provider of complete computer systems integration solutions)
- Africa Business 2000 (business opportunities in Africa into the 21st century)
- Africa.com [South Africa]
- Afrikart (African arts and crafts)
- The Alaska General Store
- Bailey Broadcasting Services (info-tainment specialists since 1983)
- Black Heritage Products
- Brenda Johnson Health and Beauty Products
- Cable and Wireless (West Indies), Ltd. [Antigua]
- Cafe Salay Gifts Boutique (designer gourmet gifts)
- Carlos A. Howard Funeral Home
- City of Austin, Texas, Department of Small and Minority Business Resources
- Cranston Software (computer hardware and software)
- Dreamality, Inc. (HTML publishing and other WWW services)
- Edgar Morris Skin Care
- Essence International (jewelry, perfume, clothes, music, electronics, and much more)
- The Good Vibe Zone (an online record store specializing in Reggae, Soul, Jazz, Jungle, House, and Dance music)
- Greener Pastures Northwest, Inc. (specializing in the recruitment and placement of people in technical fields)
- InfoChannel (Jamaica's premier access to the information superhighway)
- The Internetworking Company of Southern Africa [South Africa] (Gopher)

- IT'S A D.C. THANG
- The Ivory House (Alaskan ivory carvings, jewelry, and scrimshaw)
- JW Florence Communications
- Landrum-Brown & Associates (a consulting firm specializing in cultural and racial awareness)
- Marketing By Design, Inc. (caps and T-shirts)
- Mind, Body, & Soul Enterprises (educational services focusing on mental, physical, and spiritual development)
- Minority Enterprise Corporation (an independent non-profit organization dedicated solely to the creation and growth of minority-owned businesses within southwestern Pennsylvania)
- Motherland Artworks
- New York On-line (a bulletin board)
- One Nation Books and Art, Inc.
- Original Black South African Art
- Pangea Systems (a provider of mission-critical database applications for the biopharmaceutical and health care industries)
- Paradox (an underground late-night/after-hours restaurant/night club in Baltimore, MD)
- Products and Services on Demand (personalized products and services including books, prints, stationery, etc.)
- Queen's Palace Productions (poetry, paintings)
- Robinson Solutions, Inc. (computer consulting for small businesses)
- 3D Enterprises (providing enterprise-wide information solutions)
- 3XD (Internet consultants offering customized logos, home pages, and 3D graphics generation)
- Tribal Sentiments (authentic West African imports)
- Unite-Us Business Listings (a listing of African American-owned businesses)
- The Universal AfrICAN Writer Press
- Virgin Territory (dedicated to the creation of ecologically sound fashions for women)
- Virtual Sites (Internet service provider)
- Vision Communications (Christian books, publications, information, and electronic media)

The cost of advertising on the Net

It is becoming increasingly clear that the Internet is an important commercial tool, now and in the future. But as with any tool, you have to know how to use it correctly in order to get the most from it. At the moment, one of the best ways for businesspeople to use this Internet tool is for advertising.

There are a number of ways to advertise on the information superhighway. But the three most important words to remember when selecting and paying for Internet advertising are affordability, visibility, and effectiveness.

The cost to advertise on the Internet can be as high as $30,000 in *Hotwired Magazine* for a 30-day period, or as low as $15 for a month in a local community net. Thus, you can spend a lot of money for a high-profile location on the Internet and hope to succeed through high-volume sales, or you can go economy class, save money, and maybe get a few people to notice you and purchase your products.

Essentially, Internet advertising is much like TV or radio advertising. When you purchase time during a Redskins vs. Cowboys NFL championship game, millions of people will see your announcements—but you will spend some big bucks. If you purchase time during the 3 A.M. "Mr. Ed" reruns, your cost may be in the single digits, but only a couple of night owls or insomniacs will notice you.

The low-cost approach can work. So, don't get discouraged if instead of receiving daily 10,000 "hits" (each time someone connects to your site on the Net it is called a *hit*) on your Internet site, you only get 30 or 40. Many high-traffic sites started out as small, unnoticed areas on the Net that gradually grew. Moreover, a small number of hits can still generate a lot of money.

There are many examples of small businesspeople who had limited funds but wisely used the Internet to advertise. Small black business owners have reported that they have received large orders, sometimes as great as $50,000 or more. Often, their clients were located overseas, where U.S. products and services are scarce. For instance, in Africa, items such as pencils for schools and surgical gloves for hospitals are in short supply in many areas of the continent. The list of everyday commodities in demand there, things we take for granted here in America, could stretch from Los Angeles to Timbuktu.

By using the Internet, a small local business can blossom into an international enterprise overnight; and none of the foreign trading partners may ever know, or even care, how big or small a U.S.

operation really is as long as it can deliver. Or course, most smart businesspeople refrain from telling all their trade secrets on how to get the "best" deals and highest profit margin using the Net. Often "newbies" have to resort to basic trial and error to find the best products and services to offer as well as the best locations on the i-way to advertise. There are, however, some basic guidelines you can follow.

There are a wide variety of methods available on the Internet by which the entrepreneur can market, support, and distribute goods and services. Anything that can be bought and sold in the real world can be bought and sold on the Internet. Mail-order items such as candy, T-shirts, books, or computers are found on the Net. Numerous professional services also can be found on the Net. There are even restaurants and wineries online. Tele-medicine is gaining popularity, along with legal aid, accounting, and art galleries. Newspapers and magazines are on the Internet. Online shopping malls, classified advertising, TV-quality commercials, and music videos are on the Internet. If you can't find it on the information superhighway, it probably doesn't exist. The Internet is the marketplace of the future.

Getting the message to the consumer

Needless to say, the Internet is the hottest thing happening in the retail world. Cyberspace is rapidly attracting commercial activity. Amid all this flurry, merchants are taking a variety of routes to make sure their messages stand out in the crowd and will attract the Internet traveler. But there are no road maps for the information superhighway—it is too large to chart, to diverse to predict. Most users simply wander from site to site.

So, the i-way business owner's next objective is to persuade people to drift over to their particular Internet advertisement, and more importantly, purchase a product. A sufficiently enticing piece of bait must be used in order to hook paying customers.

According to some "Nexperts," the Internet is growing at an average rate of 10 percent per month. There are 27,000 Web sites, and this number is doubling every 53 days. That figure has been attributed to *Business Week*, which in turn was quoting someone at Sun Microsystems. IBM alone sends out more than 500 million e-mail messages a year. Add this figure to America Online, Prodigy, and CompuServe, each of which claim two to five million users. Don't forget the hundreds of freenets across the world and millions of college students and government employees with Internet access. Then there are thousands of "closed" sites that don't ever report their usage. Taken collectively, they add up to a very large number of users.

It all comes down to this: The Internet is huge and growing rapidly. Imagine what will happen when it trades its diapers in for knee pants.

With millions of newbies cruising the Net each day and looking for a fast track to all that good stuff, many companies are placing their ads in online publications, on computer bulletin boards, constructing "electronic shopping malls," "cyber cities," and other "places" in which to do business on the Net. Using the Net as classified advertising has been in practice for years. Usually, this is the most inexpensive way to make use of the Internet. Typically, your announcements are in plain text format displayed on the computer screen the same as in a print newspaper's classified advertising section.

For typical mail-order operations, the rule of thumb is to place short brief announcements in the form of e-mail in as many locations as possible for maximum exposure, in order to achieve an acceptable number of sales. However, it is not considered proper "netiquette" to randomly dump your e-mail messages indiscriminately everywhere across the Net. (They call this "spamming." If you spam, you run the risk of getting "flamed"!)

Wherever you put a message, it should be consistent with the other material in that particular area. For instance, most commercial online services such as CompuServe, Prodigy, America Online, and Genie have specific areas for classified listings. On the World Wide Web, there are areas set aside specifically for classified ads. (To find those Web sites, set your Web search function to "Classifieds.") Usually, there is either no charge at all or just a minimal monthly fee. It's the proper and correct way to list your classifieds.

Newsgroups, used appropriately, also can be a very lucrative spot to "troll for customers." Most are not appropriate for commercial purposes. Some, however, exist precisely for that reason.

There are some simple guidelines to keep in mind if you want to promote yourself on newsgroups without creating a problem with the locals. First and foremost, use only newsgroups that permit commercialization for blatant advertising. Check the FAQ for those groups to make sure you're in the right place.

Your other option is the intelligent use of a "signature" file. A signature is up to four lines of text that is automatically added to the end of every e-mail and newsgroup article you post. It is considered acceptable to mention whatever you have to sell and point people to a Web site, e-mail address, or any other place where they can find out more. As simple and subtle as this is, it can produce worthwhile results if you use it correctly. Just remember that all you are selling is a trip to your Web site or a note requesting more information. If you stay within that context, it is unlikely that anyone will take offense.

There is one catch to this approach: You must be active on one or more newsgroups to make it work. For example, let's say that you play in a Reggae band and want to promote your latest CD. Find all the newsgroups where you could logically expect to find a high concentration of people who might be interested in your music. This group might include any topic related to African-American culture as well as those related to music (okay, you can probably skip the country-western groups).

The next step is to start hanging with those groups to see what's up. When you think you have a feeling for the general flow of things, jump right in and respond to someone's posting. Offer help, ask a question, or just say "right on" to their comments. It really doesn't matter what you say. The commercial message is in your signature. It should be obvious, however, that if you are helpful, knowledgeable, and pleasant, you are going to attract a lot more of the right kind of attention. What you don't want to do is to jump in and flame someone with whom you don't agree. That will get you the wrong kind of attention.

The key ideas to keep in mind when trolling the Net with the intent of making connections are:

❶ Make yourself useful; people will appreciate your assistance.

❷ Build trust and confidence; people will respond if they trust you and believe you know what you're talking about.

❸ Be interesting; it won't matter what you say if no one reads it.

❹ Keep thorough records; anyone who responds to you privately is fair game for future announcements and offers. Write down what you talked about and when.

Of course, when you ask people to take the next step and visit your Web site or e-mail you for more information, you have to be prepared to make them an offer they can't refuse. This means a thoughtfully designed set of Web pages or a similarly effective e-mail response. Keep the hype to a minimum. Emphasize the value and benefits of your offering.

No matter how you go about it, try to come up with some kind of freebie to attract them. A free sound bite of your band, a free picture of your graphic design skills at work, whatever you have. Valuable information is always a plus. People in cyberspace are hard to fool. If you offer them something useless, not only will they not respond well, they will most likely see right through it and feel insulted. If you give them something, make it worth their while. Use your imagination.

Web pages

Until recently, using the Internet has not always been as easy as everyone claims. Sometimes, even sending a simple e-mail message could be a real test of endurance if you were not familiar with the "primitive" text editors offered by most services. Unless you were a computer programmer or a serious hacker, navigating the Net could be a frustrating and often fruitless chore. The reason for some of this confusion was that the most popular operating environment used on the Net was the infamous UNIX operating system. UNIX requires the use of many mysterious commands and obscure codes in order to get information. Even trying to understand the HELP files (they should call them "staff" files because they are often not much "help") may send users screaming into the night.

Fortunately, the Internet takes care of itself. As more universities and their students got access to the i-way, a number of helpful innovations such as Gopher, Archie, and Veronica (see Chapter 2, pages 16 and 17) were created to make the Net easier to navigate. In the evolution of the Internet, it was inevitable that pictures and sound would be integrated, as well as a more intuitive method to find information.

Thus, the World Wide Web (WWW) was born. The Web provides a colorful graphic interface to the Internet and allows the user to browse information and images through "hyper-links." A hyper-link can be either a word, phrase, or graphic image that is linked to another Web page, graphic, file, or location. That information may be physically located on another computer on the other side of the world. On the World Wide Web, anyone can "cruise" the information superhighway with the click of a mouse and never have to utter a syllable of UNIXese.

The Web allows multimedia displays using color, pictures, and sound—a pitch man's dream. Unlike, multimedia ads on television, preparing advertising for broadcast on the i-way is only a fraction of the cost of a TV production. In fact, students and home-based entrepreneurs are quite capable of creating multimedia Web presentations that can compete visually with anything the media giants prepare.

Thanks to the Web, shopping malls, cities, and other structures are possible in cyberspace. Like their real world counterparts, they are not hard to find. Using most Web directories such as Yahoo, the Universal Black Pages, or the Drum anyone can find stores by typing a few words describing what they're looking for.

The World Wide Web provides the visibility and ease of use that has made the Internet practically a household word. By a strange coincidence, it also perfectly fits advertising needs.

Your own Web site

Most Internet service providers now offer you the opportunity to post Web pages of your own. Creating a Web site is not much more difficult than writing a letter on a word processor. You must learn at least the rudiments of a coding system called html (Hyper-Text Markup Language). Don't be intimidated by that. Html is simply a way of formatting text and inserting links to other documents and graphics.

There is far more information online about using html than you will ever need or use. Here are some places that will get you off to a good start.

- The HTML Writers Guild Website *http://www.synet.net/hwg/*
- A Beginner's Guide to Html *http://www.ncsa.uiuc.edu/demoweb/html-primer.html*
- Composing Good Html *http://www.willamette.edu/html-composition/strict-html.html*
- Extensions to Html 2.0 *http://home.mcom.com/assist/net_sites/html_extensions.html*
- Extensions to Html 3.0 *http://home.mcom.com/assist/net_sites/html_extensions_3.html*
- Guides to Writing Html Documents *http://union.ncsa.uiuc.edu:80/HyperNews/get/www/html/guides.html*
- The University of Washington Web Developer's Page *http://www.ee.washington.edu/UWWeb.html*

Once you have read a bit about html, start looking at the "raw" version of some Web pages. This is easy to do. First, get the page on your screen. Most browsers will let you save a copy of the file to your disk. This is usually an option on the File menu of the browser. Many browsers also have an option (typically called "View Source") which lets you look at the raw html file right on the spot.

There are numerous software tools to make writing html easier. You can find a long list of current software at Yahoo (*http://www.yahoo.com:80/*) which you can download and try.

You can also hire someone to create your Web site for you. For that matter, there are providers who will not only create your Web site for you, but put it on their system as part of the deal. Of course, the more you farm out, the more you will pay. Whereas doing your own site will probably cost you little or nothing up front and as little as $15 a month, you can pay thousands of dollars up front and hundreds a month or more by hiring someone else to do it all for you. The choice is yours.

Having the greatest Web site in the world does you little good if no one knows about it. You must do something to generate traffic. If you have more money than time and inclination, you can just put your Web site on one of the many services that provide "homes" for businesses. These take the form of business directories, cyber-malls, and online shopping centers. The key question here is whether they will provide enough of the right kind of traffic to justify the expense. Remember too, just because someone else is setting the world on fire at a particular cyber-mall, doesn't mean that you will. They may have products that appeal to a vastly different audience or their offerings may lend themselves better to the medium.

Following are some of the properties of the ideal type of product for the Internet:

- It has a reasonably universal appeal that is culturally independent.
- It displays well in written words, color photos, sound clips, short videos—the stock in trade of the Web.
- It is easily and economically shipped anywhere in the world.
- You can give away valuable free samples at little or no expense.
- It is priced low enough that people will try it on impulse.

Now obviously, few products have all these qualities. The reason for providing this list is to give you an idea of just how ideal your products are. If they meet at least half these guidelines, you may have a good chance of finding the right formula for success. If, on the other hand, you are completely out of the ball park on one or more, maybe you need to take another look. For examples, washing machines aren't photogenic, easily shipped, inexpensive, nor do they lend themselves to free samples. You get the picture. At the other end of the spectrum, unique and valuable information—such as names and sample work from famous photographers—fits all these criteria hand in glove.

One last caveat: don't give up too easily. It is unlikely you will have an overnight success. Chances are that you will have to spend some time and effort honing your overall presentation until it works. Try anything and everything you can think of. The first order of business is to generate some traffic. Until you do that, the rest is academic. Once you have some traffic coming in, try different approaches until you see a jump in ordering. Then try to learn why the last change you made had that effect. Think of ways to enhance that. Over a period of time, you will learn more and more. Once you have found a formula that works, you have something that is little short of a money machine. It is about the cleanest way of doing business there's ever been. Every day Santa leaves money in your e-mail box. Nice work, if you have the patience and imagination to get it.

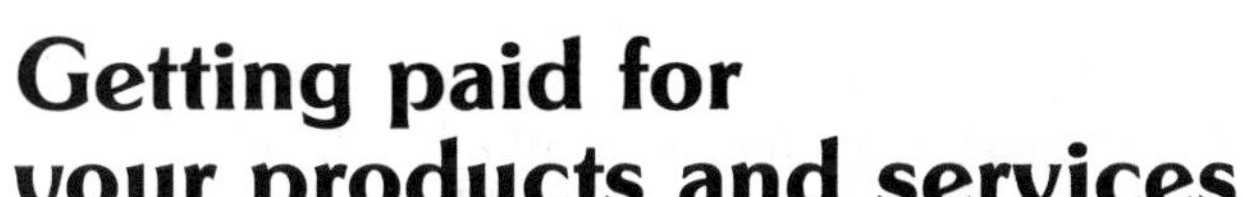

Getting paid for your products and services

One of the first questions most business owners on the Internet ask is, "How does a seller collect their money?" The most obvious answer is an embarrassingly low-tech solution—the U.S. Postal Service.

Once the customer has seen your product and decided they want to buy it, then what? There are several options available. The one most mentioned is the most basic: They can drop a check in the mail (assuming you have provided them with your mailing address and whatever other information they will need). If you have an 800-number, you may want to offer them that option as well. Credit cards are another alternative that is beginning to catch on. In fact, in a recent situation, people preferred using the credit cards almost exclusively, at least 50-to-1 over checks.

A Note about Net security

There is a lot of talk these days about security on the Internet. While it is quite true that a dedicated hacker can gain access to some systems, there are stakes much higher than stealing your credit-card information. When you think about it, you realize that the risk is actually very small and the stakes are not that high. Here are some things to consider when deciding if you should send credit-card or other sensitive information over the Internet.

- *The odds are monumentally in your favor that nothing unusual will happen. Millions of people send billions of things over the Net every day without mishap.*
- *The worst that can happen is that someone will have the information necessary to use your credit card. Granted, no one wants this to happen to them, but consider this: Every time you use that card, every employee of the company you use it with (and who knows whom else) has access to that same information. And they don't even have to go looking for it.*
- *On the Net, someone has to go to extraordinary lengths to get the same information. Wouldn't you want to make all that effort count by stealing from a big company rather than an individual?*
- *Most credit-card providers limit your liability to around $50 if someone uses your card illegally. Admittedly, $50 is $50, but it isn't exactly the national debt. What is the convenience worth to you?*
- *Internal electronic mailing systems (like Prodigy's) do not go through the Internet and are inherently much safer. If you have the option, and are concerned about security, use that method rather than Internet e-mail. That's why you have a choice here.*

Summary: While no one can guarantee that your transactions are completely safe on the Net, they can't really do that in the "real world" either. Yes, there is a small element of risk. In the end, you probably face a much greater risk of getting hit while driving down the street and that will, one way or another, cost you a lot more.

Consumers are accustomed to using credit cards for purchases. All of the commercial online services have been allowing credit-card purchases for years. In fact, before you can sign up on most online services, you must submit a valid credit-card number, so therefore, the great majority of Internet buyers have access to plastic credit.

But for many consumers, there will always be some reluctance to key in their card numbers onto the information superhighway. Most consumers' knowledge of the Internet comes from sensationalized disclosures of computer hackers and electronic abuse.

The Internet has come up with some answers of its own to facilitate the use of credit cards and ease consumer concerns. Most solutions are built around sophisticated data encryption technologies. These techniques scramble credit-card information so they can pass safely on electronic networks. Today, there are encryption procedures so effective that it would take a dedicated hacker hundreds of years to break them.

First Virtual Holdings, Inc., reportedly has an e-mail system that lets consumers use credit cards on the Internet without fearing that their account numbers will be misappropriated. The card numbers are stored away on a protected computer system and never pass over the network. Consumers register with First Virtual by phone and receive ID numbers in exchange for their card numbers. When they want to buy something electronically, they simply supply their ID number to the merchant.

Industry sources indicate that Visa and MasterCard are also working diligently to make credit cards more usable on the i-way. It has been said that Visa is developing with Microsoft a system using encryption technology that they hope will become an industry model.

Credit card-based systems have the advantage of seeming familiar to consumers, but a new form of payment is under development called "E-Cash." E-Cash, like real money, would be anonymous and have no credit limits. Using E-Cash, any organization or person could conduct business on the Net, no matter what country both parties are in or what their credit rating is—as long as the customer has possession of enough E-Cash.

According to *Businessweek* magazine, "E-Cash is money that moves along multiple channels largely outside the established network of

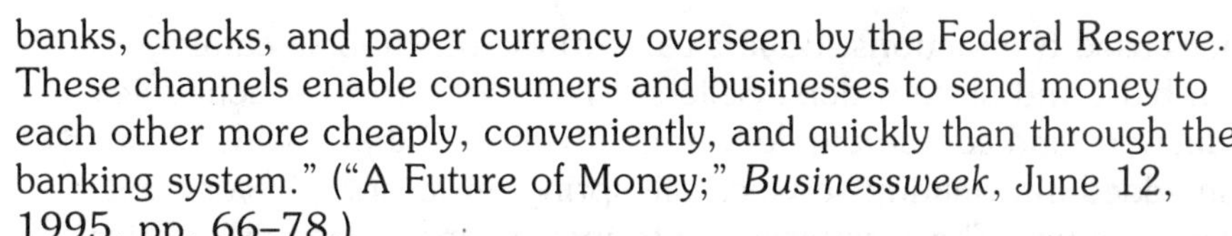

banks, checks, and paper currency overseen by the Federal Reserve. These channels enable consumers and businesses to send money to each other more cheaply, conveniently, and quickly than through the banking system." ("A Future of Money;" *Businessweek*, June 12, 1995, pp. 66–78.)

Firms such as DigiCash, Netbank, and CyberCash along with Microsoft, Xerox, Visa, and Citicorp reportedly are developing what could be called an Electronic Monetary System. Once those companies can agree on the internal workings of such a system, it could transform the way we work with money. In other words, according to the *Businessweek* article, "it could change consumers' financial lives and shake the foundations of global financial systems and even governments." Many Internet experts consider that E-Cash, which theoretically could be backed by any currency or other asset, might be the biggest revolution in currency since gold coins replaced cowry shells.

In an electronically wired world, E-Cash could replace a wad of dirty greenbacks or cumbersome coins in your pocket. A microchip placed in a plastic card, pen, button, or hand-held computer could store and transmit your digital coins and dollars at the flick of a switch.

With E-Cash or some other form of digital money you could shop online, pay for a movie and popcorn, buy a meal in a fancy restaurant, or tip the taxi driver. There are, of course, many questions about the use of E-Cash that must be resolved, such as who should be allowed to issue and regulate E-Cash. Also, how will taxes be applied in cyberspace. But perhaps the biggest issue is still security for the businesses, banks, and customers.

None of these problems is insoluble. Just as banks in the Wild, Wild West were frequently used as private cash boxes by enterprising outlaws, the future will eventually catch up and make money more secure and user-friendly on the Internet.

Enter CommerceNet

Small businesses unfamiliar with the rugged terrain of the information superhighway may want to make use of any of a number of online networks specifically set up for business operations. For example, there is CommerceNet, a consortium of Northern California technology-oriented companies and organizations whose goal is to create an electronic marketplace where companies transact business spontaneously over the Internet. According to some experts, CommerceNet will stimulate the growth of a communications infrastructure that will be easy to use, commercially oriented, and designed to expand rapidly. The CommerceNet marketplace has the potential to support all business services that normally depend on

paper-based transactions. Buyers can browse multimedia catalogs, solicit bids, and place orders. Sellers will respond to bids, schedule production, and coordinate deliveries. It is hoped that a wide array of value-added information services will spring up to bring buyers and sellers together. These services are to include specialized directories, broker and referral services, vendor certification and credit reporting, network notaries and repositories, and financial and transportation services. CommerceNet was built to provide an integrated set of services from a single source, including:

- High-speed Internet connections.
- Easy access and networking software.
- Simple point-and-click access to all CommerceNet services.

Security mechanisms to CommerceNet members' authentication, authorization, and data encryption applications made available on CommerceNet will let buyers and sellers safely exchange sensitive information such as credit-card numbers and bid amounts, sign legally enforceable contracts, maintain audit trails, and make or receive network payments through cooperating financial institutions.

The future of CommerceNet

The CommerceNet core team says it will employ state-of-the-art Internet technology to stay on the leading edge of development. Future services being explored include "shopping agents," smart computer software that can search through catalogs and negotiate deals; tools work teams that support both real-time interaction and video mail; natural language search and retrieval of information bases; and services that enable different organizations to exchange data even when they adhere to different computer and operational standards. The home page for CommerceNet appears in Fig. 6-4.

CommerceNet organizers believe that the majority of companies and organizations in the U.S. may conduct business via the Internet in five years. CommerceNet may be an important step toward a national information infrastructure capable of linking up with other electronic commerce projects in places such as Boston, Austin, and the University of Illinois. Potentially, a CommerceNet-like infrastructure could support other national efforts in the areas of education, health care, and digital libraries. You can also find more information on the CommerceNet World Wide Web server at *http://www.commerce.net/*.

Doing business with the feds

Vice President Gore and Dr. Steven Kelman, Administrator of the Office of Management and Budget's Office of Federal Procurement Policy, have unveiled an online computer service dedicated to lowering

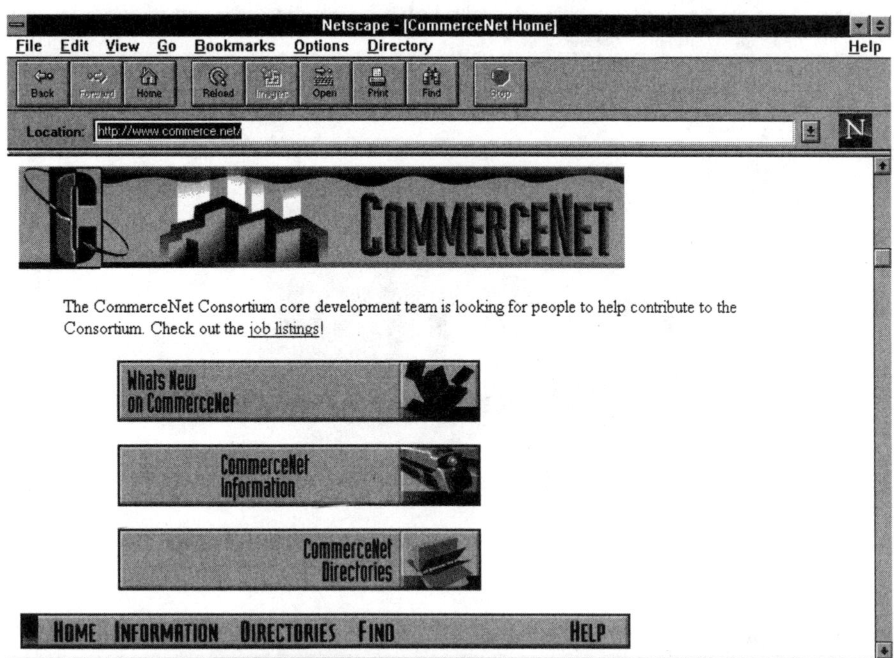

Fig. 6-4 *CommerceNet's home page*

the cost of doing business with the government through simplifying exchange of acquisition information.

Announcement of the Acquisition Reform Network was made as part of a conference on acquisition reform sponsored by the Council for Excellence in Government and *Government Executive* magazine. The Acquisition Reform Network was developed by the vice president's National Performance Review in cooperation with the Office of Federal Procurement Policy, Lawrence Livermore National Laboratory, the General Services Administration, and the Council for Excellence in Government. It provides a number of services designed to advance innovations that were developed as part of the administration's reinventing government initiative.

According to Vice President Gore, "Purchasing inefficiencies affect every government worker and by extension every American. Procurement is rarely considered glamorous work, but in an era of increased privatization, it has emerged as a key link in the chain of events from law and policy development to positive impact on the citizen. Without breakthrough reform in this area the entire reinvention movement is restrained."

The Acquisition Reform Network (see the home page in Fig. 6-5) uses the Web (*http://www-far.npr.gov*). Aside from online informal meetings for the exchange of views and general conferencing, the network will feature a collaborative workspace that will allow teams of workers from all over the country and in various positions within the

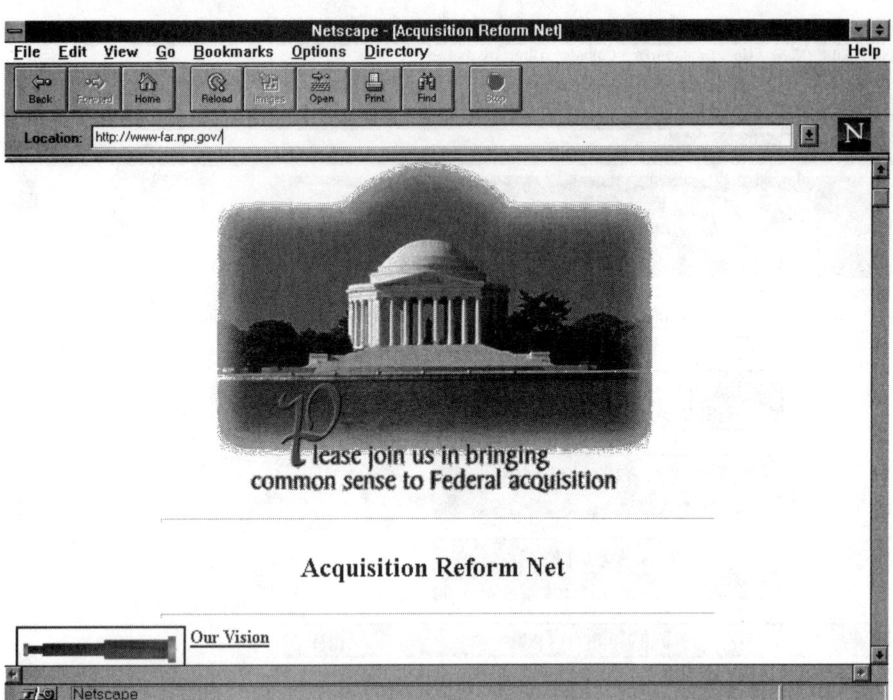

Fig. 6-5 *Acquisition Reform Network's home page*

bureaucracy to work to solve common problems. Private sector program managers will be encouraged to interact with their public sector counterparts.

Other features of the network will be a reference library of acquisition policy documents, the Federal Acquisition Regulations and their subsidiary regulations, desktop training on demand developed by the Federal Acquisition Institute, a database of promising practices that have emerged through the reinventing government process, and a single entry point for all government purchasing Internet sites.

The LEXIS-NEXIS Small Business Service

The NEXIS Small Business Service was named "Best News Service/Database" by the Information Industry Association and *Online Access* magazine in December 1994. *American Demographics* magazine named the LEXIS-NEXIS services as one of The Best 100 Sources for Marketing Information for 1995. Their home page is shown in Fig. 6-6.

Using LEXIS-NEXIS, Internet users reportedly can scan more than 8,000 ads for small businesses for sale across the U.S., with the addition of the National Business Exchange to The LEXIS-NEXIS Small Business Service. Entrepreneurs can identify businesses to

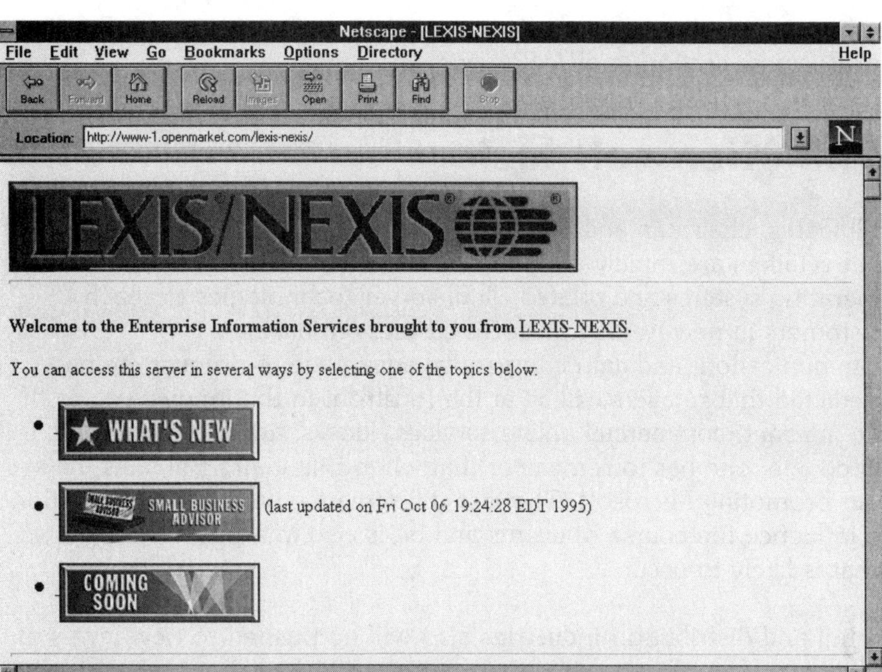

Fig. 6-6 *Enterprise Information Services of LEXIS-NEXIS*

purchase, do market and competitive research, and investigate investment opportunities. For a fee, users can order and download the contact name and telephone number that accompanies a listing.

The LEXIS-NEXIS Small Business Service provides online advice, opportunities, and reference for small business owners or those who operate a home office. In the Small Business Opportunities section, the National Business Exchange lists businesses by state and region and it is updated weekly. The National Business Exchange is a good source of businesses for sale that includes coverage of all 50 states.

Also in the Small Business Opportunities section, *The Commerce Business Daily* provides information on government contracts offered and awarded, subcontracting leads and sales of property. The information available in the Small Business Advice and Reference sections is culled from an extensive online warehouse of regional, national, and international newspapers, magazines, trade journals, and business publications. Offering 8,000 articles covering 40 different topics targeted to small businesses, LEXIS-NEXIS furnishes a collection of the practical info on how to make a small business successful. Some of these services are not cheap, but they may also help you to make or save enough money to be a bargain.

To learn more about LEXIS-NEXIS news and information products, call 800-227-4908, or send a message to *eis@lexis-nexis.com*. The Small Business Service products are available on the World Wide Web

at *http://www.directory.net/lexis-nexis*, or on Prodigy in the Prodigy for Business section at: *JUMP:nexis*.

The Microsoft factor

Bill Gates, chairman and CEO of Microsoft Corp., has stated publicly that retailers are rapidly adopting the Microsoft Windows 95 and NT operating systems and related client-server technologies to reach customers in new ways, transform business-to-business communication, and gain competitive advantage. Moreover, he has predicted that retailers will be at the forefront in the innovative use of the Internet, commercial online services, kiosks, and interactive TV. Of course, one has to remember that when Billionaire Bill talks, he's also promoting Microsoft. The fact still remains that he is in a position to influence the course of events and he is also in a position to know what is likely to occur.

Retail and distribution industries also will be pushed to new levels of efficiency. Consumers will gain greater control of shopping transactions through product and service information online. Gates has demonstrated several advanced retail applications using The Microsoft Network, CD-ROM, video-on-demand kiosks, and interactive TV. Examples included European retailer Tesco Plc's Wine Catalogue on the Internet; the "House of the Future" interactive TV shopping application, sponsored by the GIB Group (Belgium); and Best Buy's multimedia Answer Center kiosks, which let shoppers browse for product information using an interactive, full-motion video interface. QVC Inc., the world's leading electronic retail marketer, has a broad-based interactive shopping service on The Microsoft Network.

Orbis Broadcast Group

Orbis Broadcast Group (OBG), considered to be the leading independent producer of health care television, has signed an agreement with Microsoft to develop and manage a health information center for consumers and health professionals on MSN, The Microsoft Network. Operating under the brand name America's House Call Network (AHC), the health information center will be a virtual shopping mall specifically for health education, information, products, services, and a unique feature—the latest medical news, all easily accessible through The Microsoft Network.

Reportedly, unlike any other online service available, AHC on The Microsoft Network will incorporate the latest medical news and provide a place where consumers can ask questions about the news they have just seen or read. By including health news on MSN

simultaneously with broadcast distribution, MSN members will be able to access information and ask questions.

For consumers, the America's House Call Network, a virtual shopping mall of information and services, will consist of several "stores" (or "forums"), each representing a different medical condition or disease. Each store will provide a wealth of information about disease-specific services, such as a national provider referral service, patient support programs such as bulletin boards and chat groups, and a news service, a feature exclusive to AHC and MSN, that will provide users with the latest medical news.

For health care professionals, America's House Call Network will be providing MSN members with forums, interactive continuing medical education, current prescription and OTC drug information, practice guidelines, and information-supporting disease management.

Hallmark Cards, Inc.

Hallmark Cards, Inc., has begun offering greeting cards via what has been considered to be the largest, fastest-growing online network in the United States, America Online (AOL). Hallmark is forging a string of new partnerships to expand the ways consumers shop, purchase, and personalize greeting cards and related products. Hallmark is said to lead the greeting-card industry in technology-based consumer initiatives, which fall into the categories of electronic shopping, personal computer products and retail personalization. According to their online press release, their publicly stated goal is to offer "compelling solutions that make it easy and fun for people to express themselves to one another."

Hallmark Connections brand greeting cards ordered from America Online are personalized according to the sender's orders, then addressed and mailed. Hallmark Connections cards are sold through a number of alternative shopping channels, including CompuServe's Electronic Mall and IT Network's interactive television shopping channel. Hallmark will offer products on AT&T PersonaLink Market Square and will be a charter participant on U S Avenue shopping service. Hallmark also intends to offer products via The Microsoft Network and the MCI Internet service. To contact Hallmark on the Internet send an e-mail message to:

hallmarkmr@aol.com

Award-winning online businesses

The Interactive Association awards for the association's 11th Annual Awards competition was expanded to reflect the breadth of the

interactive services industry. The following companies were recognized for their innovation using the Internet and online services:

- 1-800-FLOWERS on America Online
- America Online for AOL's multimedia software
- American Express for ExpressNet
- BFD Productions for The LoopPhone Shopping Network
- CBS Marketing Interactive for CBS on Prodigy/Eye on the Net
- Chevrolet for its America's Cup application on Prodigy
- CKS Partners and MCI for internetMCI
- Donaldson, Lufkin & Jenrette Securities Corp.'s Pershing Division for PC Financial Network
- Fox Broadcasting for its Melrose Place interactive radio game
- Gannett for PI, its digital personalized information service
- Nickelodeon for its Slime Time Sweepstakes
- Phone Programs, Inc. for Lowe's Home Safety Program
- MCI for 1-900-GET-INFO
- Physicians On-line for its online service of the same name
- Prodigy Services Company for its Web Browser
- Tribune Media Services for Voice News Network
- US Order and InterVoice for SurePay
- Yahoo for Yahoo: A Guide to the Internet
- Ziff-Davis Interactive for Ziff Net On-line and Internet: Design

Past awards recipients represent a veritable "Who's Who" of the interactive industry and include:

- America Online
- CompuServe
- Checkfree
- Citibank
- GTE Main Street the ImagiNation Network
- J. Walter Thompson/On-line
- NTN Communications
- Ogilvy & Mather Direct
- Pacific Bell
- Philips Home Services
- Prodigy

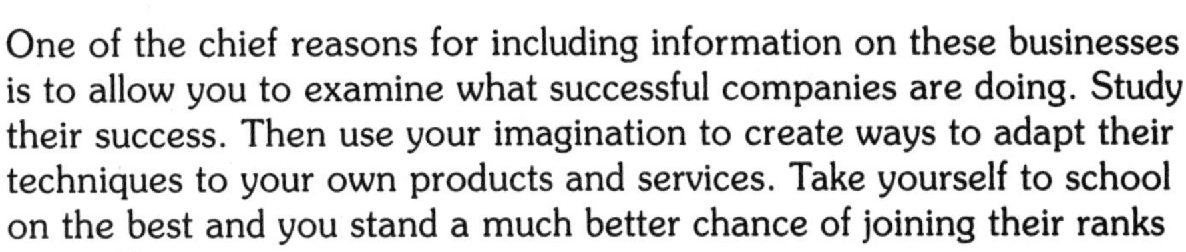

One of the chief reasons for including information on these businesses is to allow you to examine what successful companies are doing. Study their success. Then use your imagination to create ways to adapt their techniques to your own products and services. Take yourself to school on the best and you stand a much better chance of joining their ranks yourself.

The trick, of course, is trying to figure out which business on the Net are successful in cyberspace. You can't rely on the pizazz of their presentation. There are numerous Web sites that look impressive but are doing little to swell the company's coffers. One good indication is the traffic they generate. About the only way you will know this is if they have a traffic counter publicly visible on their site. Some do, some don't. Another indicator is how often you run across them when you're not looking for them. If you find yourself constantly stumbling across a reference to a site, chances are they are getting a lot of traffic. Basically, though, you just have to develop a sense of what should work and what probably shouldn't. Go back to the previous list of ideal products and other similar guidelines. Remember, you are a pioneer of sorts. You may not find all the answers you seek simply because no one really knows yet. You may be the first to discover some of it. If you're a good student and take a few chances, don't be surprised if you are first.

And before you get all intimidated by names like Microsoft and Citibank, remember this: the Internet is the most level playing field in recorded history. Your success is completely, entirely, absolutely and forever up to you and you alone! So do your homework, put on your thinking cap, and then go out there and give 'em a run for their money.

7

Reaching the Global Black Family

IN the ancient world, taking a message from the end of one continent to the end of another was a grueling ordeal involving months of physical hardships and unpredictable dangers. There were no reliable roads or sea lanes that could safely guide the courier. In fact, even the destinations sought were often shrouded with mythical references gleamed from fragments of yellowed parchment.

As transportation and communications between distant parts of the world improved, myths evaporated leaving hard kernels of fact and direction. Medieval travelers came back home with tales of long-lost tribes and totally different cultures, as well as strange and wonderful inventions. But for the average homebody, the world still remained a very big and very scary place.

In modern times, the planet Earth has not changed its physical dimensions, but now there is a wholly new perspective. Using the new perspective, the world has shrunk down to the size of a desk, and cheap, nearly instantaneous, communication is available to anyone with a telephone and a computer.

We all can be world travelers and never experience anything more discomforting than mild neck strain. Many cyber-explorers have dozens of friends and associates around the globe with whom they speak to every night. Yet the cost of these long distance interactions is only pennies a day.

The African link

Africa is the heart and soul of the global black family. Africans and Africans throughout the black diaspora are reaching across oceans to join hands via global communications. As Africa struggles for economic parity, and trading status as a full partner, the clamor for new business ventures, education reform, technology development, and cultural exchange can be heard daily in the Internet newsgroups.

African Americans and Africans throughout the black diaspora are forging important relationships to assist the ancestral homeland.

There are a number of challenges to overcome. For instance, Africa lacks a consistent telecommunications infrastructure. Often, phone calls from one neighboring African nation to another have to be routed through Europe or the United States—thousands of miles away from the callers. This causes expensive delays and lengthy interruptions. (Therefore, e-mail messages, instead of big Web pages, have the best chances of getting through.)

Governments of developing nations in Africa and elsewhere also are grappling with the problem that too many of their people don't even

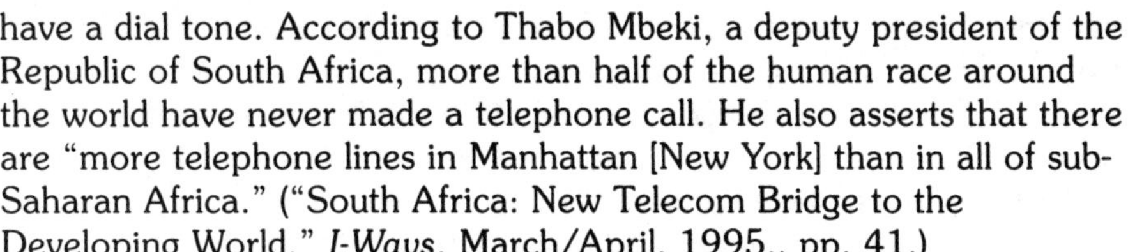

have a dial tone. According to Thabo Mbeki, a deputy president of the Republic of South Africa, more than half of the human race around the world have never made a telephone call. He also asserts that there are "more telephone lines in Manhattan [New York] than in all of sub-Saharan Africa." ("South Africa: New Telecom Bridge to the Developing World," *I-Ways*, March/April, 1995., pp. 41.)

Global Information Infrastructure Commission

Several international organizations have been set up to help bring modern communications to more parts of the world. For instance, the Global Information Infrastructure Commission (GIIC) has been established to "foster the development and utilization of information technologies and services in advancing economic growth, education, and quality of life in developing and developed countries," according to the GIIC "Agenda for Cooperation." The GII Commission which was launched in early 1995 is urging private multinational corporations to work closely with local governments to get "dial tones" in more parts of the world.

But it has been observed that more than dial tones must be implemented. Entire populations must become literate enough to benefit from Internet connections. Also, local residents must be in control of their own telecommunications infrastructure to guarantee its longevity—they must be trained as operators and builders of the hardware and software involved. It will take big corporations to start the process, but the local populace eventually must assume responsibility to maintain the systems.

Africa ONE

Already AT&T has plans to encircle Africa with the region's first high-capacity digital undersea fiber-optic network. This would link the people and businesses of Africa to each other and to the global information superhighway. William B. Carter, president of AT&T Submarine Systems, Inc., outlined the company's plan, known as Africa ONE, at a March 1995, joint hearing of the House Subcommittee on Africa and the Subcommittee on International Policy and Trade.

"Targeted investments in key technologies can help move Africa from an aid-based economy to a trade-based economy and into the mainstream of international economic prosperity—a benefit for everyone," says Carter on the Africa ONE home page. Carter also told the panel, "AT&T is committed to helping in that process by launching and leading the development of a regional telecommunications network for Africa." Carter asserted that Africa ONE would create a sophisticated telecommunications infrastructure that would boost Africa's economy, create trade and investment opportunities for multinational firms, and enhance the competitiveness of African nations by giving them "access on an international basis to technology, markets, transport, finance and information about products and resources."

The Africa ONE plan was developed by AT&T in response to a request from the International Telecommunications Union, an organization responsible for the development of global telecommunications policy, to help close the communications gap between Africa and other regions of the world.

AT&T, long recognized as a leader in building communications networks, proposed a three-tiered approach to connect Africa with the rest of the world. The first tier would focus on the populous coastal centers in Africa. These locations serve as natural gateways for international trade and, more practically, as landing points that can divert international traffic to land-based destinations throughout the continent. The second tier would connect all the nations of Africa through a regional network, integrating and supporting Africa's existing communications infrastructure. The third tier would link the Africa ONE undersea fiber-optic ring to the global information superhighway.

While AT&T Submarine Systems, Inc., would serve as the supplier of the Africa ONE network, no one is sure which African organization would handle the overall management of the communications network.

Africa ONE cable project at a glance

Length: 35,000 kilometers

Landing Points: 41 African countries plus Saudia Arabia and Italy

Technology: Optical fiber network operating at 2.5 gigabits (billion)-per-second

Anticipated: Cost-$1.9 billion

African telecommunications trends

- Africa has only 2 percent of the world's main telephone lines, despite having 12 percent of the world's population.
- In the last 10 years, Africa had the lowest annual growth of "teledensity" (main phone lines per 100 people) of any developing region in the world.

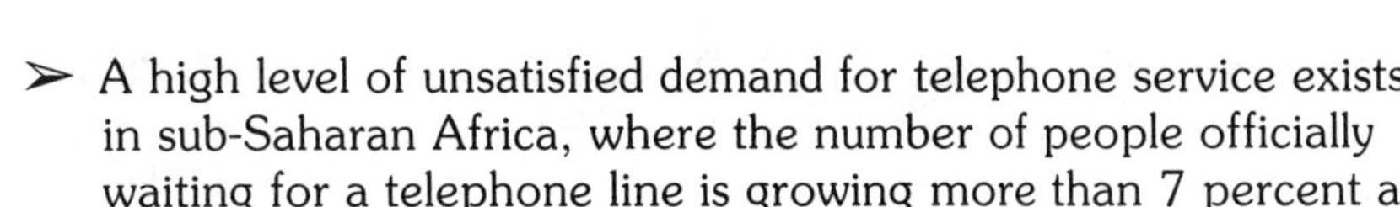

- ➢ A high level of unsatisfied demand for telephone service exists in sub-Saharan Africa, where the number of people officially waiting for a telephone line is growing more than 7 percent a year.
- ➢ The level of international telephone traffic per subscriber in the sub-Saharan Africa (over 200 minutes annually) is the highest of any region in the world. But the level of traffic per inhabitant (less than one minute) is the lowest in the world.
- ➢ The average level of pre-tax profitability of public telecommunications operators in Africa is among the highest of any region in the world. This is perhaps due to the fact that telecommunications services are available only to the richest segment of the African population and to the foreign-owned, export-oriented sectors of the economy.
- ➢ An increasing number of sub-Saharan nations have crossed the critical threshold of one telephone line per 100 inhabitants.
- ➢ The cost of installing a telephone line in Africa is the highest of any region in the world. If sub-Saharan installation costs were closer to the world's average, the region could install almost 600,000 additional lines per year.
- ➢ For many developing economies, mobile communications are a way to leap-frog into the 21st-century global marketplace. The potential for wireless communications in Africa is largely untapped.
- ➢ Privatization of telephone administrations is a growing trend in Africa. A number of African countries have announced privatization plans; many others are considering it.

Internet Africa

According to Chris Pinkham, an official with Internet Africa, 1995 would be remembered as the year of the Internet in Africa—particularly in South Africa, which reportedly accounts for 99 percent of Internet connections in sub-Saharan Africa. His prediction may not be that far off course, reflecting on the rise in public interest in the Internet during the first half of 1995. Particularly significant is the heightened awareness of the tremendous benefits of relatively low-cost, worldwide communications.

In the early stages of South African Internet development, mostly students and professors took advantage of the information superhighway to stay in touch with colleagues and friends around the world. But it didn't take long for commercial interests to grasp the potential for worldwide profits.

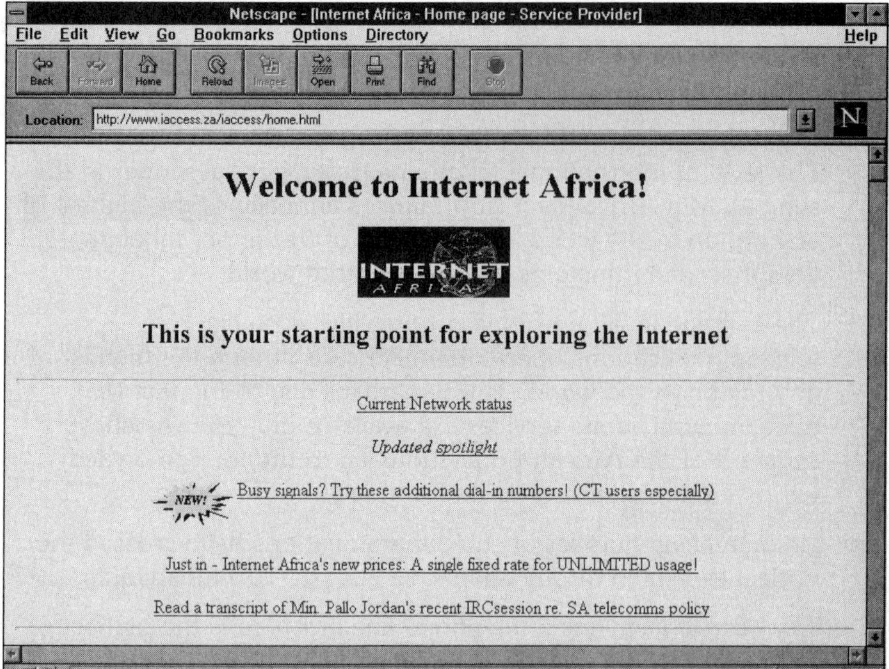

Fig. 7-1 *Internet Africa's Hope Page on the World Wide Web*

Internet Africa, which started up in 1994, has expanded throughout South and southern Africa with thousands of subscribers in Johannesburg, Pretoria, Cape Town, Durban, and Port Elizabeth. A number of South Africa's largest and best-known companies also have seen the wisdom of using the Internet as an essential business and advertising tool. Internet Africa is only one example of how Africa is moving into the information age; but other African Internet interests are forming almost daily. Internet Africa can be found on the World Wide Web at *http://www.iaccess.za/iaccess/home.html*.

AIDAT

The African Internet Development Action Team (AIDAT) is a non-profit organization set up to promote the development of the Internet in Africa. Their goals are to be the non-biased and independent voice of Internet development in Africa.

Formed at the end of 1994, AIDAT has said that it is coordinated by a group of volunteers who are highly active in the Internet industry. Although, up to now, South Africa, has been the focus of Internet and indeed, commercial activity, AIDAT reportedly is assisting with projects in other African countries. AIDAT groups its efforts into three distinct areas: public information services, industry association, and initiatives for broader Internet services. Internet-related information is available to the general public via AIDAT fax-on-demand service. This

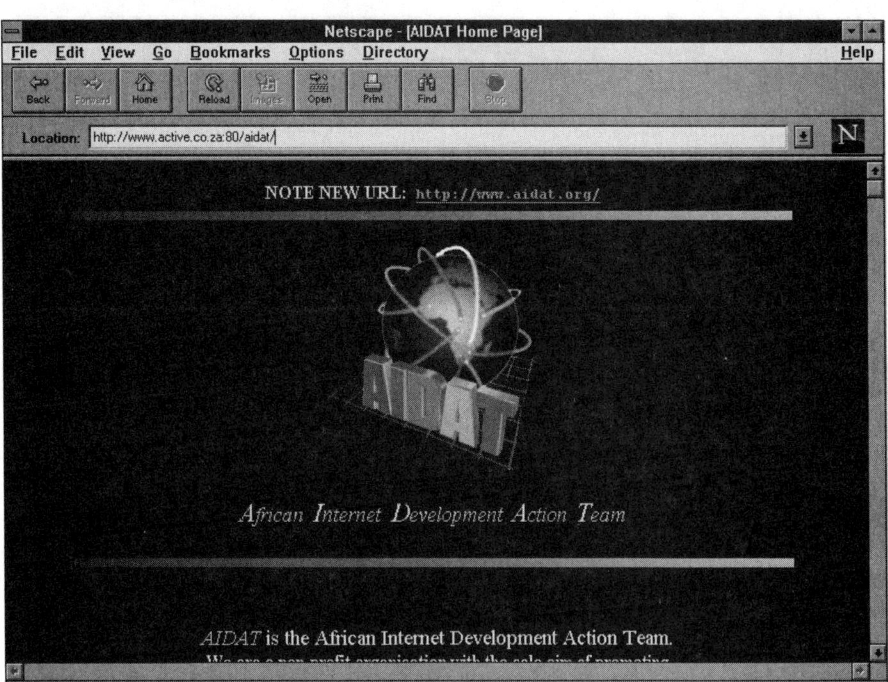

Fig. 7-2 *The African Internet Development Action Team home page*

information includes a guide to choosing an Internet service provider (ISP) and an extensive list of ISPs.

The AIDAT bulletin, which comes out approximately every three weeks, highlights interesting i-way activities in South Africa and also offers an overview of Internet happenings in the country. Quite frankly, getting reliable information about the Internet has always been a problem. AIDAT staff intends to prevent the spread of misinformation by being a dependable source of Internet news.

AIDAT can be contacted at:

Telephone: (011) 791 0410
e-mail: *brooks@odie.ee.wits.ac.za*
WWW: *http://www.active.co.za:80/aidat/*

AFRIA

Two South African information companies and a US communications firm have an alliance to bring comprehensive research and information service on Africa. AFRIA (The Africa Research & Information Alliance) is a consortium formed by Stock Press and Legi-Link from South Africa, and The Rendon Group in the USA. AFRIA offers information services on many Southern African topics, from the economy and the environment, to bills and policy shifts in the new Parliament.

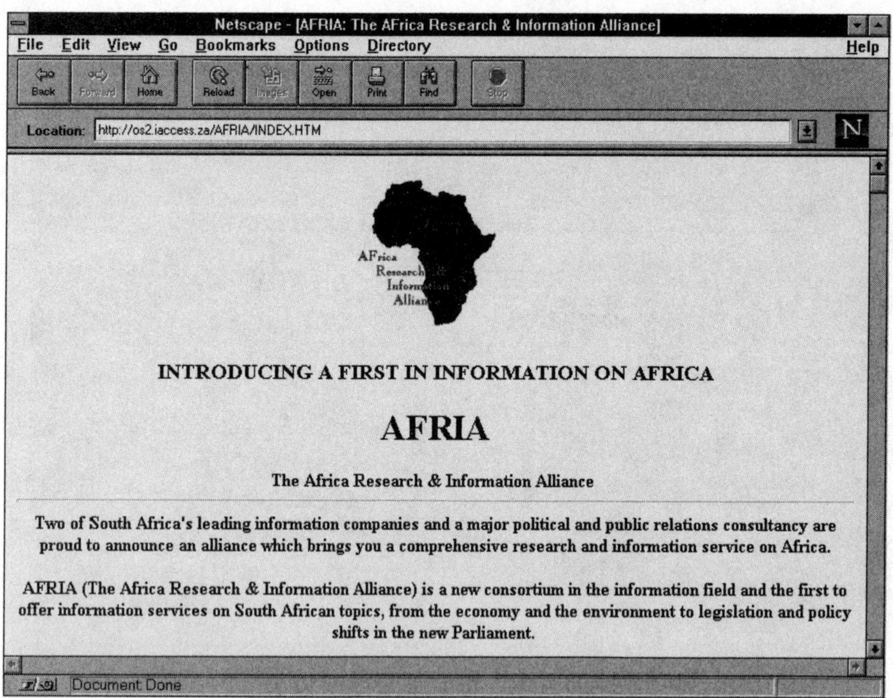

Fig. 7-3 *AFRIA's home page on the World Wide Web*

For more information about AFRIA, or to subscribe to The RDP Monitor, go to their Web site at *http://os2.iaccess.za/AFRIA/INDEX .HTM*, or send an e-mail message to: *AFRIA@leglink.co.za*

African Voices

African Voices is a quarterly newsletter providing a forum for dialogue on democratization, governance, Internet news, and civil society in Africa. It is published quarterly by the US Agency for International Development (USAID). The newsletter is available on USAID's gopher.

The gopher address is:

gopher.info.usaid.gov

The Web address is:

gopher://gopher.info.usaid.gov

To find *African Voices*, open the folder called "Documents and Publications," then "USAID Newsletters," and then "Africa Bureau Newsletters." For more information or to submit an item, please contact John Engels, Africa Bureau Information Center, USAID, SA-18, Room 203-J, Washington, DC 20523-1820; 703-312-7194; Fax: 703-312-7199. E-mail should be sent to: jengels@usaid.gov.

The African Studies Web site

Anyone interested in finding out more about Africa can access a database of African studies materials on the World Wide Web, which contains classroom materials for teachers, the business community, and other networked individuals at the University of Pennsylvania. The Web site also contains information on programs and resources at U Penn, in the US, Africa, and elsewhere.

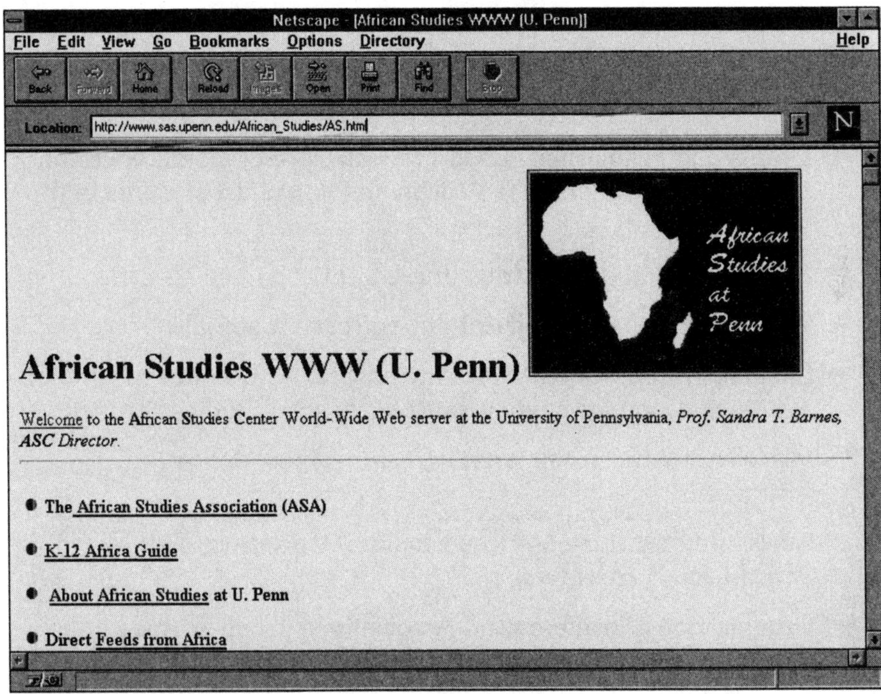

Fig. 7-4 *The African Studies WWW site at University of Pennsylvania*

The African Studies Center is part of a four-school consortium that includes Bryn Mawr, Haverford, and Swarthmore Colleges, as well as the University of Pennsylvania. The consortium promotes interdisciplinary instruction and research in African languages and area studies and exchange relationships with African institutions. The Center's outreach program, which maintains the electronic bulletin board, includes:

- Almanac & Penn News (information about the University of Pennsylvania's African Studies Consortium and the surrounding community)
- Articles & Papers (published articles, papers, and abstracts of general interest to African Studies)
- Audio-Visual Resources for African Studies (videography, film making, audio cassettes)
- Bibliography (Africa-related, Islamic, Arabic, or African-American related bibliographies)

- ➢ Books On-Line (African Studies-related monographs)
- ➢ Computer Networking (e-mail to Africa, networking and Africa, interest and discussion groups, Africa-related software, resources for academic research)
- ➢ Conferences, Colloquia and Lectures
- ➢ Current Events (announcements, new services, upcoming events)
- ➢ Electronic African News (radio and television broadcasts, online computer resources)
- ➢ GIF Images (GIF archives, Africa-related graphics)
- ➢ Governmental & Political Documents (official statements, policy papers)
- ➢ Grants and Fellowships (undergraduate, pre-doctoral, doctoral, post-doctoral, funding for African and Africanist students in the US and abroad)
- ➢ Job Opportunities (in Africa, the US, Europe and elsewhere)
- ➢ African Studies (K-12 education, outreach materials)
- ➢ Language, Courses & ASPs (African Studies programs, summer institutes, language study resources, African Studies courses)
- ➢ Miscellany (African fine arts, African recipes, African restaurants)
- ➢ Newsletters On-Line (African Studies Association, Title VI African Studies Centers)
- ➢ Organizations, Institutes and Associations (newly formed research and international organizations and institutes)
- ➢ Proceedings & Reviews (conference proceedings and book reviews)
- ➢ Products & Services (commercial products and services related to Africa)
- ➢ Publications & Publishers (newsletters, journals, monographs, African publishers and Africa-related publications)
- ➢ Travel Opportunities (employment, study, vacation, internships, and volunteer positions abroad)
- ➢ Urgent Action & Commentary (appeals for intervention, activist events and petitions)
- ➢ What's New in African Studies!! (recently posted African Studies related information)

To reach the University of Pennsylvania Web site set your browser's search engine to *http://www.african.upenn.edu/African_Studies/AS.html*.

You can also Telnet to the Web (using Lynx):

Telnet to *www.upenn.edu;*

Enter pennweb at the login prompt;

Scroll down on U. Penn's home page and choose "WWW Servers" and then "African Studies at Penn".

For more information contact: Ali B. Ali-Dinar, African Studies Program, University of Pennsylvania, 418 University Museum, Philadelphia, PA 19104-6398. The e-mail address is: aadinar@sas.upenn.edu

The Global Black Family revisited

Thanks to the Internet, the Global Black Family is now a reality. African people and related Internet activities can be found throughout the world on every continent from Europe to Asia. Before the age of the Internet, separate groups were isolated and in many cases unknown to each other. Now, Africans spread throughout this diaspora can acknowledge their common ancestral backgrounds and reunite spiritually, culturally, and economically. In a world that is rapidly developing a global economy, this unification of African people can be an advantage as similar skills and consumer desires are recognized and catered to.

Moreover, training and education can more readily be transmitted from person to person with similar views and cultural upbringings. There are also substantial benefits for non-African people.

As stated earlier, on the Internet nobody knows what color you are. Individuals with similar interests and lifestyles do seek each other out and communicate. African culture and business opportunities appeal to many different types of people. Thus, the Global Black Family will not be entirely black—it will have more of a "rainbow" hue.

The extended families

The Institute for Global Communications (IGC) provides computer networking tools for international communication and information exchange for a variety of societies and nations. IGC is the U.S. member of the Association for Progressive Communications (APC), a coalition of computer networks providing services to over 30,000 activists and organizations in more than 130 countries.

The IGC Networks—PeaceNet, EcoNet, ConflictNet, LaborNet, and WomensNet—together with APC partner networks, comprise a worldwide computer communications system dedicated to environmental preservation, peace, and human rights. New technologies are helping these worldwide communities cooperate more effectively and efficiently. IGC, located in San Francisco, California, is a division of the Tides Foundation, a 501(c)(3) tax-exempt organization.

On the Web: *http://www.sas.upenn.edu/African_Studies/Global_Comm/Global_Networking.html*. See Fig. 7-5 for a sample Web page.

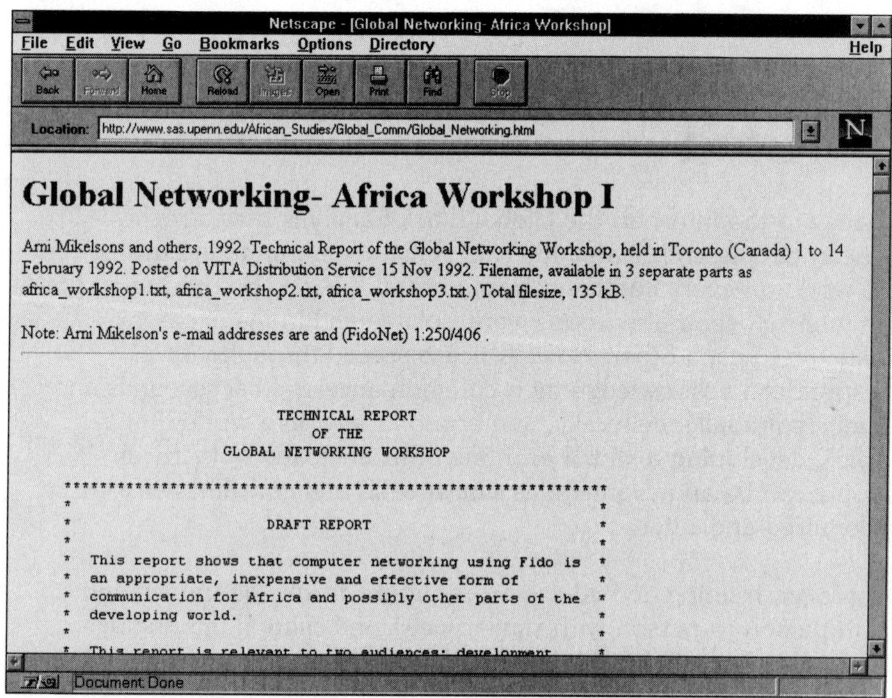

Fig. 7-5 *Web page about the Global Networking Workshop*

By subscribing to any one of the IGC Networks, you have full access to the resources of any of the other IGC Networks. Their e-mail address is *subscription@igc.apc.org*. The following is a brief description of each:

PeaceNet

PeaceNet serves peace and social justice advocates around the world in such areas as human rights, disarmament, and international relations. A number of alternative news services provide a range of information about these and other topics from around the world. Their address on the web is *http://www.peacenet.apc.org/peacenet/*.

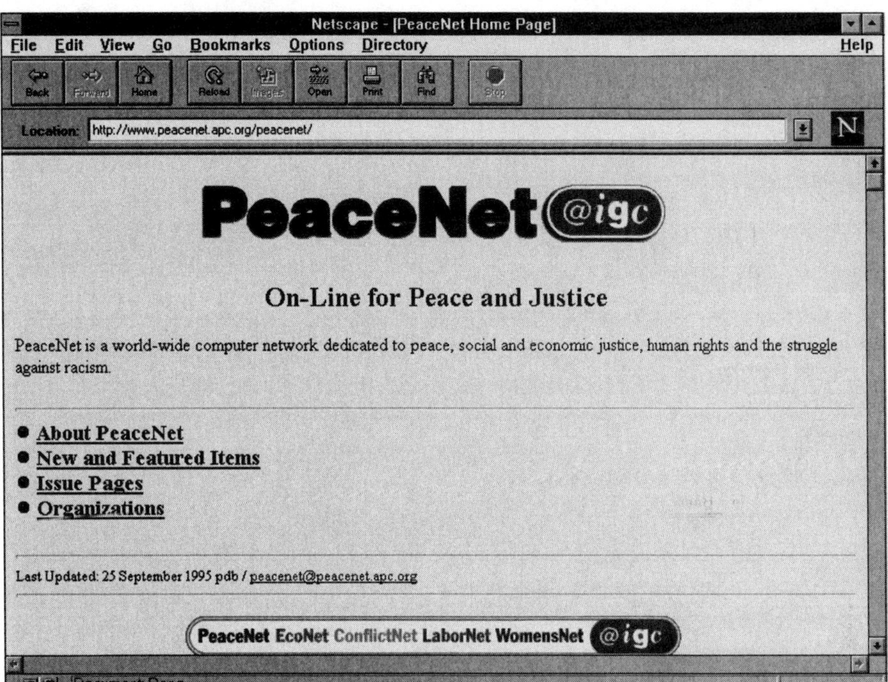

Fig. 7-6 *The PeaceNet home page*

EcoNet

EcoNet serves individuals and organizations working for environmental preservation and sustainability. Important issues covered include: global warming, energy policy, rain forest preservation, legislative activities, water quality, toxics, and environmental education.

WWW: *http://www.econet.apc.org/econet/*

ConflictNet

ConflictNet serves groups and individuals working for social justice and conflict resolution. ConflictNet's resources include guidelines for choosing a neutral third party, sample case development in conflict resolution, extensive bibliographies, legislative updates, educational materials, and newsletters from around the world.

WWW: *http://www.igc.apc.org/conflictnet/*

LaborNet

LaborNet serves groups, unions, and labor advocates interested in information sharing and collaboration with the intent of enhancing the human rights and economic justice of workers. Issues covered include

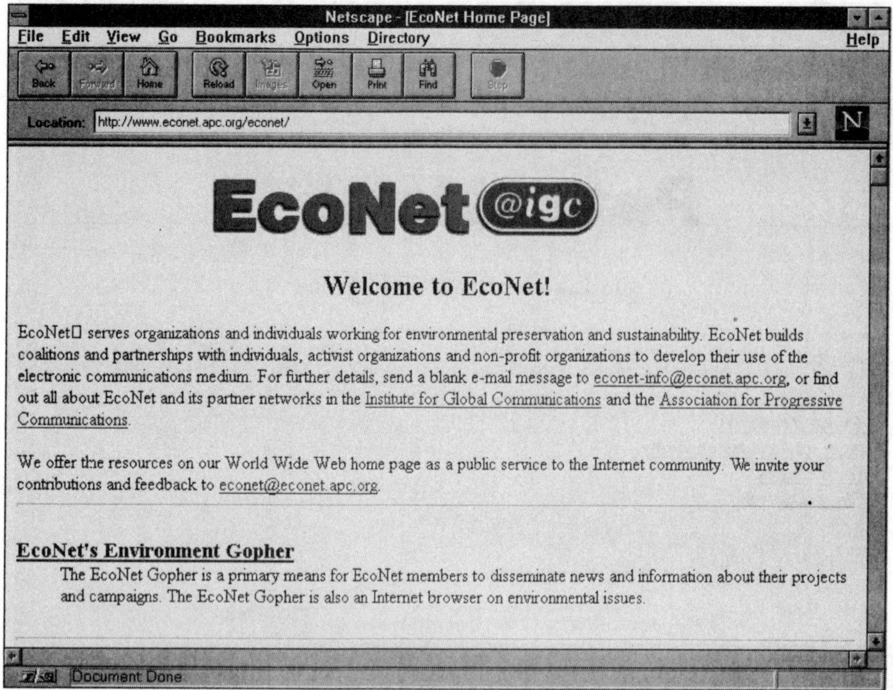

Fig. 7-7 *EcoNet's home page*

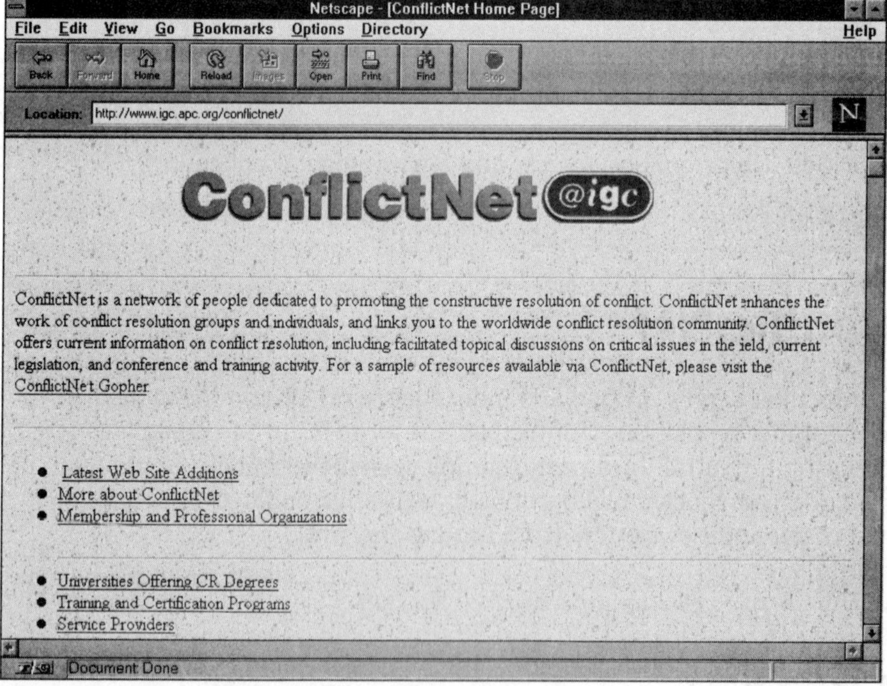

Fig. 7-8 *ConflictNet's home page*

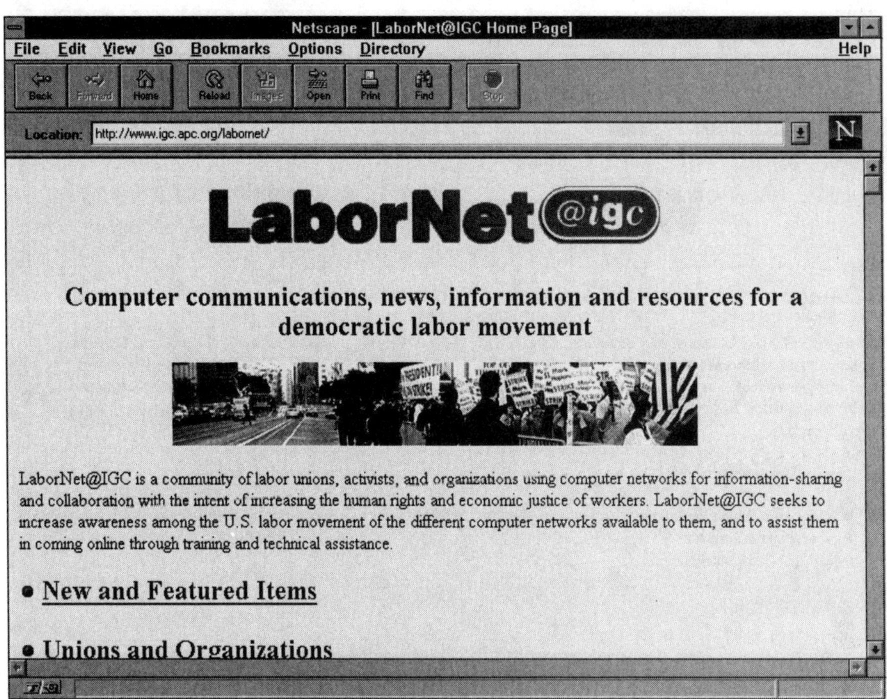

Fig. 7-9 *LaborNet's home page*

workplace and community health and safety, trade, and international union solidarity and collaboration.

WWW: *http://www.igc.apc.org/labornet/*

WomensNet

WomensNet serves women, organizations, and advocates interested in information-sharing and collaboration with the intent of enhancing the rights of women. Issues covered include health, economics, women of color, violence, women in media and communications, the Fourth World Conference on Women, development, and international news on women.

On the Web: *http://www.igc.apc.org/womensnet/*

International programs and the Association for Progressive Communications

IGC regards international cooperation and partnership as essential in addressing peace and environmental problems. IGC maintains a major program to develop low-cost access to computer networking from outside the United States, especially from non-industrialized

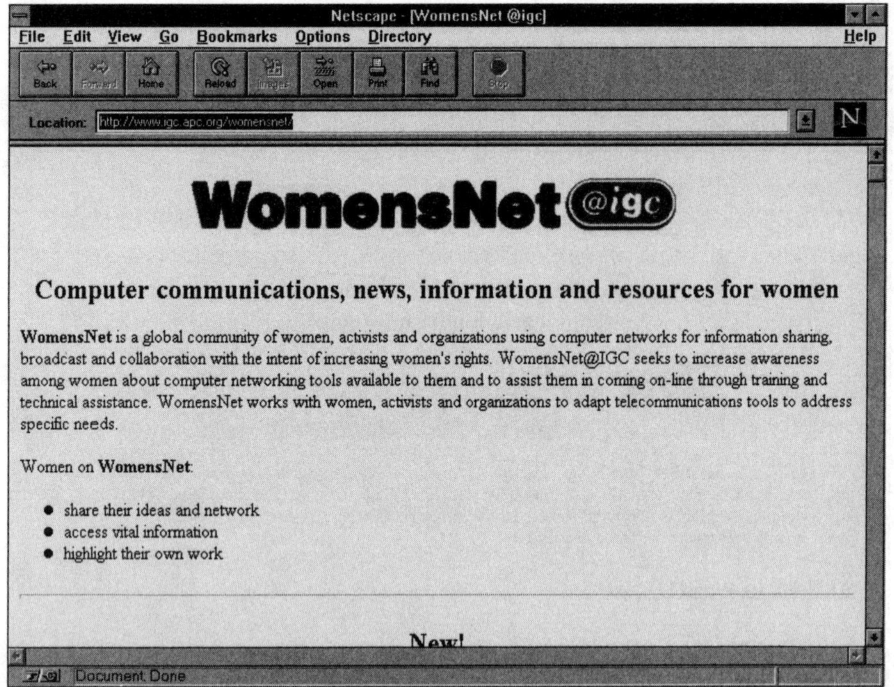

Fig. 7-10 *WomensNet's home page*

and Southern hemisphere countries. The result of this program has been the Association of Progressive Communications (APC) which now includes low-cost computer networks in sixteen countries. IGC has played a major role in starting the Alternex (Brazil), Nicarao (Nicaragua) and GlasNet (Russia) nonprofit computer networks, as well as in providing technical support to all of the member networks.

The focus of IGCs and APCs international program is to empower local, indigenous organizations by transferring expertise and capacity in computer networking. Operation and management of a local APC node becomes the full responsibility of the local organization. All APC partners are independent organizations, and retain full control over their network.

For a current list of APC member networks, send any message to *apc-info@apc.org* for an automatic reply. Anyone can join the APC global community and participate in a range of discussions and find information resources on such topics. For more information about IGC programs send e-mail to:

Art McGee
IGC Staff
amcgee@igc.apc.org

Addresses for other organizations, mailing lists, and African sites

In case none of the above references meets your needs or wishes, here are a few dozen others. The World Wide Web sites are particularly useful because virtually all of them have links to other resources. Some of those are probably not mentioned here. In your search for people, places, and things, be resourceful. Don't give up if you don't find exactly what you're looking for the first time out. Even in the unlikely event that nothing actually exists today that suits your needs, check back periodically. The number of World Wide Web sites is doubling every 53 days, so in a couple of months there will be more than twice as much as there is now. Much of this growth is taking place in Africa and other less-developed regions.

Also, don't be shy about asking people for help. Newsgroups, two-way mailing lists, and e-mail are all very useful in finding the missing pieces of your personal jigsaw puzzle. Many World Wide Web sites let you send e-mail to the person in charge just by clicking on a link right on the page you're looking at. You will find that the inhabitants of cyberspace are generally very helpful. Just be respectful and as concise as you can. If you respect their time, they will respect your needs. It's as simple as that. Many of the addresses that follow have mailing lists. For more on how to subscribe to them, see the Mailing Lists section of Chapter 4 (page 71).

Abyssinia Cyberspace Gateway:
On the Web: *http://www.cs.indiana.edu/hyplan/dmulholl/acg.html*

Africa Update:
On the Web: *http://neal.ctstateu.edu/history/africa_update/africa_update.html*

Africa-L is an Africa-wide bitnet listserv.
listserv: *listserv@vtvm1.cc.vt.edu*

African Agenda is a list from Accra and Johannesburg.
e-mail: *FAGEND@iaccess.za*

African Studies at Wisconsin:
On the Web: *http://www.wisc.edu/afr/*

African Studies Web at University of Pennsylvania:
On the Web: *http://www.sas.upenn.edu/African_Studies/AS.html*

Afrikaans is an Afrikaans discussion group:
listserv: *listproc@oliver.sun.ac.za*
On the Web: *gopher://lib.sun.ac.za/Afrikaans*

Afrlabor: A discussion group on African labor history.
e-mail: *afrlabor@acuvax.acu.edu*
Editor Carolyn Brown: *cbrown@zodiac.rutgers.edu*

Afrique is a new French-language discussion list from the Universite de Lyon.
listserv: *listserv@univ-lyon1.fr*

Afrlit is a discussion group on African literature.
e-mail: *afrlit-request@acuvax.acu.edu*

Amazigh Network:
e-mail: *amazigh-net@ensisun.imag.fr*

ANC Gopher. The ANC's newswire:
On the Web: *http://minerva.cis.yale.edu:80/`~jadwat/anc/* or
gopher://gopher://wn.apc.org
e-mail: *info@anc.org.za* or *ancdip@wn.apc.org*

Botswananet is a healthy group of several hundred members.
e-mail: *botswana@mathcs.duq.edu*

Burkina Faso:
e-mail: *aajn@catcc.bitnet*
Clari.World.Africa is a commercial USENET newsgroup devoted to African news.

DEHAI/EDIN:
e-mail: *dehai-admin@thames.stanford.edu*

Egypt-Net: A discussion group provided in daily digest form.
e-mail: *egypt-net-request@cs.sunysb.edu*

Eritrea-L:
listserv: *lists@thames.stanford.edu*

EthioList has a number of groups:
e-mail: Tadesse Tsegage at *txt4@netcom.com* or *Ethioculture @Netcom.com* or *ethiohistory@netcom.com*

Ethiopia Gateway:
On the Web: *http://www.cs.indiana.edu/hyplan/dmuholl/ ab_base.html*

Horn of Africa Bulletin:
e-mail: *enelson@nn.apc.org*

Hornet is a selection of Addis Ababa bulletin boards.
On the Web: *http://www.sas.upenn.edu/African Studies/Hornet*

H-Africa: An academic discussion on African history. Part of the H-Net family of history groups.
listserv: *listserv@msu.edu*
e-mail: *h-africa@msu.edu* or *africa@etsuarts.east-tenn-st.edu*

Indian Ocean Newsletter:
e-mail: *arm@utoronto.bitnet*

InterAfrica Group: A bimonthly résumé of regional issues:
e-mail: *IAG@padis.gn.apc.org*

Kenya-net:
e-mail: *Kenya-net@ftp.com*

Malawi-Net (a.k.a. Nyasanet):
e-mail: *nyasanet-request@unh.edu*

MISA-Net: Produced by the Media Institute of Southern Africa.
e-mail: Bruce Cohen at *wmail@is.co.za*
Their Free Press Newsletter is at *gopher:// wmail.misanet.org*
On the Web: *http://history.cc.ukans.ed u/carrie/news_main.html*

Mozambique Peace Process Bulletin:
e-mail: *misa-info@misanet.org*

Naijanet: From Nigeria:
e-mail: *naijanet@mit*

Namnet: A discussion group about Namibia.
e-mail: *namnet-request@lisse.na*

Nuafrica: It is not moderated and is therefore very freewheeling.
e-mail: *nuafrica@listserv.acns.nwu.edu*

Oromo-net:
e-mail: *makobili@netcom.com*

Rhodes University:
gopher://gopher.ru.ac.za

Rwanda: Lots of Rwandan information:
On the Web: *http://www.intac.com/Pubservice/rwanda/*

Scottish Churches Sudan Group Newsletter:
e-mail: *mam@festival.edinburgh.ac.uk*

Sudanese:
e-mail: *sudanese@crsa.bu.edu*

Sudanic Africa: An academic journal with useful book references.
On the Web: *http://www.hf-fak.uib.no/institutter/smi/sa/sahome.html*

Swahili: A list devoted to the Swahili language:
e-mail: *Swahili-l@macc.wisc.edu* or *kuntz@macc.wisc.edu*

Weekly Mail:
e-mail: *wmail-info@wmail.misanet.org*
On the Web: *http://www.is.co.za/services/wmail/wmail.html*

Zambian Post: Newspaper:
On the Web: *http://www.zamnet.com/*

Zimbabwe International Book Fair:
e-mail: *margaret.ling@geo2.poptel.org.uk*

Interesting USENET newsgroups

alt.music.african

aol.neighborhood.nation.central-african-republic

aol.neighborhood.nation.south-africa

bit.tech.africana

rec.travel.africa

soc.culture.african

soc.culture.african.american

soc.culture.berber

soc.culture.egypt

soc.culture.nigeria

soc.culture.somalia

soc.culture.south-africa

soc.culture.south-africa.afrikaans

soc.genealogy.african

t-net.chat.african-link

ww.clubs.african

za.politics (e-mail: *za-politics@quagga.ru.ac.za*)

E-mail addresses of publishers

African Imprint Library Services
e-mail: *afrcarimp@delphi.com*

Africa World Press
e-mail: *AfricaWPress@nyo.com*

Hogarth Representation (West African books)
e-mail: *100265.51@compuserve.com*

8

Connecting with the Feds

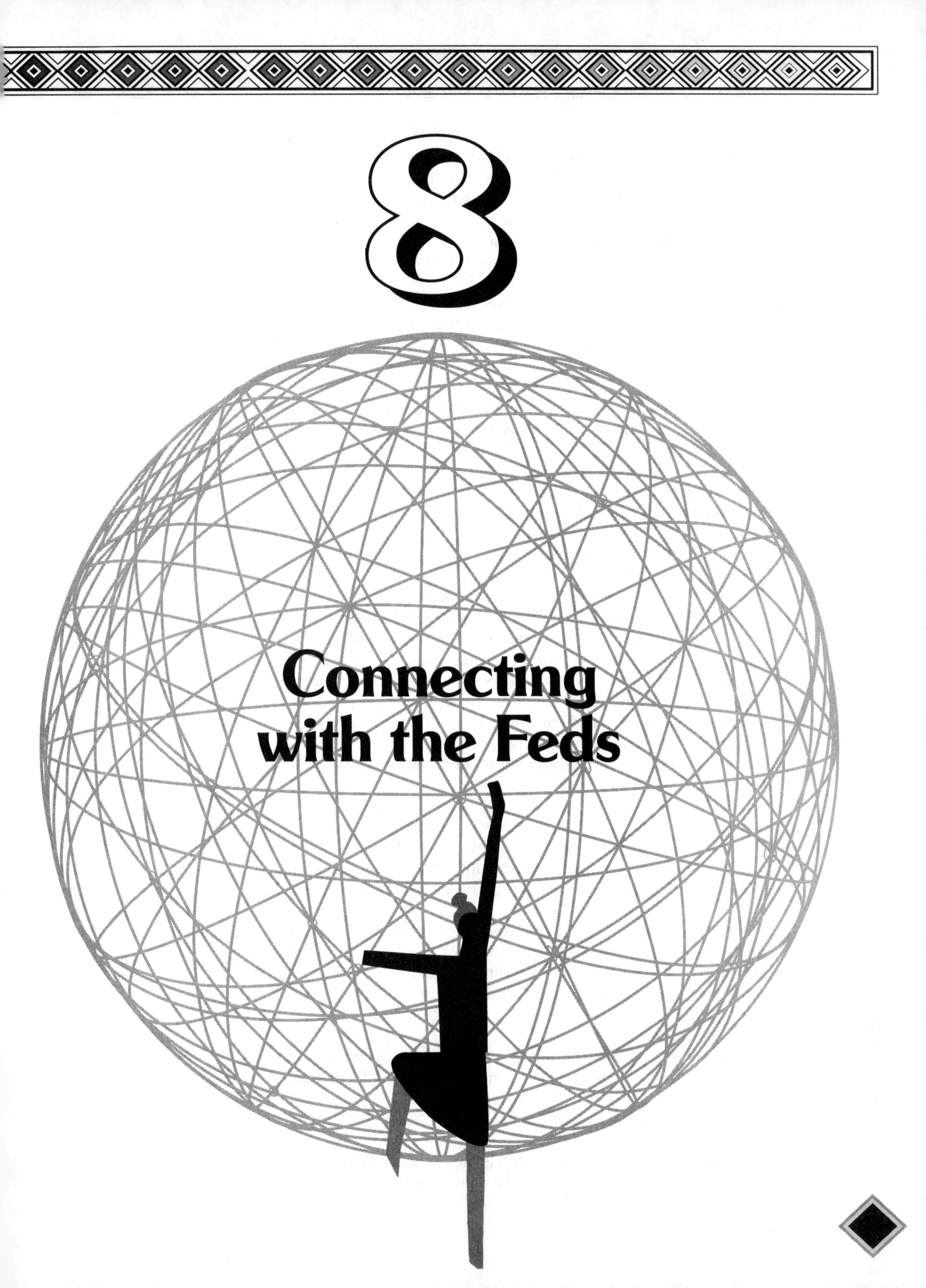

ONE of the largest employers of African Americans in the world is the United States federal government. The federal organizational structure is a labyrinth of red tape, bureaucracy, redundancy, and tons and tons of paper. But, mostly due to Vice President Al Gore's efforts to "reinvent" government, the feds have gone online to streamline their activities. Whether you want to learn how to choose the freshest fish, conduct business with the government, or find out what is required to travel to South Africa, there is a government Internet connection that can give you the information quickly and usually for free. The services are accessible virtually 24 hours a day.

Every day, more and more government assistance, information, and networking is available online. This is extremely powerful stuff. Small companies wishing to conduct business with the government can do so online. Individuals who need information about employment, social security, or the IRS can find it online. Voters who would like to keep tabs on their elected officials can do so, online.

The White House has acted to improve the accessibility of government information by opening a service called "Welcome to the White House: An Interactive Citizens' Handbook" on the World Wide Web. This service offers the public unprecedented interactive access to the federal government, from the resources of the Cabinet and independent agencies to a behind-the-scenes look at life for the First Family. In addition, the service provides a way to electronically communicate with the president and vice president, and provides improved access to thousands of White House press releases, speeches, and public documents. This multimedia interface includes photographs, audio, and "hotlinks" to other government Web sites and services.

Remember, to access any home page, you must have software that allows you to browse the World Wide Web and receive illustrations and text information. Today, any full-service Internet provider has access to the Web through a relatively easy "point and click" interface.

For users with older computers, low-speed modems (anything below 14,000 baud) or who cannot display graphics, the White House home page does support the text-only Web browser LYNX, which is software available from direct access Internet providers (see Chapter Two, page 38).

If a computer is not available to access the information provided by the White House Web service, telephone the Federal Information Center (FIC), 1-800-347-1997, to receive answers to any questions regarding the content of the service.

When a message is sent to the White House, an acknowledgment that your message has been received will be sent back to you. If a street

address is included in your message, a response will be sent by U.S. mail. The White House claims that every electronic mail message received is read and analyzed by White House staff, and public concerns and ideas are carefully recorded and reported to the president and vice president weekly.

By the way, never send jokes or any comments that could be misinterpreted as a possible threat to the president. The Secret Service reviews e-mail of a threatening nature and will act harshly upon it and the sender. Suffice it to say that nowhere in their job description is a sense of humor mentioned. To contact the White House, use the following addresses:

Basic e-mail: *President@WhiteHouse.gov*
Vice.President@WhiteHouse.gov or *Vice-President@WhiteHouse.gov*

The World Wide Web:

http://www.whitehouse.gov/White_House/Mail/html/Pres_1.html
http://www.whitehouse.gov/White_House/Mail/html/VP_1.html

White House files are named with the first four digits being the release month and day (for example 0323XXX.txt). Some standard abbreviations after the date include:

- rem   Remarks by the president
- pc   Press conference transcript
- pr   Press release
- AM   AM press briefing
- PM   PM press briefing
- sc.   The president's public schedule
- spch   Text of major speeches

These files are saved in ASCII (plain text) format. White House papers are kept in that format for up to two months. Papers more than two months old are compressed, using "PKZIP" software for the PC, into a single file that contains all of the files for that month. For instance, 0195.zip contains all papers released during January 1995.

Vice President Al Gore's National Performance Review (NPR) announced the release of "Creating a Government that Works Better and Costs Less: 1994 Status Report" in full hyper-media. The report summarizes reinvention efforts across federal agencies. It includes several hundred links to pictures and audio clips, as well as the NPR's extensive library of reinvention reference materials. The report is a complementary part of the National Performance Review's recently released ToolKit, an interactive World Wide Web home page. In the ToolKit users will find one of the best sources of reinvention information as well as important links to the people and places working to create a government that works better and costs less.

The office of Vice President Al Gore, also developed FinanceNet, which provides access to financial management documents and information pertaining to all levels of government: foreign, federal, state, and local. FinanceNet reportedly reaches across geopolitical boundaries to link financial management staff and taxpayers worldwide for continuous improvement in employee productivity and in the stewardship and accountability of taxpayer resources.

The USENET newsgroups also offer a variety of discussions that relate to government and politics:

- alt.politics.clinton
- alt.politics.org.misc
- alt.politics.reform
- alt.politics.usa.misc
- alt.news-media
- alt.activism
- talk.politics.misc

The Federal Web Locator service

Thanks to the efforts of Villanova University School of Law, there is a one-stop-shopping center at *http://www.law.vill.edu/Fed-Agency/fedwebloc.html.*

The Web pages located there are called the Federal Web Locator and are intended to offer a one-size-fits-all interface with all federal government online resources. If you have a Web browser and don't know the specific address of what you are looking for, this should be your first stop. It contains an exhaustive listing of links to federal agencies, from NASA to HUD, as well as to international organizations involved in dealings with the federal government. This one is a keeper.

Here are some other government communication locations:

- On CompuServe: GO WHITEHOUSE. Also, see the Democratic Forum: GO DEMOCRATS
- On America Online: keyword WHITEHOUSE or THE WHITEHOUSE or CLINTON

- ➢ On Prodigy: JUMP:WHITE HOUSE MEMO
- ➢ On The WELL: type whitehouse
- ➢ On MCI: type VIEW WHITE HOUSE

The National Telecommunications and Information Administration

The National Telecommunications and Information Administration (NTIA), an agency of the U.S. Department of Commerce, is the president's principal voice on domestic and international telecommunications and information policy. NTIA activities cover the entire range of telecommunications including domestic and international telecommunications policy, spectrum management, telecommunications research, and application projects funded by telecommunications grants.

An 800-number has been established to answer questions about the National Information Infrastructure (NII) initiative, commonly referred to as the information superhighway or simply i-way. The number is 1-800-NII-8818. The 800-number is part of the administration's public education campaign to urge Americans to "get connected to the Information Age." The campaign, which was launched in March, 1995, by Secretary of Commerce Ronald H. Brown and Acting Secretary of Agriculture Richard Rominger, is targeting those Americans who are less likely to own computers. At the campaign launching, NTIA released census data that showed a correlation between income level, race, and educational background and computer ownership.

The study confirmed that minority households, households with incomes less than $30,000, and households headed by persons without a college education are the least likely to own computers. For minority households with incomes of $75,000 or more, the percentage of families with computers is nearly identical to mainstream families (about 44 percent of which have home computers.)

"It is critical that all Americans understand the importance of new telecommunications and information technologies. As we enter the Information Age, more and more jobs will depend on computer literacy and technical expertise," said Larry Irving, Assistant Secretary of Commerce for Communications and Information, and Administrator of NTIA, at a press conference.

"Through the one-eight-hundred number, we will answer citizens' questions or refer them to places that can answer their questions on this important topic. Our goal is to help narrow the gap between

information 'haves' and 'have nots'," added Irving. Information about NTIA and the NII is available on the Internet:

- *ftp.ntia.doc.gov*
- *gopher.ntia.doc.gov*
- *http://www.ntia.doc.gov*

The congressional connection

The House and the Senate also are constantly improving their electronic public-access links. Anyone can access congressional information via the protocols listed below. For additional information, please contact the local offices of U.S. Representatives or Senators.

U.S. House of Representatives

e-mail: *Congress@hr.House.gov*
gopher: *Gopher.House.gov*
On the Web: *http://www.house.gov*

U.S. Senate

gopher: *Gopher.Senate.gov*
FTP: *FTP.Senate.gov*

Library of Congress

gopher: *Marvel.loc.gov*
FTP: *seq1.loc.gov*
Telnet: *locis.loc.gov*

FEDWORLD

One of the most comprehensive sites to visit for federal information on the Internet is FEDWORLD, operated by the National Technical Information Service. On FEDWORLD, you will be rewarded with vast resources and will spend hours in this large body of important knowledge.

FEDWORLD offers another relatively easy means of access to information about the federal government. There is no need to hire expensive consulting services or spend weeks learning exotic command procedures; FEDWORLD is like having a branch office of the feds in your own backyard. Internet users plugged into this vast

computer network can access hundreds of sources of current government information from around the world: census data, Supreme Court decisions, world health statistics, company financial reports, weather forecasts, United Nations information, daily White House briefings, and much more. Government agencies daily are distributing increasingly large amounts of information electronically. You can reach the FedWorld Computer System's traditional "BBS" file library by using your modem to dial (703) 321-3339; set your telecommunications software protocols to (N-8-1).

You can also reach FedWorld using the World Wide Web, FTP, Telnet, and Gopher, though the Web is by far the easiest and best way. Use your favorite Web browser "search" option, and type in the word "Fedworld." After a few seconds, an image of the Official Fedworld government seal should appear (be patient; sometimes it may take a few seconds for the full image to materialize). This Web site will allow you to access hundreds of other government Web pages and on-line documents.

The Web URL is *http://www.fedworld.gov.* The Telnet command to FedWorld is *fedworld.doc.gov* or *fedworld.gov.* FTP to FedWorld by using *ftp.fedworld.gov.*

Copyright info on government documents

Federal government information (including press releases, speeches, etc.) is not copyrighted. Even when they are incorporated into a copyrighted article, the government's words themselves are not copyrighted, only the editorial content of the article is.

Anyone is free to post government press releases and other published material anywhere. If, however, you are posting a newspaper report of a government press release without the newspaper's permission, you could be infringing on copyright and subject to a lawsuit.

Other government sources

Government documents:
gopher: *esusda.gov*
gopher: *sunsite.unc.edu*

Americans Communicating Electronically (ACE):
gopher: *ace.esusda.gov*

Federal Publications BBS:
voice: (202) 512-1387

National Archives:
gopher: *gopher.nara.gov*
On the Web: *http://www.nara.gov*
voice: (202) 501-5525

National Institutes of Health (NIH):
BBS: (301) 480-5144
gopher: *gopher.nih.gov*

National Institute for Science and Technology:
gopher: *gopher.nist.gov* (login: gopher)

National Oceanic and Atmospheric Adm. (NOAA):
gopher: *gopher.noaa.gov*

National Science Foundation (NSF):
gopher: *gopher.nsf.gov*

U.S. Geological Survey:
gopher: *gopher.usgs.gov*

Department of Education:
gopher: *gopher.inet.ed.gov*

Federal Information Exchange (FEDIX):
gopher: *fedix.fie.com*

FEDIX Dial-in (modem) BBS: 1-800-783-3349
Smithsonian Institution Natural History:
gopher: *gopher.smithson.si.edu*

Brookhaven National Laboratory—Protein Data Bank (PDB):
gopher: *gopher.bnl.gov*

Bureau of the Census:
gopher: *gopher.census.gov*

The *Clinton@Marist* log files, which contain all the official administration releases distributed through the MIT servers, are available via anonymous FTP. These logs contain, in addition to the official releases, the Internet posts that comprise the ongoing discussion conducted by the list subscribers. To obtain the logs, FTP *maristb.marist.edu*—the logs are in the CLINTON directory and are named CLINTON LOG9208 through CLINTON LOGyymm (where yymm stands for the current year and month). Problems should be directed to:

urls@maristc.bitnet or *urls@vm.marist.edu*.

Computer Professionals for Social Responsibility is providing all Clinton documents on technology and privacy at the CPSR Internet Library, available via FTP/WAIS/Gopher at *cpsr.org/cpsr/clinton* (and in other folders as relevant). For e-mail access, send a message with the word "help" at the first line of text to *listserv@cpsr.org*.

The Texas A&M University Gopher Server makes available White House press releases and other documents. This archive includes information from 1992 until the present time and is updated as new documents are released. Gopher users can reach the Texas A&M server by choosing it from their local server's list of other gophers, or by pointing their gopher clients to *gopher.tamu.edu*.

The White House Communications office is distributing press releases over an experimental system developed during the campaign at the MIT Artificial Intelligence Laboratory. You can obtain copies of all the press releases from a wide variety of online services or discussion groups devoted to either national politics in general or President Clinton in particular.

Federal Information Exchange, Inc., is a private company located in Gaithersburg, Maryland, which operates several multi-agency information services, including: FEDIX U.S. Federal Agency Opportunities, an online information service that links the higher education community and the federal government to facilitate research and education. FEDIX contains the latest information from the Commerce Business Daily, Federal Register, and other sources for participating federal agencies.

The U.S. Department of Commerce Information Locator Service links to each of the department's agencies, including the National Trade Data Bank and the National Economic, Social, and Environmental Data Bank.

The National Institute of Standards and Technology (NIST) promotes U.S. economic growth by working with industry to develop and apply technology, measurements, and standards—providing the basic technical infrastructure needed by U.S. industry.

The U.S. National Information Infrastructure Virtual Library is an information-sharing resource for both users and developers of the national information infrastructure, or information superhighway. The library is co-sponsored by the president's Information Infrastructure Task Force and the Council on Competitiveness.

The National Oceanic and Atmospheric Administration (NOAA) Network Information Center (NIC) provides network services to the NOAA community under the Network Advisory Review Boards-supported NIC project. The NOAA/NIC was created to support NOAA in the appropriate use of the Internet by providing a wide range of network services to regional campuses, Network Operations Centers and to the NOAA networking community at large. The Telemetering Ocean and Atmospheric Data (TAO) Project, at NOAA's Pacific Marine Environmental Laboratory, maintains the TAO array of moored ocean buoys. A major component of the global climate monitoring system, the TAO array is supported by an international consortium and consists of 70 moored ocean buoys spanning the Equatorial Pacific Ocean, [telemetering ocean and atmospheric data] to shore-based computers in real-time via satellite. The TAO Web pages include descriptions of the project, pictures of the buoys, scientific publications on the data, graphics of the real-time TAO data, and access to TAO data in ASCII files.

Also available are the Web pages "What is an El Nino?", written for the layman and suitable for use in the classroom. The Climate Prediction Center (CPC) provides climate products and services consisting of operational prediction of climate variations, monitoring of the climate system, development of data bases for determining current global and regional climate anomalies and trends, and analysis of their origins and linkages to the complete climate system. These services cover climate time scales ranging from weeks to seasons, extending into the future as far as technically feasible, and over the domain of land, ocean, and atmosphere, extending into the stratosphere.

Officially mandated

The National Marine Fisheries Service home page includes links to National Marine Fisheries Science Centers and NMFS-related sites. In addition, the books *Our Living Oceans*, *Annual Report 1993*, and *Index for Fisheries of the US* are available online. There are also home pages for certain NMFS offices, including the Office of Protected Resources, containing a brochure called "Protecting the Nation's Marine Species" which gives a listing of endangered and threatened species. This page also has various marine sounds and MPEG movies.

The Northwest Fisheries Science Center, located in Seattle, Washington, has also opened a Web home page. NWFSC is a research facility of the northwest region of the National Marine Fisheries Service, NOAA, and is responsible for providing scientific and technical support for the management, conservation, and development of the Pacific Northwest region's anadromous and marine fishery resources.

Department of Defense, Defense Construction Supply Center (D.C.S.C.) is one of the largest procurement activities for the Department of Defense. DefenseLINK is the official source for public online defense information and provides links to the public Web

services of the military departments, and other military organizations. It also provides up-to-the-minute news releases and access to a range of publications.

The Defense Logistics Services Center (DLSC), Battle Creek, Michigan, provides logistics information products and services to all military and civilian government services and agencies. The server provides information on the full range of DLSC products and services, including clickable maps.

The Information Technology Standards site provides standards and information about standards, and related information for the development of programs for the Department of Defense.

The USAF Web Server provides information on the Air Force Internet (AFIN). The U.S. Army Home Page is the master home page for the U.S. Army.

The purpose of the USACE Geospatial Data Infrastructure site is to organize and make available to the federal government, business, researchers, and the general public data from the Corps of Engineers. It is part of the National Spatial Data Initiative.

Data is stored in ftp-accessible directories. A WAIS index server can be employed to search for keywords of interest to the user. Included in the data are points of contact to access the actual data.

The Naval Research Laboratory (NRL) Home Page contains links to other NRL facilities including the Backgrounds Data Center United States Naval Observatory General information about the Observatory, star catalogs, earth orientation information, precise time, and time interval information, and more.

The Lawrence Livermore National Laboratory (LLNL) Home Page, LLNL Biology and Biotechnology Research Program (BBRP), contains information about research projects and centers, including a detailed map of human chromosomes. Research projects include DNA repair, molecular toxicology and human risk assessment, and structural biology and technology development. Centers include the Human Genome Center and the Center for Healthcare Technology.

The National Renewable Energy Laboratory server provides information about the laboratory and its research. Anyone can access information on renewable energy research, development, and applications; accumulated energy data and resource maps; publications; business and job opportunities; and links and directions to other energy resources. It is located in Golden, Colorado.

The Department of Health and Human Services Web server provides information on the mission, programs, organization, institutions, and

impact of the U.S. Department of Health and Human Services on the health and well-being of the American public. Topics listed include:

- ➢ Administration for Children and Families
- ➢ Aid to Families with Dependent Children Program Division
- ➢ Public Health Service
- ➢ Agency for Toxic Substances and Disease Registry (ATSDR)
- ➢ Centers for Disease Control and Prevention

The Mobility and Mortality Weekly Report (MMWR) Series is prepared by the Centers for Disease Control and Prevention (CDC) and is available free of charge in electronic format from CDC's World Wide Web server at *http://www.cdc.gov/* or from CDC's file transfer protocol server at *ftp://ftp.cdc.gov/pub/mmwr/mmwr_wk ftp.cdc.gov*.

Data in the weekly MMWR are provisional, based on weekly reports to CDC by state health departments. The reporting week concludes at close of business on Friday; compiled data on a national basis are officially mandated to the public on the following Friday. Information provided includes:

- ➢ Food and Drug Administration
- ➢ Center for Food Safety and Applied Nutrition
- ➢ Health Resources and Services Administration
- ➢ Indian Health Service
- ➢ National AIDS Program Office
- ➢ National Institutes of Health
- ➢ Extramural Invention Information Management System (EIIMS)
- ➢ Laboratory of Structural Biology
- ➢ National Cancer Institute Metabolism Branch
- ➢ Division of Computer Research and Technology
- ➢ National Library of Medicine (NLM)
- ➢ Lister Hill National Center for Biomedical Communications

The National Library of Medicine is considered the world's largest library dealing with a single scientific/professional topic. It cares for more than 4.5 million holdings (including books, journals, reports, manuscripts and audio-visual items).

The Bureau of Indian Affairs, Division of Energy and Mineral Resources has a World Wide Web server. The division provides special services to the Indian mineral owner that are unique within the Department of the Interior. A program overview of the National Indian

Oil and Gas Evaluation and Management System has been developed. Information online includes:

- Office of Acquisition and Property Management
- Office of Administrative Services
- United States Fish and Wildlife Service
- United States Geological Survey

The U.S. Geological Survey's Cascades Volcano Observatory also has a Web server. Some information on volcanically induced geologic and hydrologic hazards as well as images of volcanoes and volcanic phenomena are available.

USGS provides Atlantic Marine Geology Geologic and oceanographic displays, reports, and data, mostly about the U.S. Exclusive Economic Zone (EEZ) off the east coast and Gulf of Mexico, including many links to geologic and oceanographic colleague institutions or data and information sites.

The U.S. Bureau of Labor Statistics' LABSTAT database contains a wide range of statistics in the broad area of labor economics, including employment and unemployment figures, consumer price index, producer price index, wages, productivity, etc. Data is provided in the form of news releases with high-level aggregates, as well as detailed historical time series.

A collaborative effort with the University of Illinois-Chicago, DOSFAN provides access to official U.S. foreign policy information—speeches, statements, and testimony by the president, secretary of state, and other senior officials; Dispatch; background notes on countries and international organizations; country briefings; congressional reports on trade, human rights, terrorism, narcotics, and other subjects; daily press briefing transcripts; directories; consular and travel information; and much more.

Diplomatic Security Service, Counter-Terrorism Rewards Program (HEROES) offers rewards of up to $4 million for information preventing acts of international terrorism against the United States, or leading to the arrest or conviction of terrorist criminals responsible for such acts.

The HEROES Web home page profiles examples of specific cases and provides information about wanted individuals related to those cases.

The official World Wide Web site for FEMA, the Federal Emergency Management Agency, contains hundreds of pages of information about FEMA regarding preparedness for all types of natural and man-made disasters. Visitors to the site may read and download many different publications, photos, and forms.

People interested in becoming a standby disaster assistance employee may send an automated inquiry form. If you want to be better prepared for emergencies, or learn how the federal, state, and local governments plan for, train, and respond to emergencies, this is a good place to start.

The United States General Services Administration provides online ordering for government agencies from The Federal Supply Service, documents are provided by the Consumer Information Center, National Performance Review, Federal Acquisition Regulations and much, much more.

The National Aeronautics and Space Administration (NASA) World Wide Web Root home page acts as the primary document to all other NASA center home pages. Many, many centers are represented. Science buffs will find the NASA Web sites particularly interesting.

The Ames High Performance and Communications Center (HPCC) office is the lead center for the NASA/HPCC Computational Aerosciences program, and is involved in interdisiplinary research for the aerospace and high performance computing communities. On the Ames HPCC server you will find information on research participation in various HPCC projects, as well as a comprehensive listing of educational computing resources designed to assist the K-12 online community.

NASA's Astrophysics Data System offers the Einstein Archive Service. This service provides query and retrieval capability for the Einstein X ray Observatory's processed data archive. The archive includes about 5000 X ray observations taken between 1978 and 1981.

Other fascinating Web sites include:

- Harvard-Smithsonian Center for Astrophysics NASA Headquarters
- Jet Propulsion Laboratory
- Johnson Space Center
- Kennedy Space Center
- Langley Research Center
- Lewis Research Center
- The Marshall Space Flight Center (MSFC)
- Procurement Office NASA Scientific & Technical Information Program
- The National Academy of Sciences is a private, nonprofit, self-perpetuating society of distinguished scholars engaged in scientific and engineering research, dedicated to the furtherance of science and technology and to their use for general welfare.

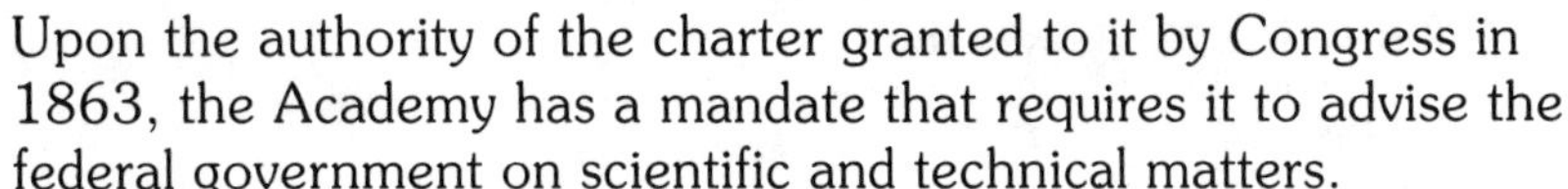

Upon the authority of the charter granted to it by Congress in 1863, the Academy has a mandate that requires it to advise the federal government on scientific and technical matters.

- The Institute of Medicine was established in 1970 by the National Academy of Sciences to secure the services of eminent members of appropriate professions in the examination of policy matters pertaining to the health of the public. The Institute acts under the responsibility given to the National Academy of Sciences by its congressional charter to be an adviser to the federal government and, upon its own initiative, to identify issues of medical care, research, and education.
- The National Academy of Engineering was established in 1964, under charter of the National Academy of Sciences, as a parallel organization of outstanding engineers. It is autonomous in its administration and in the selection of its members, sharing with the National Academy of Sciences the responsibility for advising the federal government. The National Academy of Engineering also sponsors engineering programs aimed at meeting national needs, encourages education and research, and recognizes the superior achievements of engineers.
- The National Research Council was organized by the National Academy of Sciences in 1916 to associate the broad community of science and technology with the Academy's purpose of furthering knowledge and advising the federal government. Functioning in accordance with general policies determined by the Academy, the Council has become the principal operating agency of both the National Academy of Sciences and the National Academy of Engineering in providing services to the government, the public, and the scientific and engineering communities.
- National Science Foundation's home page includes the Guide to Programs and the Grants Proposal Guide. These documents provide information on program initiatives at NSF, along with instructions for preparing and submitting proposals. The Home Page also includes biographies of NSF officials and a feature on the Alan T. Waterman Award winners. Weekly "What's New" pages provide a summary of new items.

The following is a partial list of U.S. Federal Government Agencies on the Internet. This list is subject to change daily as more federal government agencies go online.

Executive branch

- The White House
- Bureau of Economic Analysis (BEA) Bureau of the Census
- Department of Agriculture
- Department of Defense

- Department of Education
- Department of Energy
- Defense Programs
- Energy Efficiency and Renewable Energy Network
- Energy Information Administration
- Energy Research
- Energy Sciences Network (ESnet)
- Environment, Safety, and Health Environmental Management
- Fissile Materials Disposition
- Fossil Energy
- Fusion Energy
- Human Resources and Administration Procurement and Assistance Management
- Science Education and Technical Information Laboratories and Facilities
- Argonne National Laboratory (ANL)
- Brookhaven National Laboratory
- Continuous Electron Beam Accelerator Facility (CEBAF)
- Energy Efficiency and Renewable Energy Network (EREN)
- Fermi National Accelerator Laboratory (Fermilab)
- Idaho National Engineering Laboratory
- Kansas City Plant
- Lawrence Berkeley Laboratory (LBL)
- Lawrence Livermore National Laboratory
- National Energy Research Supercomputer Center
- Los Alamos National Laboratory (LANL)
- Advanced Computing Laboratory
- National Renewable Energy Laboratory Nevada Operations Office
- Oak Ridge National Laboratories
- Center for Computational Sciences
- Pacific Northwest Laboratory (PNL)
- Princeton Plasma Physics Laboratory
- Sandia National Laboratories
- Department of Health and Human Services Administration on Aging

- Administration for Children and Families Health Care
- Financing Administration Public Health Service (PHS)
- Agency for Toxic Substances and Disease Registry
- Case Studies in Environmental Medicine
- Centers for Disease Control (CDC)
- National Center for Chronic Disease Prevention and Health Promotion
- National Center for Environmental Health
- National Center for Health Statistics
- National Center for Infectious Diseases
- National Center for Injury Prevention and Control
- National Center for Prevention Services
- National Institute for Occupational Safety and Health
- Epidemiology Program Office
- International Health Program Office
- Public Health Practice Program Office
- National Immunization Program Childhood Immunization Initiative
- National Center for Food Safety and Applied Nutrition (CFSAN)
- National Center for Toxicological Research (NCTR) Gopher
- Indian Health Service (IHS)
- National Institutes of Health (NIH)
- Advanced Laboratory Workstation Project
- Division of Computer Research and Technology (DCRT)
- BioInformatics Molecular Analysis Section (BIMAS)
- BioMagResBank Database Gateway
- GenoBase Database Gateway
- Division of Research Grants (DRG) National Cancer Institute (NCI)
- CancerNet
- National Center for Human Genome Research (NCHGR)
- National Eye Institute
- National Heart, Lung, and Blood Institute (NHLBI)
- National Institute for Allergy and Infectious Diseases (NIAID)
- National Institute of Diabetes and Digestive and Kidney Disease (NIDDK)

- National Institute of Drug Abuse
- National Institute of Environmental Health Sciences (NIEHS)
- National Institute of General Medical Sciences (NIGMS)
- National Institute of Mental Health (NIMH)
- National Institute of Nursing Research National Institute on Aging
- National Library of Medicine (NLM)
- National Center for Biotechnology Information (NCBI) at NLM
- Social Security Administration (became independent March 31, 1995)
- Substance Abuse and Mental Health Services Administration
- Department of Housing and Urban Development (HUD)
- Department of the Interior
- Department of State
- Department of State Foreign Affairs Network (DOSFAN)
- Department of Transportation
- Department of the Treasury
- Internal Revenue Service
- United States Customs Service
- Bureau of Alcohol, Tobacco, and Firearms
- Financial Management Service
- United States Secret Service
- Office of Thrift Supervision United States Mint
- Department of Veterans Affairs

Judicial branch

- Courts of Appeals
- Eleventh Circuit
- Federal Judicial Center Federal Judiciary
- Supreme Court Decisions

Independent Agencies African Development Foundation

- Central Intelligence Agency (CIA)
- Commission on Civil Rights
- Commodity Futures Trading Commission

- Consumer Product Safety Commission (CPSC)
- Defense Nuclear Facilities Safety Board
- Environmental Protection Agency (EPA)
- Equal Employment Opportunity Commission
- Export-Import Bank of the United States
- Farm Credit Administration
- Federal Aviation Administration (FAA)
- Federal Communications Commission (FCC)
- Federal Deposit Insurance Corporation (FDIC)
- Federal Election Commission
- Federal Emergency Management Agency (FEMA)
- Federal Housing Finance Board
- Federal Labor Relations Authority
- Federal Maritime Commission
- Federal Mediation and Conciliation Service
- Federal Mine Safety and Health Review Commission
- Federal Reserve System
- Federal Reserve Bank of Chicago
- Federal Retirement Thrift Investment Board
- Federal Trade Commission (FTC)
- Federal Information Center Public Building Service
- Federal Supply Service
- Information Technology Service
- Concept Development Record (CDR)—FTS 2000 Inter-American Foundation
- Interstate Commerce Commission
- Merit Systems Protection Board
- National Aeronautic and Space Administration (NASA)
- Ames Research Center
- Dryden Flight Research Center
- Goddard Institute for Space Studies
- Goddard Space Flight Center
- Jet Propulsion Laboratory
- Johnson Space Center

- Kennedy Space Center
- Langley Research Center
- Lewis Research Center
- Marshall Space Flight Center
- Stennis Space Center
- Wallops Flight Facility
- National Archives and Records Administration (NARA)
- National Capital Planning Commission
- National Credit Union Administration
- National Foundation on the Arts and the Humanities
- National Labor Relations Board
- National Mediation Board
- National Railroad Passenger Corporation (Amtrak)
- National Performance Review (NPR)
- FinanceNet
- National Science Foundation (NSF)
- National Transportation Safety Board
- Nuclear Regulatory Commission (NRC)
- Occupational Safety and Health Review Commission
- Office of Government Ethics
- Office of Personnel Management
- Office of Special Counsel
- Panama Canal Commission
- Peace Corps
- Pennsylvania Avenue Development Corporation
- Pension Benefit Guaranty Corporation
- Postal Rate Commission
- Railroad Retirement Board
- Resolution Trust Corporation
- Securities and Exchange Commission (SEC)
- EDGAR Database
- Selective Service System
- Small Business Administration (SBA)
- Social Security Administration (SSA)

- Tennessee Valley Authority
- Thrift Depositor Protection Oversight Board
- Trade and Development Agency
- United States Arms Control and Disarmament Agency
- United States Information Agency
- Voice of America (VOA)
- United States International Development Cooperation Agency
- Agency for International Development
- United States International Trade Commission (USITC)
- United States-Israel Science and Technology Commission
- United States Postal Service (USPS)

Quasi-official agencies

- Electronic Commerce Resource Center Program
- National Center for Atmospheric Research Mesa Laboratory
- Foothills Laboratory
- Smithsonian Institution
- Center for Earth and Planetary Studies
- Harvard-Smithsonian Center for Astrophysics
- National Air and Space Museum
- National Museum of American Art
- National Museum of Natural History

Other government indexes

- EIT Alphabetical Directory
- Federal Information Exchange Annotated
- Government Information Locator Service (GILS) Demonstration
- National Technology Transfer Center
- UC Irvine-Gophers
- Villanova Center for Information Law and Policy
- The Federal Web Locator

U.S. Government Information Servers

U.S. Government Information Servers have been sorted into main subject categories. On the Web, you can move to an alphabetic location in the subject category list by selecting a category in the

following index or by scrolling through the list specific subjects shown below.

Index of subject categories

A - Admin., Aeronautics, etc.

B - Behavior, Business, etc.

C - Chemistry, Computers, etc.

E - Education, Energy, etc.

G - Government Inventions

H - Health Care

I - Industrial Engineering

J - Jobs, Justice, etc.

L - Legislature, Library, etc.

M - Manufacturing, Military, etc.

N - Natural Resources, Navigation, etc.

O - Ocean Technology, Ordnance, etc.

P - Photography, Physics, etc.

S - Space Technology

T - Transportation

U - Urban and Regional Technology

List of subject categories

A

Administration and Management
Aeronautics and Aerodynamics
Agriculture and Food
Astronomy and Astrophysics
Atmospheric Sciences

B

Behavior and Society
Biomedical Technology and Human Factors Engineering Building
Industry Technology and Housing
Business, Commerce and Economics

C

Chemistry
Civil Engineering
Combustion, Engines, and Propellants
Communication
Computers, Control, and Information Theory

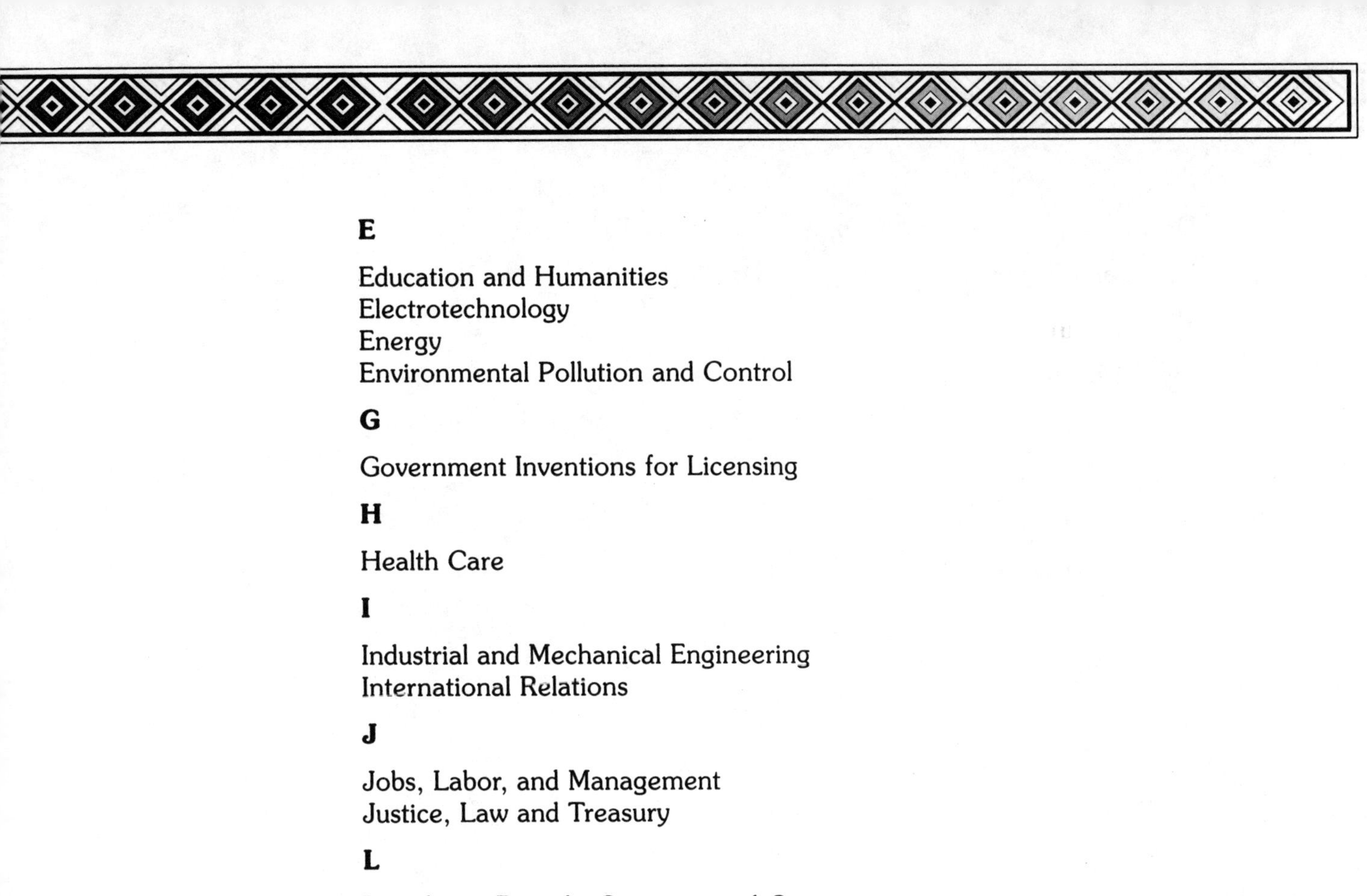

E

Education and Humanities
Electrotechnology
Energy
Environmental Pollution and Control

G

Government Inventions for Licensing

H

Health Care

I

Industrial and Mechanical Engineering
International Relations

J

Jobs, Labor, and Management
Justice, Law and Treasury

L

Legislative Branch, Congress and Committees
Library and Information Sciences

M

Manufacturing Technology
Material Science
Mathematical Sciences
Medicine and Biology
Military Sciences and Defense

N

Natural Resources and Earth Sciences
Navigation, Guidance, and Control
Nuclear Science and Technology

O

Ocean Technology and Engineering

P

Photography and Recording Devices
Physics
Problem Solving Information for State and Local Governments

S

Space Technology

T

Transportation

U

Urban and Regional Technology and Development

V

Veterans Affairs

A

African Internet Connections by Country

Angola (AO)

GreenNet FidoNet node
ANGONET
Development Workshop
Rua Rei Katyavala, 113
Luanda
Voice: +244-2-348-371 / 396-107
Fax: +244-2-393-445
Haymee Perez Cogle <hperez@angonet.gn.apc.org>
Node Name: angonet.gn.apc.org

Burkina Faso (BF)

Orstom UUCP node in Ouagadougou
UUCP over X.25—2 hosts—25 users
Dominique Remy
<remy@ouaga.orstom.bf>
Node Name: brouaga.orstom.bf
Dialup: +226 31 4748
Voice: +226 30 67 37 / 30 67 39
Fax: +226 31 03 85
Post: ORSTOM—01 BP 182—Ouagadougou

Orstom UUCP node in Bobo-Dioulasso
UUCP/g/v24bis to ouaga.orstom.bf—1 host—8 users
Dominique Remy
<remy@ouaga.orstom.bf>
Voice: +226 97 12 69
Fax: +226 97 09 42
Post: Antenne ORSTOM -01 BP 171 Bobo-Dioulasso 01

Republic of Botswana (BW)

University of Botswana, Gabarone
Mobuto Drive, Gaborone
Voice: +267 35-1151/35-6364
Fax: +267 35-7573
Thula Segokgo <segokgot@pula.ub.bw>
Node Name: pula.ub.bw or motswedi.ub.bw

University of Botswana
Mobuto Drive, Gaborone
Voice: +267 351151 x2318
Fax: +267 301594
Mark Stobbs <stobbs@noka.ub.bw>

Public FidoNet node, 5:7001/1 John Case
Big Mathata's Fido
Gaborone
Data: +267 373461 9600,CM,XR,V32b,V42b

Public FidoNet node, 5:7021/1 ELNET—Windhoek
Alex Boll
Data: +27 61-239623

Republic of the Congo (CG)

Orstom UUCP node in Brazzaville
UUCP dialup using Telebit modem—1 host—25 users
Node Name: brazza.orstom.fr
Christophe Brun <brunchri@brazza.orstom.fr>
Voice: +242 83 26 80 / 81 / 82
Fax: +242 83 29 77
Post: ORSTOM—BP 181—Brazzaville

Republic of Cote d'Ivoire (CI)

Orstom UUCP node in Abidjan
Name: abidjan.orstom.fr
UUCP over X.25—about 15 users
Brou Mian <brou@abidjan.orstom.fr>
Dialup: +225 35 1180
Voice: +225 24 37 79
Fax: +225 24 65 04
Post: ORSTOM—15 B.P. 917—ABIDJAN 15

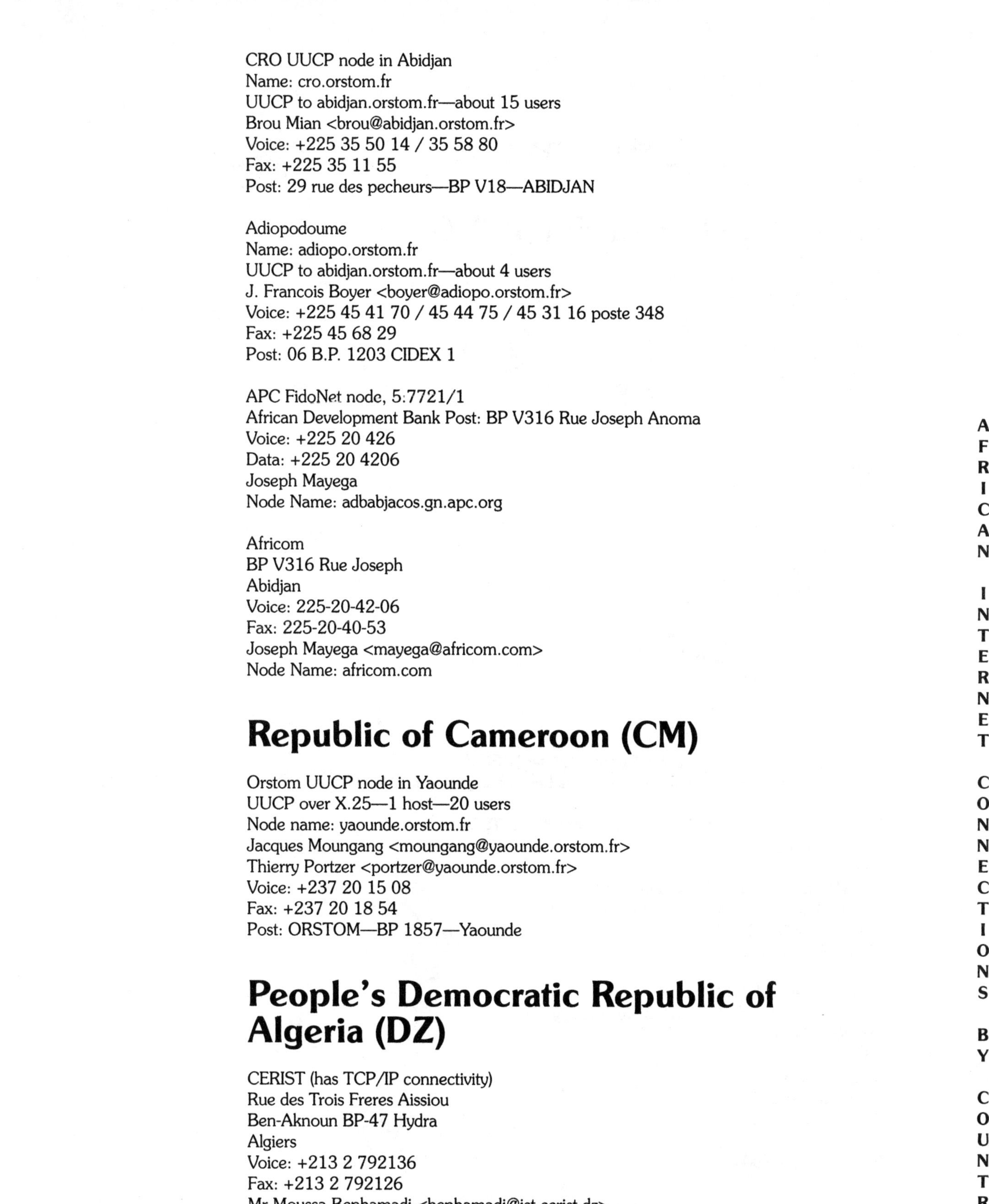

CRO UUCP node in Abidjan
Name: cro.orstom.fr
UUCP to abidjan.orstom.fr—about 15 users
Brou Mian <brou@abidjan.orstom.fr>
Voice: +225 35 50 14 / 35 58 80
Fax: +225 35 11 55
Post: 29 rue des pecheurs—BP V18—ABIDJAN

Adiopodoume
Name: adiopo.orstom.fr
UUCP to abidjan.orstom.fr—about 4 users
J. Francois Boyer <boyer@adiopo.orstom.fr>
Voice: +225 45 41 70 / 45 44 75 / 45 31 16 poste 348
Fax: +225 45 68 29
Post: 06 B.P. 1203 CIDEX 1

APC FidoNet node, 5:7721/1
African Development Bank Post: BP V316 Rue Joseph Anoma
Voice: +225 20 426
Data: +225 20 4206
Joseph Mayega
Node Name: adbabjacos.gn.apc.org

Africom
BP V316 Rue Joseph
Abidjan
Voice: 225-20-42-06
Fax: 225-20-40-53
Joseph Mayega <mayega@africom.com>
Node Name: africom.com

Republic of Cameroon (CM)

Orstom UUCP node in Yaounde
UUCP over X.25—1 host—20 users
Node name: yaounde.orstom.fr
Jacques Moungang <moungang@yaounde.orstom.fr>
Thierry Portzer <portzer@yaounde.orstom.fr>
Voice: +237 20 15 08
Fax: +237 20 18 54
Post: ORSTOM—BP 1857—Yaounde

People's Democratic Republic of Algeria (DZ)

CERIST (has TCP/IP connectivity)
Rue des Trois Freres Aissiou
Ben-Aknoun BP-47 Hydra
Algiers
Voice: +213 2 792136
Fax: +213 2 792126
Mr Moussa Benhamadi <benhamadi@ist.cerist.dz>
Mrs Aouaouche El-Maouhab <elmaouhab@ist.cerist.dz>

Algeria Net
06 Rue Frederic MISTRAL Telemly
Algiers
Voice: +213-2-612-715
Sid-Ali Bettache <sbettache@algeria.gn.apc.org>
Node Name: algeria.gn.apc.org

Arab Republic of Egypt (EG)

Egyptian Universities Network (EUN)
FRCU Computer Center
Supreme Council of Universities
Cairo University, Egypt
Nashwa AbdelBaki nashwa@frcu.eun.eg
Voice: +202 5735 405
Fax: +202 5728 174

Prof. M.A.R. Ghonaimy
EUN Director
FRCU Computer Center
Supreme Council of Universities
Cairo University, Egypt
adeeb@frcu.eun.eg
Voice: +202 5735 405
Fax: +202 5728 174

Prof. Aly El-Din Hilal, Executive Director
FRCU Supreme Council of Universities
Cairo University, Egypt
execdir@frcu.eun.eg
Voice and fax: +202 5728 174

Cabinet Information and Decision Support Center (IDSC)/
Regional Information Technology & Software Engineering Center (RITSEC)
Dr. Tarek Kamel
Head Communications and Networks group IDSC/RITSEC
11 A Hassan Sabry Street
Zamalek, Cairo, Egypt
tkamel@ritsec.com.eg (Tarek Kamel, admin)
ohadary@ritsec.com.eg (Ossama Elhadary tech)
Voice: +202 35 51551 & 34 03538
Fax: +202 34 12139

Egyptian National STI Network
Academy of Scientific Research & Technology
101 Kasr Al-Ainy St.
Cairo, Egypt
Maged Boulos
mb@estinet.uucp
P.O. Box 1522 Cairo 11511
Voice: +202 3557253
Fax: +202 3547807

Ethiopia (ET)

APC FidoNet node, 5:751/1
Hornet
Post: Box 3001
Addis Ababa
Lishan Adam <lishan@padis.gn.apc.org>
or <padis@padis.gn.apc.org>
Data: +251 1 514534
Voice: +251 1 517200
Fax: +251 1 514416
Node Name: hornet.gn.apc.org

Republic of Ghana (GH)

APC FidoNet node, 5:781/2
FOE-Ghana
Accra
Voice: +233 21-225-963
Gifty Annan <foe@foe-ghana.gn.apc.org>
Node Name: foe-ghana.gn.apc.org

APC FidoNet node
Ghastinet
Council for Scientific & Industrial Research
P.O. Box M32
Accra
Voice: +233 21 77352
William Anim Dankwa <William_Anim-Dankwa@ghastinet.gn.apc.org>
Node Name: ghastinet.gn.apc.org

Association of African Universities Accra, Ghana
Voice: +233 21 774495
Fax: +233 21 774821
2400 baud UUCP to Rhodes University in RSA
John Bart-Plange <jbp@aau.org>
Node name: aau.org

Republic of Gambia (GM)

APC FidoNet node
African Centre for Human Rights
Raymond Sock
Okairaba Ave
Banjul
Voice: +220-94525
Hannah Forster <hforster@achrds.gn.apc.org>
achrds.gn.apc.org

Medical Research Council
Box 273
Banjul
Voice: 220-495-442
Fax: 495-919; Modem: 497-012
Joe Bangali <jbangali@gam.healthnet.org>

Republic of Guinea (GN)

Moussa Kourouma <kourouma@pades.ac.gn>
Ministry of Higher Education and Scientific Research
Conakry, Guinea
Voice: +224-41-41-41
Fax: +224-41-41-41
Tech: Sekou Kande <sekou@net.gn>

Republic of Kenya (KE)

Public FidoNet node, 5:731/1
Environment Liaison Centre
International Post: Box 72461 Nairobi
Doug Rigby <drigby@elci.gn.apc.org>
Data: +254 2-567043
Voice: +254 2 562 015
Node Name: elci.gn.apc.org

Public FidoNet node, 5:731/4
University of Nairobi, Computer Science
Dr G.M. Macharia <gmacharia@unics.gn.apc.org>
Data: +254-2-444919
9600,CM,XA,PEP
Node Name: unics.gn.apc.org

Public FidoNet node, 5:731/10
ARSO (African Regional Standards Organisation)
Box 57363
Nairobi
Voice: +254-2-224561
Edward Chonelwa <sysop@arso.gn.apc.org>
Node name: arso.gn.apc.org

African Regional Center for Computing
P. O. Box 58638, Nairobi
Voice: +254 2 723552 or 728351
Fax: +254 2 727810
Shem Ochuodho <shem@arcc.kaact.kenya-net.org>
ThornTree, Omega Micro Systems
Box 38941, Nairobi
Voice: +254-2-229-650/215-095
Fax: 229-650
Data: 332-596/244-200
Ronald Nunn/Crispin Sikuku <thorntree@tt.gn.apc.org>

Kingdom of Lesotho (LS)

UUCP site off of UNINET-ZA
National University of Lesotho
PO Roma 180; Maseru
Lebeko, Sello <lls@isas.nul.ls>

Voice: +266 340601
Fax: +266 340000
Fido point off worknet Transformation Resource Centre trc@wn.apc.

Morocco (MA)

APC FidoNet node in Rabat
ENDA MAGHREB
JJ Guibbert <jjg@endamag.gn.apc.org>
FidoNet 5:7951/2
Telephone: +212 (7) 75 64 14
Fax: +212 (7) 75 64 13
Post: ENDAMAG; 196 Quartier O.L.M.; Rabat

Madagascar (MG)

Orstom UUCP node in Antanarivo
Name: tana.orstom.fr
UUCP over X.25 to France—0 host (UUCP on DOS)—7 users
Jeannette Razanamiadana <razanami@orstom-tana.rio.org>
Voice: +261 23 30 98
Fax: +261 23 30 98
Post: ORSTOM—BP 434—101 Antananarivo

Republic of Mali (ML)

Orstom UUCP node in Bamako
Name: bamako.orstom.ml
UUCP over X.25—2 hosts—20 users
Eric Stevance
<stevance@bamako.orstom.ml>
Voice: +223 22 43 05 / 22 27 74
Fax: +223 22 75 88
Post: ORSTOM—BP 2528—Bamako

CNRST in Bamko
Name: cnrst.ml
UUCP/g/V22bis to bamako.orstom.ml
Mamadou Diallo Iam <mdiallo@cnrst.ml>
Voice: +223 22 90 85
Post: CNRST—BP 3052 Bamako MALI

ISFRA in Bamako
Name: isfra.ml
UUCP/g/V22bis to bamako.orstom.ml Patrick Baudot <baudot@isfra.ml>
Institut d'Economie Rurale (IER) in Bamako
Name: ier-bamako.ier.ml
UUCP/g/V22bis to bamako.orstom.ml
Tim Schilling <schillin@ier-bamako.ier.ml>

AGETTIPE in Bamako
Name: aget-bko.agetipe.ml
UUCP/g/V22bis to bamako.orstom.ml
Lamine Ben Barka <benbarka@aget-bko.agetipe.ml>
Voice: +223 22 06 60

Save the Children (US) in Bamako
Name: sc-bko-save.ml
UUCP/g/V22bis to bamako.orstom.ml
Peter Laugharn <laugharn@sc-bko.save.ml>
Voice: +223 22 61 34

Institut d'Education Populaire in Kati
Name: iep-kati.iep.ml
UUCP/g/V22bis to bamako.orstom.
Maria Keita <mkeita@iep-kati.iep.ml>

Mauritius (MU)

Orstom UUCP node in Maurice
dialup UUCP
Maurice CAYRE <cayre@maurice.orstom.fr>
Voice: +230 233 47 29
Post: Fisheries research center—Alsion-Petite Riviere

Public FidoNet node, 5:726/1
University of Mauritius Computer Centre
Reduit
Michael Dewson
Data: +230 464-1773
2400,CM
APC node name: umcc.gn.apc.org

AGAnet
183 Morcellemont Montreal
Beau Bassin
Voice: +230-233-5326 / 465-1421
Fido/BBS:465-1336
Altaf Dossa <adossa@aganet.wn.apc.org>
Node Name: aganet.wn.apc.org

Malawi (MW)

user%nyasa@hippo.ru.ac.za
University of Guelph, Malawi
Steve Huddle
user%nyala@hippo.ru.ac.za

Chancellors College
FidoNet node 5:7231/1
University of Malawi
Post: Chancellor College; Zomba
Data: +265 52241
Paulos Nyirenda <Paulos_Nyirenda@f1.n7231.z5.fidonet.org>
Node Name: f1.n7231.z5.fidonet.org

[note from llk@kepler.unh.edu]
Mathematics and CS dep'ts address:
user@p4.f1.n7231.z5.fidonet.org (usernames take the form Pnyirenda)

People's Republic of Mozambique (MZ)

University of Eduardo Mondlane
Center for Informatica
Maputo, Mozambique
2400 baud UUCP to Rhodes Univ in RSA
postmaster@dzowo.uem.mz Americo Muchanga
venancio@dzowo.uem.mz, Venancio Massingue
Voice: +258 1 491557

APC node in Nampula nndc@ugccoop.frcs.alt.za
Voice (off.) +258-6-213980
Telefax: +258-6-213975
Post: C/O COCAMO Box 185
Maputo, Mozambique

Public FidoNet node, 5:7221/1
Maputo
Data: +258 1-415303
Helder Santos
9600 V32bis up 24hrs on a good line

Public FidoNet node, 5:7221/2
Maputo
Data: +258 1-425745
Anibal Maques
9600 V32bis

Republic of Namibia (NA)

Department of Computer Science
bill@grumpy.cs.unam.NA
(administrative contact)
tim@grumpy.cs.unam.NA
(technical contact)

University of Namibia
Private Bag
Windhoek
Voice: + 27 61 307 2428/9
Fax: +27 61 307 2286
94.04.24 Mail to some addresses in NA continues to bounce.

Republic of the Niger (NE)

Orstom UUCP node in Niamey
Name: niamey.orstom.fr
UUCP over X.25—3 hosts—over 20 users
Julien Bonfort <bonfort@niamey.orstom.fr>

Voice: +227 73 20 54 / 72 31 15
Fax: +227 72 28 04
Post: ORSTOM—BP 11 416—

Nigeria (NG)

APC FidoNet node, 5:7861/103
Post: Lagos/Ile-Ife, Nigeria Chuma Agbodike
Data: +234-36-231262
Node Name: lixy.gn.apc.org

Public FidoNet node, 5:7861/104 Lagos
Iyabo Odusote
Data: +234 1-860754 9600,CM,PEP,XA,V32b,V42b

Public FidoNet node, 5:7861/105 Lagos
David Obi
Data: +234 1-523189 9600,CM,XA,V32b,V42b

Public FidoNet node, 5:7861/106 Lagos
Bennett Agbodike
Data: +234 1-832009 9600,CM,XA,V32b,V42b

Unconfirmed UUCP node
Yaba College of Technology, Department of Computer Science, Lagos
UUCP to Italy
Mrs. Iyabo Odusote <root@yaba.cnuce.cnr.it>
Post: P.O. Box 2011, Yaba Lagos, Nigeria
Voice: +234 1-860754
Fax: +234 1-823062/860211

Republic of Senegal (SN)

Public FidoNet node, 5:7711/1 ENDA-Dakar
Moussa Fall <mfall@endadak.gn.apc.org> Data: +221-21-7627
9600,CM,PEP,V32
Voice: +221 21 6027
APC node name: endadak.gn.apc.org

Orstom UUCP node in Dakar
Name: dakar.orstom.sn
Christophe Brun <brunchri@dakar.orstom.sn>
Edem Fianyo <fianyo@dakar.orstom.sn>
Voice: +221 32 34 76 / 32 34 80
Fax: +221 32 43 07
Post: ORSTOM—BP 1386—Dakar

Ecole Nationale Superieure Universitaire de Technologie in Dakar
Name: ensut.ensut.sn
Christian Clercin <clercin@ensut.ensut.sn>
Voice: +221 25 75 28
Fax: +221 25 55 94
Post: ENSUT BP 5085 Dakar-Fann SENEGAL

Ecole Nationale Superieure Universitaire de Technologie in Dakar
Name: lpa.ensut.sn
UUCP to dakar.orstom.sn—1 host 5 users
Simeon Fongang <fongang@lpa.ensut.sn>
Voice: +221 25 93 64
Fax: +221 25 55 94
Post: LPA-ENSUT BP 5085 Dakar-Fann SENEGAL

ISRA-CRODT (Centre Recherche Oceanographique de Dakar Thiaroye)
Name: isra.isra.sn
UUCP to dakar.orstom.sn—4 hosts 15 users
Ramadane Sarr <sarr@isra.isra.sn>
Voice: +221 34 54 89
Fax: +221 34 27 92
Post: ISRA/CRODT—BP 2241 Dakar

UCAD (Universite de Cheikh Anta Diop)
Name: anta.univ-dakar.sn
UUCP to orstom.sn—1 host 5 users
Ndiaye Samba <ndiayesa@anta.univ-dakar.sn>
Voice: +221 24 19 32
Post: Centre de calcul—UCAD BP 5005 DAKAR-Fann
Also: Bibliotheque Universitaire
Thioune Alioune <thioune@bucad.univ-dakar.sn>

USL (Universite de Saint Louis) Mathematiques Appliquees et Informatique
Name: louis.univ-stl.sn
UUCP to orstom.sn—1 host 5 users
Voice: +221 61 19 06
Fax: +221 61 18 84
Post: Universite Saint-Louis—UER M.A.I. BP 234 Saint-Louis
Also: Bibliotheque Universitaire
NDOYE <ndoye@bu.univ-stl.sn>
MET (Ministere de la Modernisation et de la Technologie)
CNDST (Centre National de la Documentation Scientifique et Technique)
Name: mmet.rinaf.sn
UUCP to orstom.sn—1 host 5 users
Ndiaye Moustapha <ndiayem@mmet.mmet.sn>
Voice: +221 23 70 68
Fax: +221 22 97 64
Post: CNDST—BP 218 Dakar
Also: DPS (Direction de la Prevision et des Statistiques)
Fall Babacar <bfall@dps.mmet.sn> +221 23 00 50
Also: DAST (Direction des Affaires Scientifiques et Techniques)
A Ousseynou <oba@dast.mmet.sn>

CSE (Centre de Suivi Ecologique)
Name: cse.orstom.sn
UUCP to orstom.sn—1 host 5 users
Jorgen Holm <holm@cse.cse.sn
Voice: +221 25 80 66
Fax: +221 25 81 68
Post: CSE BP 154 Dakar

Institut Pasteur
Name: pasteur.pasteur.sn
UUCP to dakar.orstom.sn—1 host 5 users
Jean Pierre Digoutte <digoutte@pasteur.pasteur.sn>

Voice: +221 23 51 81
Post: Institut Pasteur—BP 220 Dakar

MEN (Ministere de l'Education Nationale)
Ecole Nationale d'Economie Appliquee
Name: enea.men.sn
UUCP to dakar.orstom.sn—1 host 2 users
Gaye Ibrahima <igaye@enea.men.sn>
Voice: +221 25 25 48
Fax: +221 24 42 06
Post: ENEA BP 5084 Dakar
Also: Bureau d'Anglais pour le Ministere de l'Education Nationale
MBAYE Aymerou <ambaye@elto.men.sn> +221 22 35 90

PANA (Agence Panafricaine d'Information)
Name: pana.pana.sn
UUCP to dakar.orstom.sn—1 host 5 users
Amadou Mahtar BA <baam@pana.pana.sn>
Voice: +221 24 13 95
Post: PANA BP 4056 Dakar

CORAF (Conference des Responsables Africains en Agronomie)
Name: senegal.coraf.sn
UUCP to dakar.orstom.sn—1 host 1 user
Ndiaga Mbaye <mbaye@senegal.coraf.sn>
Voice: +221 25 55 69
Fax: +221 25 55 69
Post: CORAF—BP 3120 Dakar

CCA (American Culturel Centre)
Regional English Language Teaching Officer
Name: cca.usis.sn
UUCP to dakar.orstom.sn—1 host 1 user
Timothy Robinson <robinson@cca.usis.sn>
Voice: +221 23 11 85

Conference des Ministres de l'Education ayant le Francais en partage
Name: confemen.rio.org
UUCP to dakar.orstom.sn—1 host 5 users
Paul Coustere <coustere@confemen.rio.org>
Voice: +221 21 60 22
Fax: +221 21 32 26
Post: BP 3220 Dakar

South Zone Water Management
Project Name: proges.rio.org
UUCP to dakar.orstom.sn—1 host 5 users
Terry Hart <terry@proges.rio.org>
Voice: +221 91 22 68
Fax: +221 91 22 63
Post: South Zone Water Management Project BP 24 Ziguinchor

FAO Dakar
Name: fao-dakar.rio.org
UUCP to dakar.orstom.sn—1 host 1 user
Antonio Tavares de Pinho <tavares@fao-dakar.rio.org>
Voice: +221 23 58 91

Fax: +221 23 58 97
Post: FAO—BP 3300 Dakar

ISRA—Office in BAMBEY
Name: ceraas.orstom.sn
UUCP to dakar.orstom.sn—1 host—1 user
Daniel Annerose <annerose@ceraas.orstom.sn>

Seychelles (SC)

Victoria / ORSTOM
Seychelles Fishing Authority Headquarters Rue des Frangipaniers—
BP 570 Victoria-Mahe
Voice: +(248) 247 42
Fax: +(248) 245 08
Marc Bartholme <bartho@seychel.orstom.fr>
Node Name: seychel.orstom.fr

Kingdom of Swaziland (SZ)

There is a UUCP link from Rhodes, reported to be reliable as of 93.11.01. In the interim, one can write to the admin of the nascent domain:

Vriezekolk, Eelco
University of Swaziland Department of Computer Science
Phone Number: +268 84545/ +268 84011 ext 211 Fax: +268 85276
Eelco Vriezekolk <eelco@attic.alt.sz>

Togolese Republic (TG)

Orstom UUCP node in Lome
Name: lome.orstom.fr
UUCP over X.25—1 host—8 users
Richard Gozo <gozo@lome.orstom.fr>
Voice: +228 21 43 44 / 21 43 46 Fax: +228 21 03 43
Post: ORSTOM—BP 375—Lome

Tunisia (TN)

Internet 192.68.138.0
Admin: Makni, Mondher <mondher@tunisia.eu.net>
Tech: Saadaoui, Kamel <saadaoui@tunisia.eu.net> IRSIT
BP 212, Rue Ibn Nadime Cite Mahrajane, Tunis 1082
Voice: +216 1-787-757
Fax: +216 1 787 827

Public FidoNet node, 5:7911/1
ENDA Inter-Arabe
6 Impasse de le mer Rouge, ARIANA
Michael Cracknell

Data: +216 1 70 1827
2400, CM, PEP
Voice: +216 1-718-340
APC node name: endaarabe.gn.apc.org

BITNET
Abida, Nejib <abida@tnearn.bitnet>
IRSIT
BP 212, Rue Ibn Nadime Cite Mahrajane, Tunis 1082
Voice: +216 1-787-757
Fax: +216 1 787 827

United Republic of Tanzania (TZ)

APC FidoNet node
Council for Science and Technology Epidemiology & Biostatistics dept.
Muhimbili Medical Centre
P.O. Box 65015, Dar es Salaam
Voice: +255-51-26211
William Sangiwa <bsangiwa@costech.gn.apc.org> costech.gn.apc.org

CGNET has one user online from Tanzania (PLAN-SALAAM @CGNET.COM). They are the Foster Parents Plan office in that country; they log on via phone calls to KENPAC's x.25 node in Nairobi, Kenya.

HNET TAN Council for Science and Technology
Epidemiology & Biostatistics dept.
Muhimbili University College of Health Sciences
P.O. Box 65015
Dar es Salaam
Voice: +255-51-27081 ext 240 Fax: 46163
William Sangiwa ID: bsangiwa
Node Name: hnettan.gn.apc.org

Republic of Uganda (UG)

Public FidoNet node, 5:7321/1
Makerere University, Institute of Computer Science Box 7062, Kampala
Charles Musisi <cmusisi@mukla.gn.apc.org>
Data: +256 41-532440
Voice: +256 41-559-712
APC node name: mukla.gn.apc.org

Republic of South Africa (ZA)

IP, UUCP, and FidoNet networking too ubiquitous to enumerate.

Alan Barrett—barrett@daisy.ee.und.ac.za (South African UUCP and Internet)
Chris Pinkham—chris@aim1.aztec.co.za (commercial TCP/IP network)
Paul Nash—paul@frcs.alt.za (African NGOs)
Mike Lawrie—ccml@hippo.ru.ac.za (university TCP/IP network)
Dave Wilson—ccdw@hippo.ru.ac.za (FidoNet in Africa)

Republic of Zambia (ZM)

Zambia became the fifth country in Africa to have a full time connection to the Internet of 94.11.22.

rip% ping -s 196.7.240.1
PING 196.7.240.1: 56 data bytes
64 bytes from 196.7.240.1: icmp_seq=0. time=5029. ms
University of Zambia Computer Centre Box 32379; Lusaka
Neil Robinson
Voice: +260 1 252 507
Node name: puku.unza.zm

Public FidoNet node, 5:761/1
University of Zambia Computer Centre Box 32379; Lusaka
Mark Bennett <mbennett@unza.gn.apc.org>
Data: +260 1 252 892
Voice: +260 1 252 507
Node Name: unza.gn.apc.org
94.08.04 Contact made using aesl@f1.n761.z5.fidonet.org

APC FidoNet node
ZANGONET
Zambia Association for Research and Development (ZARD) Lusaka
zango.gn.apc.org

Republic of Zimbabwe (ZW)

UUCP node off UNINET-ZA
University of Zimbabwe
John Sheppard <postmaster@zimbix.uz.zw>
Voice: +263 4 303211 x1378
Node Name: zimbix.uz.zw

Public FidoNet node, 5:7211/1 Mango
PO Box 7069; Harare
Rob Borland <rborland@mango.apc.org> Data: +263-4-738692
Voice: +263 4 303 211 ext 1492
Node Name: mango.apc.org

B

U.S. Public Libraries on the Internet

If you are in one of the areas served by these libraries, you may be able to get free or inexpensive Internet services through them. Check your local phone book for their phone numbers. Some of these services are excellent.

Public libraries on gopher servers

Allen County Public Library Gopher (Ft. Wayne, IN)
Boston Public Library Gopher (Boston, MA)
Chester County Library and District Center (Chester County, PA)
Cleveland Public Library Gopher (Cleveland, OH)
Delaware's Public Library Gopher (Dover, DE)
Denver Public Library (Denver, CO)
Kitsap Regional Library Gopher (Bremerton, WA)
Metro Net Library Consortium Gopher (Detroit, MI)
Pasadena Public Library Gopher (Pasadena, CA)
Pikes Peak Library's MaggNet (Colorado Springs, CO)
Queensborough Public Library Gopher (Jamaica, NY)
Salt Lake City Public Library Gopher (Salt Lake City, UT)

Seattle Public Library Gopher (Seattle, WA)
Public Library of Youngstown and Mahoning County (Youngstown, OH)

Public libraries on Web servers

Abbot Public Library (Marblehead, MA)
Alachua County Library District (Gainesville, FL)
Allen County Public Library (Ft. Wayne, IN) under construction
City of Anacortes Public Library (Anacortes, WA)
Ann Arbor Public Library (Ann Arbor, MI)
Appleton Public Library (Appleton, WI) 1st public library in Wisconsin to put up a Web server
Atlanta/Fulton Public Library (Atlanta, GA)
Austin Public Library (Austin, TX)
Baldwin Public Library (Birmingham, MI)
Baltimore County Public Library (Towson, MD)
Bedford Free Public Library (Bedford, MA)
The Berkeley Public Library (Berkeley, CA)
Birmingham Public Library (Birmingham, AL)
Bloomfield Township Public Library (Bloomfield Hills, MI)
Boston Public Library (Boston, MA)
Boulder Public Library (Boulder, CO)
Burlington County Library (Westampton, NJ) 1st public library in New Jersey to provide Web access to its customers
Cambridge Public Library (Cambridge, MA)
Camden Public Library (Camden, ME)
Carnegie Library of Pittsburgh (Pittsburgh, PA)
Carnegie-Stout Public Library (Dubuque, IA)
Canton Public Library (Canton, MI)
Carroll County Public Library (Westminster, MD)
Cedar Falls Public Library (Cedar Falls, IA)
Public Library of Charlotte & Mecklenburg County (Charlotte, NC) "1995 Library of the Year"
Chicago Public Library (Chicago, IL)
Clark Public Library (Clark, NJ) 1st public library system in New Jersey to put up a Web server
Dayton & Montgomery County Public Library (Dayton, OH)
Delaware Public Library (Dover, DE)
Public Library of Des Moines (Des Moines, IA)
Douglas Public Library District (Castle Rock, CO)
El Dorado County Library (Placerville, CA)
Ellsworth Public Library (Ellsworth, ME)

Eugene Public Library (Eugene, OR)
Evansville-Vanderburgh County Public Library (Evansville, IN)
Farmingham Community Library (Farmingham, MI)
Farmington Hills Library (Farmington Hills, MI)
Fayetteville Public Library (Ozark Regional Library, AR)
The Ferguson Library (Stamford, CT)
Flint Public Library (Flint, MI)
Farmington Community Library (Farmington, CT)
Glenview Public Library (Glenview, IL)
Hawaii State Public Library System (HI)
Hollis Social Library (Hollis, NH)
Houston Public Library (Houston, TX)
Indianapolis-Marion County Public Library (Indianapolis, IN)
Jackson County Public Library (Seymour, IN)
Kansas City Public Library (Kansas City, MO)
Kinderhook Regional Library (Lebanon, MO)
Kokomo-Howard County Public Library (Kokomo, IN)
Lawrence Public Library (Lawrence, KS)
Longmont Public Library (Boulder, CO)
Mahopac Public Library (Mahopac, NY)
Mead Public Library (Sheboygan, WI)
Metro Net Library Consortium, Inc. (a virtual consortium of eight Detroit suburban public libraries, MI)
Mideastern Michigan Library Cooperative (MI)
Millicent Library (Fairhaven, MA)
Milton Public Library (Milton, MA)
Monroe County Public Library (Bloomington, IN)
Monroe County Public Library (Rochester, NY)
Montgomery-Floyd Regional Library (Christiansburg, VA)
Mount Arlington Public Library (Mount Arlington, NJ)
Mount Prospect Public Library (Mount Prospect, IL)
Moscow Free Library (Moscow, ID)
Moscow-Latah County Library District (Latah County, ID)
Public Library of Nashville and Davidson County (Nashville, TN)
New Castle-Henry County Public Library (New Castle, IN)
New Orleans Public Library (New Orleans, LA) (World Wide Web)
New York Public Library (New York, NY)
Norfolk Public Library (Norfolk, VA)
Novi Public Library (Novi, MI)
City of Palo Alto Libraries (Palo Alto, CA)

Bibliotheque publique d'information (BIP)—public
Pasadena Public Library (Pasadena, CA) (World Wide Web)
The Free Public Library of Philadelphia (Philadelphia, PA)
Provincetown Public Library (Provincetown, MA)
Provo City Library (Provo, UT)
Richardson Public Library (Richardson, TX)
Riverside City and County Public Library (Riverside, CA)
Rochester Hills Public Library (Rochester, MI)
Sacramento Public Library (Sacramento, CA)
St. Charles City-County Library District (Saint Peters, MO)
St. Joseph County Public Library (South Bend, IN)
Saint Paul Public Library (St. Paul, MN)
St. Petersburg Public Library System (St. Petersburg, FL)
San Francisco Public Library (San Francisco, CA)
Santa Cruz Public Libraries (Santa Cruz, CA)
Santa Fe Public Library (Santa Fe, NM)
Seattle Public Library (Seattle, WA) (World Wide Web)
SELCO (Southeastern Libraries Cooperating); regional agency for 30 public libraries in Southeastern Minnesota, including: Albert Lea, Austin, Blooming Prairie, Brownsdale, Caledonia, Cannon Falls, Chatifield, Dodge Center, Faribault, Grand Meadow, Harmony, Hokah, Kasson, Kenyon, LaCrescent, Lake City, Lanesboro, LeRoy, Mabel, Northfield, Owatonna, Pine Island, Plainview, Preston, Red Wing, Rochester, Rushford, St. Charles, SELCO Bookmobile (Owatonna), SELCO Bookmobile (Winona), Spring Valley, Stewartville, Wabash, West Concord, Winona, Zumbrota Public Libraries
Sharon Public Library (Sharon, MA)
Southeastern Ohio Public Libraries home page
Southfield Public Library (Southfield, MI)
Spokane Public Library (Spokane, WA)
Taylor Public Library (Taylor, TX)
Topeka and Shawnee County Public Library (Topeka, KS)
Waldoboro Public Library (Waldoboro, ME)
Washoe County Library (Reno, NV)
Westerville (OH) Public Library Web server
Wicomico County Free Library (Salisbury, MD)
Willard Library (Evansville, IN)

Bibliography

Resources on African Americans, business, and the economy

Bauchum, Rosalind G. *The Black Business and Professional Woman: Selected References of Achievement: A Tribute to the 50th Year of the National Association of Negro Business and Professional Women's Clubs, Inc.* Monticello, Ill.: Vance Bibliographies, 1985.

Davis, Lenwood G. *Poverty and the Black Community: A Preliminary Survey*. Monticello, Ill.: Council of Planning Librarians, 1976.

Davis, Lenwood G. *The Black Family in Urban Areas in the United States: A Bibliography of Published Works on the Black Family in Urban Areas in the United States*, 2d Ed. Monticello, Ill.: Council of Planning Librarians, 1979.

Nordquist, Joan. *African Americans: Social and Economic Conditions: A Bibliography*. Santa Cruz, CA: Reference and Research Services, 1992.

Obudho, Robert A. *Afro-American Demography and Urban Issues: A Bibliography*. Westport, Conn.: Greenwood Press, 1985.

Williams, D. F. (Darrell Fisher). *The Political Economy of Black Community Development: A Research Bibliography*. Monticello, Ill.: Council of Planning Librarians, 1973.

Worsham, John P. *A Bibliographical Guide to the Black Literature in Planning and Urban Studies Periodicals, 1970-1978.* Monticello, Ill.: Vance Bibliographies, 1979.

Recent works on African Americans in the U.S. economy

Blacksheare, Edward. *The Black Family: Impact of Economics & Health Care,* 1st ed. Detroit: PC Print Pub., 1990.

Blackwell, James Edward. *The Community: Diversity and Unity,* 3rd ed. New York: Harper Collins, 1991.

Burman, Stephen. *The Black Progress Question: Explaining the African-American Predicament.* Thousand Oaks, Calif.: Sage Publications, 1995.

Butler, John S. *Entrepreneurship and Self-help among Black Americans: A Reconsideration of Race and Economics.* Albany: State University of New York Press, 1991.

Carnoy, Martin. *Faded Dreams: The Politics and Economics of Race in America.* Cambridge [England]; New York, NY, USA: Cambridge University Press, 1994.

Craig, Russell, M.S. *The Socio-economic Truth of Black America.* Decatur, GA: Remnant Pub., 1992.

Green, Shelley. *Black Entrepreneurship in America.* New Brunswick, NJ: Transaction Publishers, 1990.

Henderson, Perry E. *The Black Church Credit Union,* 1st ed. Lima, Ohio: Fairway Press, 1990.

Jencks, Christopher, and Paul E. Peterson, eds. *The Urban Underclass.* Washington, D.C.: Brookings Institution, 1991.

Jennings, James. *Race, Politics, and Economic Development: Community Perspectives.* New York: Routledge Chapman & Hall, 1992.

Jones, Jacqueline. *The Dispossessed: America's Underclasses from the Civil War to the Present.* New York: Basic Books, 1992.

Kimbro, Dennis Paul. *Think and Grow Rich: A Black Choice.* 1st ed. New York: Fawcett Columbine, 1991.

Kunjufu, Jawanza. *Black Economics: Solutions for Economic and Community Empowerment.* 1st ed. Chicago, Ill.: African American Images, 1991.

Lumumba, Chokwe. *Reparations Yes: The Legal and Political Reasons Why Negroes, Afrikans, Black People in the United*

States, Should be Paid Now for the Enslavement of our Ancestors and for War Against Us after Slavery: Articles, 3rd ed. Baton Rouge, LA: House of Songhay, Commission for Positive Education, 1993.

Mandle, Jay R. *Not Slave, Not Free: The African American Economic Experience Since the Civil War.* Durham: Duke University Press, 1992.

Reed, Wornie L., ed. *Critiques of the NRC Study: A Common Destiny: Blacks and American Society.* Boston: William Monroe Trotter Institute, University of Massachusetts at Boston, 1990.

Reed, Wornie L. *Social, Political, and Economic Issues in Black America.* Boston: William Monroe Trotter Institute, University of Massachusetts at Boston, 1990.

Forthcoming on African Americans in the U.S. economy

Blacks in Rural America. New Brunswick: Transaction Publishers, 1995.

Kenman, George Frost. *At a Century's Ending: Reflections 1982-1995.* New York: W.W. Norton, 1996.

Reparations, the Cure for America's Race Problem: A Collaborative Effort in Reparations Advocacy by the Founding Members of C.U.R.E. 1st ed., Hampton, VA: U.B. & US Communication Systems, 1994.

Recent works on African-American business

Bates, Timothy Mason. *Banking on Black Enterprise: The Potential of Emerging Firms for Revitalizing Urban Economics.* Washington, DC: Joint Center for Political and Economic Studies, 1993.

Butler, John S. *Entrepreneurship and Self-help among Black Americans: A Reconsideration of Race and Economics.* Albany: State University of New York Press, 1991.

Carroll, John M. (Martin). *Fritz Pollard: Pioneer in Racial Advancement.* Urbana: University of Illinois Press, 1992.

Diggs, Anita Doreen. *Success at Work: A Guide for African-Americans.* Fort Lee, NJ: Barricade Books; Emeryville, CA: Distributed by Publishers Group West, 1993.

Fraser, George C. *Success Runs in our Race: The Complete Guide to Effective Networking in the African-American Community.* 1st ed., New York: W. Morrow, 1994.

Greenberg, Jonathan D. *Staking A Claim: Jake Simmons and the Making of an African-American Oil Dynasty.* New York, NY: Plume, 1990. 1991 printing.

Harry, Lois. *Stressors, Beliefs, and Coping Behaviors of Black Women Entrepreneurs.* New York: Garland Pub., 1994.

Ingham, John N. *African-American Business Leaders: A Biographical Dictionary.* Westport, Conn.: Greenwood Press, 1994.

Lewis, Reginald F. *Why Should White Guys Have All the Fun?: How Reginald Lewis Created a Billion-dollar Business Empire.* New York: Wiley, 1995.

Pierce, Joseph A. (Alphonso). *Negro Business and Business Education: Their Present and Prospective Development.* New York: Plenum Press, 1995.

Simms, Darrell D. (Dean). *Black Experience, Strategies, and Tactics in the Business World: A Corporate Perspective: A Handbook for Professionals.* Beaverton, Ore.: Management Aspects, 1991.

Spivey, William R. *Corporate America in Black and White.* New York, NY: Carlton Press, 1993.

Spivey, William R. *Succeeding in Corporate America: A Case Study of a Black American Against the Odds.* 1st ed., New York: Vantage Press, 1991.

Thomas, William. *How to Build Wealth in the Bottom-half of the Black Community.* Oakland, Calif.: Marsh-Wentworth Pub., 1994.

History

Harris, Abram Lincoln. *The Negro as Capitalist: A Study of Banking and Business Among American Negroes.* College Park, MD: McGrath Pub. Co., 1968.

Johnson, Whittington Bernard. *The Promising Years, 1750-1830: The Emergence of Black Labor and Business.* New York: Garland Pub., 1993.

Katz, Michael B., ed. *The "Underclass" Debate: Views from History.* Princeton, NJ: Princeton University Press, 1993.

Matney, William C. *America's Black Population, 1970 to 1982: A Statistical View.* Washington: U.S. Dept of Commerce, Bureau of the Census, 1983.

Records of the National Negro Business League [microform]. Bethesda, MD: University Publications of America, 1994. Microfilm reels.

Schweninger, Loren. *Black Property Owners in the South, 1790-1915.* Urbana: University of Illinois Press, 1990.

Smith, J. Owens. *The Politics of Ethnic and Racial Inequality: A Systematic Comparative Macro-analysis from the Colonial Period to the Present,* 2nd ed., Dubuque, Iowa: Kendall/Hunt Pub. Co., 1992.

Weisbrot, Robert. *Freedom Bound: A History of America's Civil Rights Movement.* New York, NY: Plume, 1990.

Recent works on discrimination

Burstein, Paul, ed. *Equal Employment Opportunity: Labor Market Discrimination and Public Policy.* New York: Aldine de gruyter, 1994.

Darity, William A. *The Black Underclass: Critical Essays on Race and Unwantedness.* New York: Garland Pub., 1994.

Donahoe, Myrna Cherkoss. *Resolving Discriminatory Practices Against Minorities and Women in Steel and Auto, Los Angeles, California, 1936-1982.* Los Angeles: Center for Labor Research and Education, Institute of Industrial Relations, University of California, Los Angeles, 1991.

Leiman, Melvin M. *Political Economy of Racism.* Boulder: Westview, 1993.

Tomaskovic-Devey, Donald. *Gender & Racial Inequality at Work: The Sources and Consequences of Job Segregation.* Ithaca: ILR Press, 1993.

Index

Illustrations are in **boldface**.

B

C

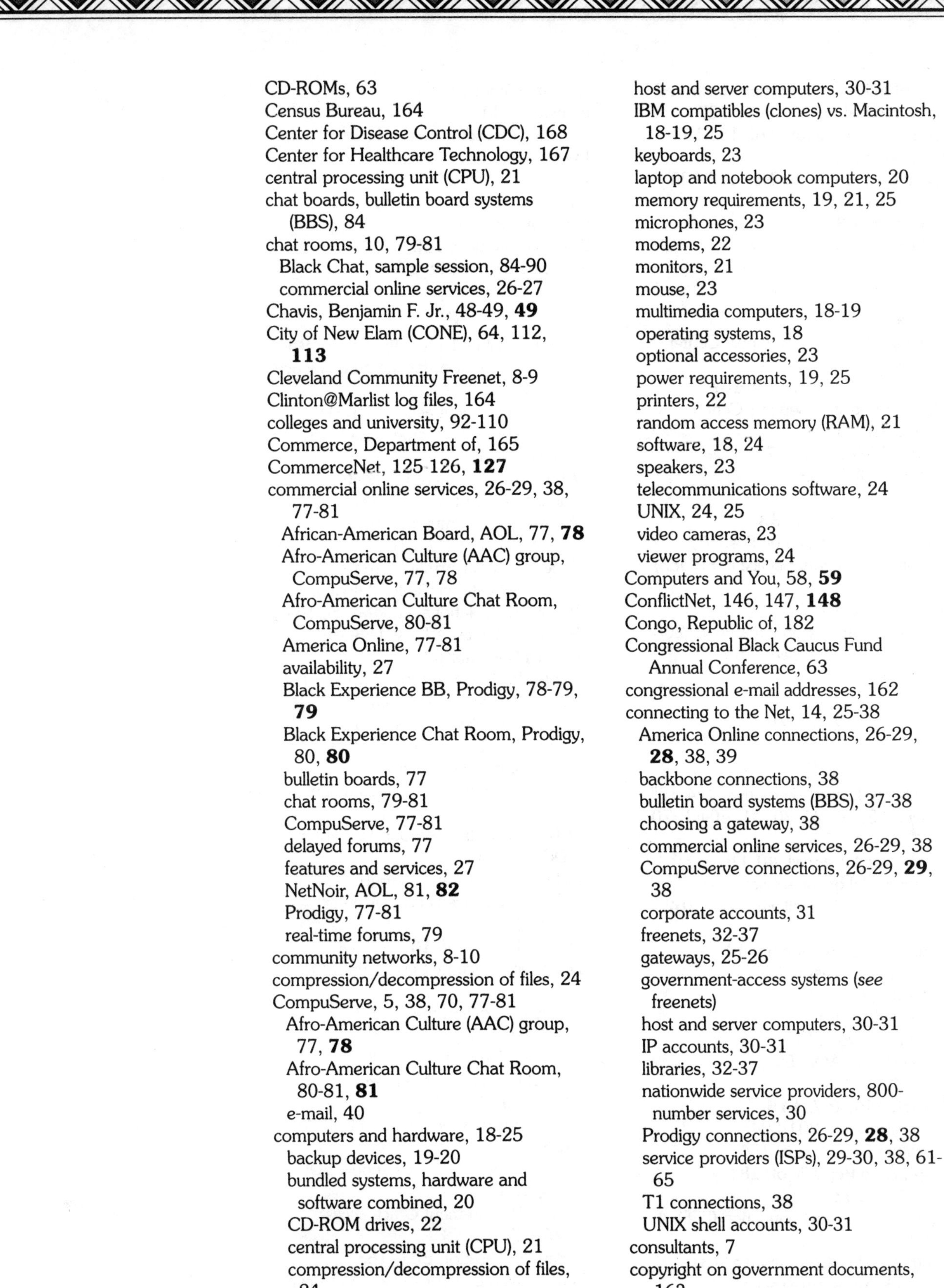

D

E

F

G

H

Y

Z

About the authors

Stafford L. Battle is cofounder and president of The City of New Elam, Inc., an online Internet company whose target market is a nontechnical audience. Battle serves as Webmaster for The City of New Elam and editor-in-chief of *ElamWorld Technology Review*, a technology-related online publication for nontechnical people. He has also written dozens of magazine and journal articles about computers for nontechnical readers. He received a B.A. from Brandeis University and completed Stanford University's Professional Publishing Course and Howard University's Book Publishing Institute.

Reynold O. Harris is cofounder of The City of New Elam, Inc. Harris has a background in sales and marketing, public speaking, and training and development. He has conducted leadership training seminars for youth, seminars for employment and training professionals, and career-development courses for special populations. Currently an adjunct faculty member at the University of the District of Columbia (UDC), he received a B.S. from Delaware State University, an M.A. from Central Michigan University, and will receive a Ph.D. in adult education from UDC in the spring of 1996.

About the author